44771
338.5

MICROECONOMICS
NEW OLD

J

Graham D Fitzpatrick

H 000038

215475

OXFORD UNIVERSITY PRESS

Oxford University Press, Walton Street, Oxford OX2 6DP

Oxford New York Toronto
Delhi Bombay Calcutta Madras Karachi
Petaling Jaya Singapore Hong Kong Tokyo
Nairobi Dar es Salaam Cape Town
Melbourne Auckland

and associated companies in
Beirut Berlin Ibadan Nicosia

Oxford is a trade mark of Oxford University Press

ISBN 0 19 913296 8

© Oxford University Press 1986
First published 1986
Reprinted 1987

00d1512

To my parents

Phototypeset by Oxford Publishing Services

Printed in Great Britain by William Clowes Ltd, Beccles, Suffolk

Contents

Preface

This book sets out to achieve two basic objectives within each chapter. Firstly, it covers traditional microeconomics in a concise but comprehensive way, providing students studying for A level economics and equivalent examinations with a full understanding of the basic theory.

The second objective involves filling a gap that exists in the present literature. By questioning the assumptions upon which the traditional theory is based, alternative approaches have been developed. In many A level books these newer theories are often ignored or outlined in such a superficial way as to be of little use. This makes it necessary for students to turn to specialist texts that cover them in great detail and depth or even original texts and articles that present them in such a rigorous form that they are often beyond the requirements of students at this level.

In this book we aim to make these new theories and approaches accessible to the average student. The basic ideas behind many of the new approaches are conveyed in a simple manner that will usefully extend A level students while acting as a sound introduction for undergraduates.

The questions that follow each chapter are all taken from recent examination papers and provide evidence that examiners are increasingly expecting at least some knowledge of these recent developments. Each set of questions is made up of one data response question and twelve essay questions taken from examinations set by all the examining boards. Emphasis has been placed on choosing questions that require an understanding of these new ideas.

Acknowledgements

It is impossible to overemphasize the contribution made by Michele Weisslinger with whom I collaborated closely. If the book provides a clear, orderly presentation it is largely due to her expertise as a linguist and the skill with which she edited the original drafts. Her detailed research and comments led to a great deal of restructuring and rewriting, some of which she undertook herself.

I would also like to acknowledge the help and encouragement that I received from those around me. This includes all my colleagues in the economics department at Luton Sixth Form College and in particular Barrie Gore who read and commented on the draft copies of each chapter.

Appreciation is due to the following examining boards for permission to use the examination questions that appear at the end of each chapter: Associated Examining Board; Joint Matriculation Board; Oxford and Cambridge Schools Examination Board; Oxford Colleges Admissions Office; Scottish Examination Board; Secretary to the Cambridge Colleges' Examination; University of Cambridge Local Examinations Syndicate; University of London Entrance and School Examinations Council; University of Oxford Delegacy of Local Examinations (OLE); Welsh Joint Education Committee.

Introduction

What is economics?

Economics is a social science. It employs a scientific method of study to examine the economic behaviour of people in society. What constitutes economic behaviour? In order to answer this we need to make a few observations about the world in which we live.

Firstly, we have needs in terms of necessities such as food, shelter, and clothing; and desires in terms of luxuries such as jewellery, Persian rugs, and music centres. What concerns economists is the fact that these wants appear to be never-ending — insatiable. Secondly, the economic resources that are available to produce these goods and services are **scarce**. By economic resources, or **factors of production**, we mean the labour, capital, and natural resources that are combined in order to produce goods and services. By referring to them as scarce we are merely highlighting the fact that there are never enough economic resources to satisfy the insatiable wants of people.

Economic behaviour is that aspect of behaviour that stems from a person's attempt to satisfy as many of his wants as possible, given the fact that the resources at his disposal are limited in supply, or scarce. This inevitably involves making **choices**. If all the available resources are being used and a person wants more of good A, then he must choose between more of good A and the sacrifice of, say, good B. If more of good A is to be produced, scarce resources must be directed away from the production of good B, thereby reducing the amount of good B available for consumption. This introduces a further economic idea, that of **opportunity cost**. An individual with a limited income, that is with scarce resources, may have to choose between a holiday abroad and a new stereo. If he chooses the holiday the stereo is the opportunity cost, and vice versa. Governments too have scarce resources. They may have to choose between a new hospital and a new school. In this case the opportunity cost of the hospital would be the school and vice versa.

In other words, the subject matter of economics is those aspects of the behaviour of individuals, firms, and governments that stem from the choices that have to be made due to the scarcity of resources. For the individual this involves choices about what work to do and what goods to consume. For the firm this involves choices about what to produce and how to produce it. For the government this involves choices about how much to raise from taxation and what to spend it on.

Microeconomics and macroeconomics

The study of economics is divided into two parts — microeconomics and macroeconomics. Microeconomics is the area of study to which this book is devoted. It deals with the economic behaviour of individual decision-making units such as consumers, workers, and firms. Macroeconomics deals with the behaviour of aggregates or collections of decision-making units such as the total expenditure of all consumers, the total amount of income earned by all workers, and the total output of all firms. These aggregates are considered in terms of their effects on inflation, unemployment, growth, and the balance of payments.

Microeconomics tries to focus our attention on the way in which the decisions of consumers, producers, and resource owners interrelate so as to determine the relative prices of goods and factors of production. These prices in turn serve as the mechanism by which scarce resources are allocated among alternative uses. This is called the **price mechanism**. It is the analysis of this allocating or choice-making mechanism that is at the heart of microeconomic theory. Choices have to be made about what, how, and where to produce as well as about the distribution of the final product. All of this may sound very abstract, but as we shall see, it can throw a great deal of light on many practical problems confronted by individuals, firms, and governments as they face up to the basic economic problem of scarce resources.

By asking how well economic systems perform in deciding how to allocate resources, several of the following chapters will move into the field of microeconomics known as **welfare economics**. In effect, we are asking: 'Does the price mechanism do a good job?' 'Are resources being allocated so as to maximize economic efficiency?' At this stage two points must be made. Firstly, in economies such as Britain government intervention is widespread, affecting many aspects of economic behaviour. We are not therefore judging a **market** economy where activities of consumers and producers interact freely, but a **mixed** economy. This is an economy where some of the resources are allocated in accordance with the price mechanism, while others are allocated by the state, as in a **command** or **planned** economy. Note also that a government's behaviour might be difficult to analyse in terms of purely economic criteria — social and political motives may well be at work. Secondly, we have the problem of deciding by what criteria an economy's performance should be judged. If our aim is to allocate resources so as to maximize human welfare for the community as a whole, we must be able to quantify 'welfare', but attempts to do this are surrounded by controversy. For example, how can the effects of pollution, unemployment, increased leisure time, and so on be quantified? These problems will be returned to in the following chapters.

Positive and normative economics

The two difficulties just outlined bring us to a further distinction often made by economists, that between positive and normative economics. **Positive** economics is confined to an analysis of facts, while **normative** economics considers value judgements. Positive economics makes statements about what is the case, while normative economics makes statements about what ought to be. The following is a positive statement: 'If the government reduces expenditure as planned, unemployment will increase to four million.' If on the other hand someone were to say, 'four million unemployed is unacceptable', then this would be a normative statement.

The reason for mentioning the distinction at this stage leads on from the two difficulties mentioned earlier regarding welfare economics. It is an assumption of many economics textbooks that they should confine themselves to positive economics. However, the behaviour of individuals, firms, and governments is often based on value judgements as much as facts. The entrepreneur may decide against an industrial location, not on cost grounds, but on some preconceived notion about the quality of life in that part of the country. More generally, government intervention exists and is motivated in part by social and political attitudes that are more normative than positive. Despite all this, the assumptions upon which much of traditional microeconomic theory is based involve 'rational economic behaviour' as this is more easily adapted to a positive approach. By insisting on this, many of the theories are not as complete as they could be. For this reason, along with the fact that attempts to analyse economic welfare must incorporate normative economics, the following chapters will not tie themselves solely to the positive approach.

New theories and old

Having explored some basic definitions we are now in a position to clarify the scope and structure of the book. Each chapter takes a major aspect of microeconomics and begins with a comprehensive outline of the appropriate traditional theory. Some of the assumptions on which the traditional theories have been built will then be questioned. For example:

1 Will the forces of supply and demand always produce a price?
2 Can consumer satisfaction be measured?
3 Is the size of your income the only factor that determines your level of consumption?
4 Do firms aim to maximize their profits?
5 Are wage levels the only factor to influence employment decisions?

The questioning of these traditional assumptions will lead to doubts about the validity of the traditional theories. By facing up to these doubts the new theories attempt to provide a more realistic analysis of economic behaviour. A discussion of these newer theories will constitute the second part of each chapter.

A point that will be returned to is that these new theories and approaches invariably add to the analysis provided by the more traditional ones. They complement the older theories; in no way do they render them obsolete. Also it is hoped that an introduction to these newer theories will develop a deeper understanding of the more traditional ideas.

Chapter 1   *The price mechanism*

A study of the price mechanism or market system involves an analysis of the interaction between the behaviour of consumers and producers. This interaction takes place within a market situation. Wherever buyers and sellers are in contact a market situation can be said to exist.

The price mechanism is basically a system of resource allocation. The first part of this chapter will provide a brief outline of the traditional explanation of how this system works. Such an explanation is built upon very restrictive assumptions. It provides an idealized picture of how a market economy is supposed to lead to an 'optimum' allocation of resources.

The second part of the chapter will focus on the fact that in the real world the price mechanism does not work quite so smoothly. Firstly, there are many frictions and imperfections that undermine the restrictive assumptions upon which the traditional analysis is based. Secondly, there are certain circumstances where even with all the traditional assumptions the price mechanism fails to allocate resources efficiently. Finally, when the market system fails there would seem to be a case for government intervention, and it is worth remembering that increases in government intervention signify a movement away from the market economy in the direction of the mixed type of economic system.

Chapters 2, 3, and 4 look in more detail at certain aspects of the behaviour of consumers and producers. An argument could be made for reading Chapters 2, 3, and 4 before Chapter 1. However, the advantages of a broad overview of the price mechanism from the outset probably outweigh the advantages to be gained from beginning with a detailed scrutiny of its component parts. By way of a compromise the reader is referred forward to Chapters 2, 3, and 4 whenever points being made now are expanded later.

Part 1   *The traditional price mechanism*

Resources and, therefore, the goods and services they produce are scarce. As a result choices have to be made regarding what to produce, what methods of production to use, and how to distribute the goods and services once they have been produced. The price mechanism provides a system whereby these choices can be made.

The traditional analysis assumes that there is a market for every good and every factor of production. Consumers will create the demand within each market, while producers will supply the product.

A further assumption is that each market will be a competitive or perfect market. By this it is meant that there will always be so many buyers and sellers that no single one can influence the overall market conditions. All buyers are trying to maximize their satisfaction, while all suppliers are trying to maximize their profit. The traditional analysis also assumes perfect knowledge, certainty, and mobility within the market.

The crucial outcome of these assumptions is that all firms within the market will be price-takers: all firms will charge the same price for a particular good and all consumers, therefore, will pay the same price. For a more detailed outline of what constitutes a perfect market see Chapter 4, p.80.

Within each market the behaviour of consumers and producers will determine a price. These prices will in turn determine the quantities to be produced in each market and, therefore, the use of resources. The case for this system of resource allocation tries to show that it will result in an 'efficient' or 'socially optimum' allocation of resources. Before looking at how the market system determines prices and at what exactly is meant by an 'efficient' outcome, it will be necessary to examine in more detail the behaviour of consumers (**demand theory**) and the behaviour of producers (**supply theory**).

1 Consumers' demand

1.1 The law of demand and the demand curve

When an economist talks of demand he does not mean the wants or needs of people, but their **effective demand**, that is the quantity that they actually consume at a given price over a given period of time. It is possible to identify either a single consumer's demand, or the demand of all consumers in the market (**aggregate demand**). This is simply arrived at by the horizontal summation of individual demand curves (see below).

The **law of demand** expresses an important relationship between the price of a good and the demand for it. It states that there is an inverse relationship between the price of a good and the quantity demanded, assuming that all other factors are held constant. If price rises less will be bought, while if price falls more will be bought. Chapter 2 will study this relationship in more detail. For the time being, it is enough to assume that at a lower price

present consumers will feel able to consume more, non-consumers may feel able to undertake consumption, and those consuming cheaper substitutes may feel able to switch to 'the real thing'.

If the demand for a given good is calculated over a range of prices and expressed as a table, this is called a **demand schedule** (Table 1.1). If such a schedule is represented graphically with price on the vertical axis and quantity demanded on the horizontal axis, this gives us a **demand curve** (Fig. 1.1).

Points to notice about the demand curve

1 Given the law of demand, the demand curve will always slope downwards from left to right. There is an inverse relationship between the price of tea and the number of packets consumed.
2 If the curve is prolonged to the left, it will eventually cut the vertical axis. At this point the good will have priced itself out of the market: none would be demanded. No tea would be sold.
3 If the curve is prolonged to the right, it will eventually cut the horizontal axis. This point will indicate the amount of the good that could be given away. There is a limit to the number of packets of tea that would be demanded if they were free.

Table 1.1   A demand schedule

Price of tea (pence per packet)	Packets demanded per day (000s)
250	100
200	160
150	250
100	450
50	800

Fig. 1.1   A demand curve

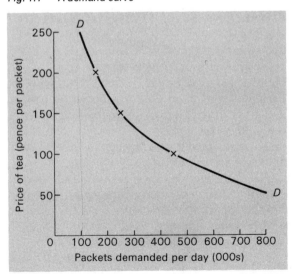

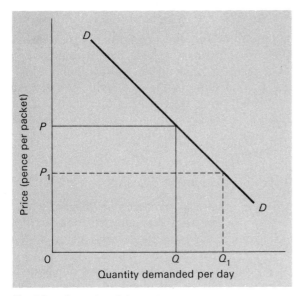

Fig. 1.2   Extension of demand

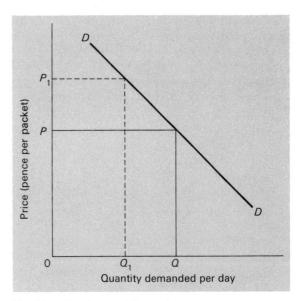

Fig. 1.3   Contraction of demand

4 The whole curve must have a time dimension. It must show the quantity demanded
per day, week, month, year, or whatever.
Without this, it is meaningless.

1.2 Changes in demand

It is possible to distinguish between two types
of change. On the one hand there are extensions and contractions, and on the other
increases and decreases.

Extensions and contractions

These refer to changes in the quantity demanded that result from changes in the price of
the good itself. When more packets of tea are
demanded at a lower price, this is an extension
of demand (Fig. 1.2). When less packets are
demanded at a higher price, this is a contraction of demand (Fig. 1.3). The demand curve
itself does not move.

Increases and decreases

When the demand for a good increases, more
will be consumed at the given price. As this
will be the case for any price on the vertical
axis, the whole curve will shift outwards to the
right from D to D_1 (Fig. 1.4). For example,

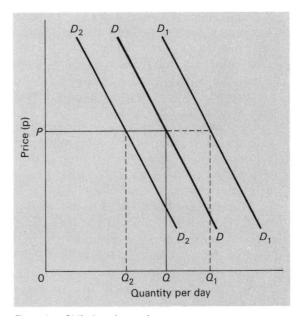

Fig. 1.4   Shifts in a demand curve

where 100 000 packets of tea per day were
consumed at a price of 250p a packet before the
increase in demand, 150 000 will be bought
after the increase in demand. The reverse is
true for a fall in demand. Less will be bought at
each of the given prices. The demand curve
shifts from D to D_2 on Fig. 1.4.

There are a number of reasons why demand might increase or decrease.

1 Changes in real income (Note 1, p.140): If real incomes were to increase, it would seem reasonable to assume that more packets of tea would be consumed per day. Without trying to confuse the issue, it is worth pointing out that some people might consume less tea as a result of an increase in their income. The explanation of this could be that they consumed tea, despite the fact that they preferred coffee, because it was cheaper. Their higher income now enables them to drink coffee. In their eyes, they have switched from an **inferior** to a **superior** product.

2 Changes in the price of other goods: Coffee might be thought of as a substitute for tea. The two goods are in **competitive demand**. The price of coffee might rise so as to cause a contraction in its demand. Some of those consumers no longer drinking coffee would switch to tea, thereby causing an increase in the demand for tea. Tea-pots and tea, on the other hand, are complementary goods. They are in **joint demand**. If the price of tea were to rise significantly, causing a contraction in its demand, the demand for tea-pots would tend to decrease.

3 Changes in taste: A heavy advertising campaign for tea would, if successful, result in an increase in the demand for tea. A successful advertising campaign for coffee would tend to decrease the demand for tea. The introduction of a new hot drink on to the market could decrease the demand for tea. These could all be thought of as changes in taste.

4 Changes in population: A fall in the birthrate might result in a fall in the total population. This could result in a decrease in the demand for tea.

5 Changes in the availability of credit: Packets of tea are not normally bought on credit. You would not take out a mortgage, ask for hire-purchase facilities, or even use your credit card in order to pay. However, the availability of credit would affect the demand for houses, televisions, wall-to-wall carpeting, and so on. As credit becomes more available, demand for such products would increase.

1.3 Elasticity of demand

Elasticity of demand is an attempt to measure the responsiveness of the quantity demanded to changes in other variables. The demand for a given good will change as a result of a change in its own price, the price of other goods, or the real incomes of consumers. Elasticity measures the extent to which the quantity demanded changes.

Types of elasticity of demand

1 **Price elasticity of demand** measures the responsiveness of the quantity demanded of a good to changes in its own price. If the price of a packet of tea goes up by 10p, what will happen to the quantity of tea demanded?

2 **Cross elasticity of demand** measures the responsiveness of the quantity demanded to changes in the price of other goods. If the price of a jar of coffee goes up by 10p, what will happen to the quantity of tea demanded?

3 **Income elasticity of demand** measures the responsiveness of the quantity demanded of a good to a change in the real income of consumers. If, on average, real incomes increase by £1000 a year, what will happen to the quantity of tea demanded?

Types of coefficients of elasticity

The **coefficient of elasticity** provides a precise measure of elasticity and is given by the following formula:

$$\frac{\text{Percentage (\%) change in quantity demanded}}{\text{Percentage (\%) change in the variable}}$$

If the coefficient is greater than one (i.e. the percentage change in the quantity demanded is greater than the percentage change in the variable), demand is said to be **elastic**.

If the coefficient is less than one (i.e. the percentage change in the quantity demanded is less than the percentage change in the variable), demand is said to be **inelastic**.

If the coefficient is equal to one (i.e. both percentage changes are equal), demand is said to be **unitary**.

The direction of the changes $(+,-)$ will

determine the sign of the coefficient. The two extreme types of elasticity are where the coefficient equals zero (**perfectly inelastic demand**) and infinity (**perfectly elastic demand**). As there are three types of elasticity, there are three coefficients.

1 The **coefficient of price elasticity of demand** equals:

$$\frac{\text{Percentage (\%) change in quantity demanded}}{\text{Percentage (\%) change in price}}$$

Given the law of demand, the coefficient will always be negative, with a positive change in price resulting in a negative change in the quantity demanded and vice versa. However, the minus sign is often ignored. Whether or not demand is elastic, inelastic, or unitary for a particular price change has important implications for how the change will affect total expenditure on the good. The consumer's total expenditure is calculated by multiplying the price by the quantity consumed. From the producer's point of view this is the same as his **total revenue** (see Chapter 4, p.78).

If demand is elastic a rise in price will result in a fall in total revenue, while a fall in price will result in an increase in total revenue. If demand is inelastic a rise in price will result in an increase in total revenue, while a fall in price will result in a decrease in total revenue. If demand is unitary, the change in price will leave total revenue unaltered.

Consider Fig. 1.5. If the price falls from *a* to *d*, total revenue increases (*def0 > abc0*). For this price change, the demand curve is elastic. If the price falls by the same amount, but this time from *g* to *j*, total revenue decreases (*jkl0<ghi0*). For this price change the demand curve is inelastic.

Price elasticity of demand will vary along the length of the demand curve in all but three cases:
a) The perfectly elastic demand curve (horizontal) will have a coefficient of infinity throughout its length.
b) The perfectly inelastic demand curve (vertical) will have a coefficient of zero throughout its length.

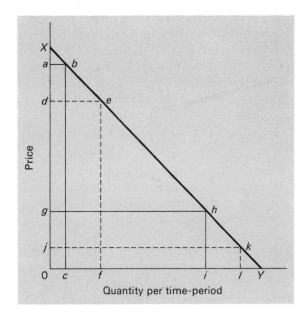

Fig. 1.5   Elasticity along a demand curve

c) The unitary demand curve (rectangular hyperbola) will have a coefficient of one throughout its length.

Rather than calculate price elasticity for a particular price change, it is possible to calculate it for a point on the demand curve. The coefficient for a given point on a straight-line demand curve is given by dividing the distance down the curve to the quantity axis by the distance up the curve to the price axis from the point in question. For example, the coefficient at point *h* on the demand curve in Fig. 1.5 is equal to $Yh \div hX$. Clearly this will be less than one, making demand at this point inelastic. Note 4 (p.140) provides an explanation of this although the mathematical proof is avoided.

What factors determine the degree of price elasticity of demand for a good? The most important is the **availability of close substitutes** in the relevant price range. The more close substitutes there are available for a good whose price changes, the more elastic its demand will be. Another important factor is the proportion of a consumer's income spent on the good. The smaller the proportion is, the more price inelastic demand will be. Other factors might be considered. For example, the demand for addictive goods

13

will usually be price inelastic, while the demand for most goods tends to be more price elastic in the long run. However, factors such as these are little more than extensions of the first.

2 The **coefficient of cross elasticity of demand** equals:

Percentage (%) change in quantity demanded of good *A*
———————————————————————
Percentage (%) change in price of good *B*

The coefficient may be positive or negative. Goods in competitive demand will have positive cross elasticities. For example, an increase in the price of coffee will increase the demand for tea.

Goods in joint demand will have negative cross elasticities. For instance, an increase in the price of record-players will reduce the demand for records. The coefficient will be high for goods that are very close substitutes or complements and low when they are neither substitutes nor complements.

3 The **coefficient of income elasticity of demand** equals:

Percentage (%) change in quantity demanded
———————————————————————
Percentage (%) change in real income

The coefficient can be either positive or negative. Consumers will usually react to an increase in real income by consuming more; hence a positive coefficient. However, in the case of **inferior goods** the opposite will be true. Potatoes might be thought of as an inferior good. People on low incomes may eat a lot of them as they are cheap and filling. An increase in income will result in them consuming fewer potatoes and more expensive food such as steak.

1.4 Summary

In looking at the theory of demand, we have explained what economists mean by the demand for a product. We have also considered what factors might affect the level of demand and how responsive demand might be to changes in these factors. Similar questions will now be answered regarding the behaviour of producers (the theory of supply).

Chapters 2 and 3 will provide more detail about certain aspects of consumer demand.

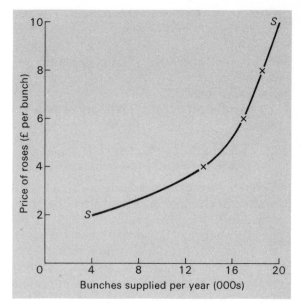

Fig. 1.6   A supply curve

2 Producers' supply

2.1 The law of supply and the supply curve

As with demand it is **effective supply** that is important. This is the quantity that producers would supply at a given price over a given period of time. Supply figures can be provided for a single firm or in the case of **aggregate** or **market supply** for all the firms in a given industry.

The relationship between price and the quantity supplied is given by the **law of supply**: the higher the price is, the greater will be the quantity offered for sale, all other factors being held constant. A detailed explanation of this positive relationship is given in Chapter 4 (Fig. 4.11, p.83). For the time being it is enough to assume that, in the market as a whole, higher prices will result in higher profit levels, and higher profit levels will act as an incentive to present producers to produce more and to new firms to enter the market. Such a reaction is in accordance with the basic assumption that firms are profit maximizers.

If supply is calculated over a given price range and expressed as a table, this is called a **supply schedule** (Table 1.2). When this schedule is plotted graphically, this gives us a

Table 1.2   A supply schedule

Price of roses (£ per bunch)	Bunches supplied per year (000s)
10	20·0
8	18·5
6	17·0
4	13·5
2	4·0

supply curve (Fig. 1.6). Given the law of supply, the supply curve will always slope upwards from left to right.

2.2 Changes in supply

An increase in price will result in an **extension** in supply, while a decrease will result in a **contraction**. For example, an increase in the price of a bunch of roses from £6 to £8 will cause an extension in supply of 1500 bunches per year. The supply curve itself does not move; the movement is along the curve.

Increases and **decreases** in supply will cause the position of the supply curve to shift to the right and left respectively. Different quantities will be supplied at each price. Consider Fig. 1.7. A shift in the supply curve from SS to S_1S_1 represents an increase in supply: at price A, the quantity supplied has increased from X to Z. Returning to the original supply curve SS, price would have had to increase from A to B in order to bring about an extension in supply equal in size to the above increase, i.e. XZ.

A shift in the supply curve from SS to S_2S_2 represents a decrease in supply: at price A, the quantity supplied has deceased from X to Y. A fall in price from A to C would have been necessary for supply to have contracted by the same amount.

Causes of increases or decreases in supply

The basic factor influencing the willingness and ability of producers to supply is the costs of production: the money they have to pay in order to employ the factors of production or resources they need. At any given price, as costs increase so the profitability of the product

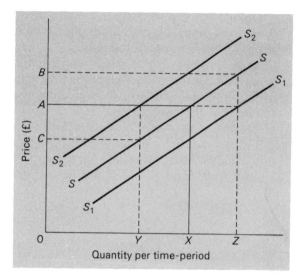

Fig. 1.7   Movements along and shifts in a supply curve

decreases. Producers will react to lower profits by either producing less or leaving the industry. Therefore, the quantity supplied will decrease.

Several of the following factors relate to changes in the firm's costs (Fig. 1.7).

1 Changes in the price of factors of production: For the firms producing roses, an increase in their workers' wages constitutes an increase in the price they pay for labour and, therefore, their costs. This would shift the supply curve from SS to S_2S_2. A fall in the cost of fertilizer, on the other hand, would shift the curve from SS to S_1S_1. Given that profit is the price of enterprise, even changes in profit margins would cause the supply curve to shift.

2 Changes in technology: The introduction of a new and more efficient cultivation technique would reduce costs and shift the supply curve to the right from SS to S_1S_1.

3 Changes in government policy: There are several circumstances where government policy will influence supply. Perhaps the most significant is through the imposition of indirect taxation. If a tax were imposed on roses, producers would react as if this were a new additional cost. The supply curve would shift to the left from SS to S_2S_2. Legal restriction on the production of a good

15

would shift its supply curve to the left, while the subsidizing of a good's production would shift its supply curve to the right.

4   Changes in the price of other goods: If the price of another good increases this will increase its profitability, thus making the production of it more attractive. If the price of carnations increases, resources may shift from the production of roses to the production of carnations. The supply curve for roses would shift from SS to S_2S_2. Roses and carnations are said to be in competitive supply. Beef and hides are in joint supply so that if an increase in the price of beef caused an extension in its supply, this would in turn cause an increase in the supply of hides. The supply curve for hides would shift from SS to S_1S_1.

5   Other factors: The supply of some goods varies with natural circumstances such as the weather. Human factors such as wars and strikes affect the supply of others.

Fig. 1.8   Elastic supply

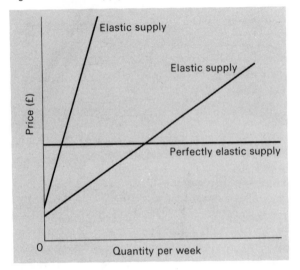

Fig. 1.9   Unitary supply

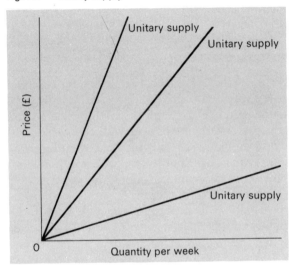

Fig. 1.10   Inelastic supply

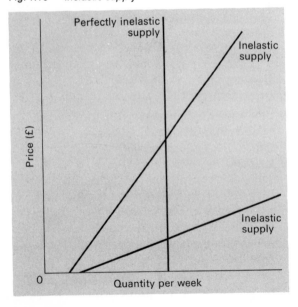

Fig. 1.11   Non-linear supply

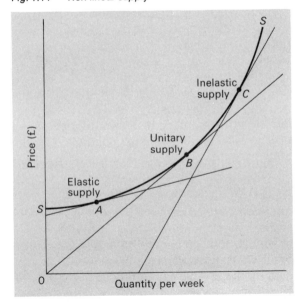

2.3 Elasticity of supply

Unlike our approach to demand elasticity, we are only interested in the responsiveness of the quantity supplied to changes in one variable: the price of the good itself. **Price elasticity of supply** can be measured arithmetically, using the following formula:

$$\frac{\text{Percentage (\%) change in quantity supplied}}{\text{Percentage (\%) change in price}}$$

If this coefficient of elasticity is greater than one, supply is **elastic**. If it is less than one, supply is **inelastic**. If it is equal to one, supply is **unitary**.

A vertical supply curve is said to be **perfectly inelastic** and the coefficient would be zero. A horizontal supply curve is said to be **perfectly elastic** and the coefficient would be infinity.

The law of supply means that the price elasticity of supply will always be **positive**.

Consider Figs. 1.8 to 1.11:

1 In Fig. 1.8 all straight-line supply curves that intersect the vertical axis are elastic.
2 In Fig. 1.9 all straight-line supply curves that pass through the origin have unitary elasticity.
3 In Fig. 1.10 all straight-line supply curves that intersect the horizontal axis are inelastic.
4 In Fig. 1.11 elasticity at a point on a curve is found by drawing a tangent and finding the point of intersection with the axis.

A mathematical background may enable you to find the explanation of these diagrams, but such a mathematical proof is beyond the scope of this book.

Factors determining elasticity of supply

Clearly, the ease with which output can be increased in response to changes in price will determine the elasticity of supply. This will depend upon the degree of **flexibility of productive resources**. Where stocks can be fed on to the market easily, where excess capacity exists, and where additional resources are readily available, supply will be elastic.

In any assessment of elasticity of supply the time-period is crucial. It is useful to distinguish

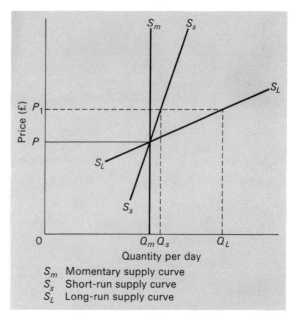

S_m Momentary supply curve
S_s Short-run supply curve
S_L Long-run supply curve

Fig. 1.12   Elasticity of supply and the time-period

between the very short run (momentary), the short run, and the long run (Fig. 1.12).

Consider a fisherman who sells his catch on the quayside at the end of each day's fishing. In the very short run (S_m), supply is fixed, i.e. perfectly inelastic. Whatever price his fish fetch on a given day, he cannot increase the amount made available to the market that day. The quantities of all factors of production employed are fixed and, therefore, supply is fixed.

If the price on a particular day is high, and if the fisherman expects it to remain so, he may want to supply more the following day. The flexibility of the resources available to him will determine to what extent he can do this. He could quickly hire extra hands and set out earlier. Such options are open to him in the short run (S_s). During this time-period the quantities of certain factors may be variable, but the supply of at least one factor remains fixed.

However, to increase his daily supply even further, he may need to buy a second fishing-boat and find enough labour to man it. All this will take time – the long run (S_L). In the long run all factors are variable. Unfortunately for the fisherman, he has to contend with further factors such as the weather, EEC regulations, and luck.

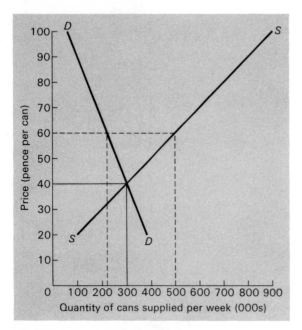

Fig. 1.13   The equilibrium price

Table 1.3   Demand and supply schedules

Price (pence per can)	Cans demanded per week (000s)	Cans supplied per week (000s)
100	60	900
80	140	700
60	220	500
40	300	300
20	380	100

3 The price mechanism

Having outlined demand theory and supply theory, we shall now bring together the behaviour of consumers and producers in the form of the **price mechanism**.

3.1 Price determination

The equilibrium price

The information in Table 1.3 relates to the market for dog food. From this information the supply and demand curves can be plotted on the same graph (Fig. 1.13). At a price of 60p dog owners will demand only 220 000 cans per week. This is 280 000 short of the quantity that the firms have put on to the market. An **excess supply** of 280 000 cans will be left unsold.

During the following weeks the firms will lower their price and, therefore, the quantity they are willing to supply. As the price is lowered there will be an extension in demand. For this reason, the firms will not need to lower their weekly supply by the full 280 000 cans. When the weekly supply is down by 200 000 cans to 300 000, demand will have extended to the point where it equals supply at a price of 40p. This is the **equilibrium price**: the price at which the quantity demanded by consumers is exactly matched by the quantity supplied by the firms. As long as the conditions of supply and demand remain unchanged, there will be no tendency to move away from this price. The effect of excess supply is clearly to put downward pressure on the price.

Had the initial price been set at 20p, the firms would have placed 100 000 cans on the market, only to find a demand for 380 000 cans. There would therefore have been an **excess demand** of 280 000 cans. This time the firms would increase output, thereby increasing price and reducing demand until the equilibrium price of 40p is once again reached.

The effects of shifts in supply and demand

We have seen that various factors can cause the demand and supply curves to shift to the right

Fig. 1.14   Shifts in supply and demand

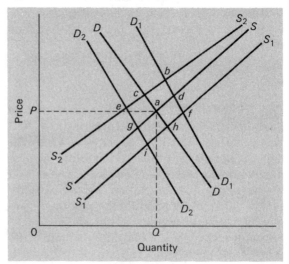

or to the left. Such shifts signify increases and decreases in demand and supply. We are now in a position to analyse the effects of such changes in conditions on price and quantity within the market.

Consider Fig. 1.14 and Table 1.4. In each case take equilibrium point *a* as representing the original situation. The table specifies the product being sold in the market and the changes in market conditions. Cover the right-hand column and work out each new equilibrium point. Then check that your answers are correct.

3.2 *Resource allocation*

There are three interrelated aspects of resource allocation — three areas in which decisions have to be made. Given the conditions of perfect competition, the price mechanism solves all three problems simultaneously.

1 Firstly, a decision has to be made about **what** goods and services to produce with the available resources.
2 Secondly, a decision has to be made about **how** to combine the available resources in order to produce each type of good or service.

3 Finally, a decision has to be made about **for whom** different goods and services are produced.

These are sometimes thought of as **allocative**, **productive**, and **distributive** choices respectively.

How, then, does the price mechanism make these choices? Within a market economy everything has a price. Every good, every service, and every factor of production has a price. Each commodity is sold within a market where the forces of supply and demand interact to determine these prices (see paragraph 3.1 above).

What to produce

If more of a commodity is demanded at its present market price, the increased demand will shift the demand curve to the right. This will create excess demand which will put upward pressure on the price. The higher price will attract extra resources to the industry and more will be supplied. Extra resources could also be attracted to a specific industry as a result of lower costs. A reduction in costs would shift the supply curve to the right. This would result in lower prices, thereby causing an extension in demand.

Table 1.4   The effects of changing supply and demand conditions

Product	Changes in conditions	New equilibrium point
Holidays in Brighton	A successful advertising campaign by the Brighton Tourist Board	*d*: both price and quantity go up
Beer	An increase in the tax on beer	*c*: price goes up, quantity goes down
Books	An increase in printing costs	*c*: price goes up, quantity goes down
Dog food	Improved techniques reduce cost of canning	*h*: price goes down, quantity goes up
Record players	An increase in the price of records due to an increase in the cost of materials	*g*: both price and quantity go down
Tea	An increase in the price of coffee due to a bad coffee harvest	*d*: both price and quantity go up
Houses	A fall in the cost of a mortgage and an increase in the price of land	*b*: both price and quantity go up
Hides	An increase in the quantity of beef consumed and leather becomes an increasingly fashionable material	*f*: price stays the same, quantity goes up
Fish	A fall in the price of meat due to a government subsidy and a fall in the wages of fishermen	*i*: both price and quantity go down
Plastic flowers	A fall in the price of real flowers due to an increase in supply and an increase in the price of plastic	*e*: price goes up, quantity goes down

In this way changes in supply and demand alter the relative prices of commodities, which in turn determine the relative quantities of goods and services to be produced. The price mechanism has made a choice about what to produce, and has thereby determined to which industries and in what relative quantities resources should be allocated.

How to produce

In order to maximize profits under conditions of perfect competition, costs must always be minimized. Scarce resources must be employed so as to maximize possible output. At any point in time a cheaper method of production will always replace a more expensive one. Those producers who can meet the demand of consumers at the lowest price will expand, while those who cannot will go out of business. This price competition between producers or firms has determined how commodities are produced. The price mechanism has made a choice regarding the combination of factors that should be used in each industry.

For whom to produce

The forces of supply and demand in the market for factors of production determine for whom goods and services are produced. In such markets the price of the factor constitutes the income of the owner of the factor. The size of each individual's income determines his potential claim on the goods and services that are available. Some individuals are in a position to provide land, capital, and enterprise and depending on the market conditions, these will earn them varying amounts of income in the form of rent, interest, and profit.

For most people all they have to sell is their labour. What it earns them will depend upon the market conditions that exist for the type of labour they have to sell. The demand for computer programmers may be increasing while the demand for office clerks is falling. The price or wage of the computer programmer will tend to rise while that of the office clerk will tend to fall. The computer programmer will be able to consume more of the available goods and services while the office clerk will consume less. Not surprisingly, more people will want to become computer programmers and fewer will want to be office clerks. Chapter 5 provides a more detailed analysis of productive and distributive choices.

Summary

The whole system operates so as to reconcile the demand for goods by individuals and the demand for factors by firms with the supply of goods by firms and the supply of factors by individuals. Individuals as consumers interact with firms in the markets for goods and services. Individuals as owners of factors of production interact with firms in the markets for factors of production. The interaction establishes prices and, along with the resulting profits and losses, they act as signals to both consumers and producers. By responding to these signals, choices are made about what, how, and for whom to produce.

3.3 Efficiency

Does the price mechanism result in an **efficient** allocation of resources? Before answering the question, it is necessary to consider the meaning of 'efficient' in this context. In trying to establish a meaning, the subject of **welfare economics** will be introduced. As a starting-point we can assume that the aim of an economic system should be to satisfy as many of the insatiable needs of the community as possible given the scarce resources at its disposal. The aim should be to maximize the level of satisfaction or 'welfare' within the community. We are now faced with the problem of defining and even measuring welfare.

Welfare could be defined in terms of the quantity of goods made available to the community: the greater the quantity, the higher the level of welfare. However, this is a very materialistic approach, and satisfaction or welfare can often be achieved through activities other than the consumption of economic goods — a swim in the sea, prayer, job satisfaction, and so on. Increased production of goods and services may indirectly decrease welfare. Increased pollution may make the sea a less pleasant place to swim, increased levels of noise may interrupt the tranquillity of prayer, increased specialization of workers may increase output but reduce job satisfaction as work becomes repetitive and monotonous.

Trying to arrive at a precise measurement of changes in welfare introduces further difficulties. Consider a situation where an economy has increased its output of cigarettes by one million. Can we take this increase in quantity as a positive measure of the increase in welfare? The subjective nature of satisfaction or welfare means that we cannot. Amongst smokers the consumption of more cigarettes will give some more satisfaction than others. If a particular individual were to double the number he smokes, this would not necessarily double his satisfaction. Amongst non-smokers, at best their satisfaction will be unaltered, at worst the additional pollution of the atmosphere may reduce their welfare. Problems such as these make the measurement of total levels of welfare and changes in welfare very difficult.

In order to 'judge' the price mechanism we shall ignore many of the above difficulties and define welfare as the satisfaction or benefit gained from the production and consumption of economic goods. Producers and consumers are involved in such economic activity. It is their gain in benefit that must be maximized for an efficient allocation of resources to exist.

Whenever it is possible to increase someone's benefit without reducing that of someone else, then total welfare can be increased. Under such circumstances the existing resource allocation is not yet an efficient one. Welfare is maximized when it is impossible to increase the benefit gained by any one person without reducing that of someone else. This is called the **Pareto criterion** and was originally formulated by the Italian economist Vilfredo Pareto.

Taking this definition of welfare maximization, it is now necessary to show that the price mechanism will result in such an outcome. In order to do this two further concepts relating to the benefit gained by consumers and producers will be introduced.

Consumer surplus

Consider the demand curve in Fig. 1.15. Assume that the price is P. This will be the amount paid for each of the Q units consumed. In fact consumers would have been willing to pay more. For unit Q_1 they would have paid P_1, and in the same way the demand curve shows the price they would be prepared to give for each individual unit. The difference between what consumers actually pay (PBQO) and what they would have been willing to pay (ABQO) is called **consumer surplus** (ABP). This represents the benefit or welfare gained by consumers in excess of what they have paid for.

Producer surplus

Consider the supply curve in Fig. 1.16. Assume that the market price is P. This will be the amount received for each of the Q units supplied. In fact producers would have been willing to accept less. Unit Q_1 would have been supplied for a price of P_1, and in the same way the supply curve shows the price at which they would have been willing to supply each individual unit. The difference between the total revenue that producers actually receive (PBQO) and the total revenue that they would

Fig. 1.15   Consumer surplus

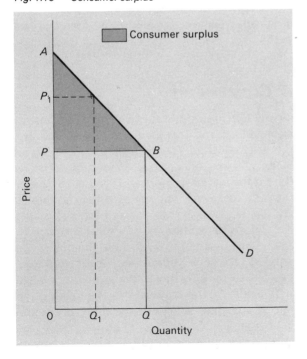

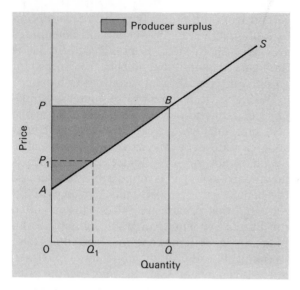

Fig. 1.16   *Producer surplus*

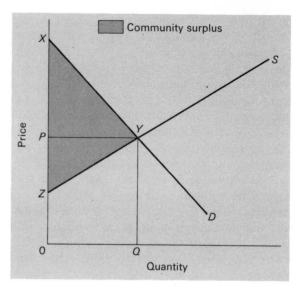

Fig. 1.17   *Community surplus*

have been willing to accept (*ABQO*) is called **producer surplus** (*PBA*). This represents the benefit or welfare gained by producers and is in fact equal to their profit.

The argument in favour of the price mechanism

Remembering that consumers and producers are the only people involved in economic activity, consider Fig. 1.17 in terms of consumer and producer surplus. The diagram represents the market supply and demand conditions in a given perfect market. From our previous analysis:

$$\text{Consumer surplus} = XYP$$
$$\text{Producer surplus} = ZYP$$

Therefore:

Community surplus = consumer surplus +
producer surplus
= *XYP* + *ZYP*
= *XYZ*

The argument in favour of the price mechanism rests on the fact that it can be shown geometrically that *no* other price/quantity combination will result in as much surplus benefit for the community. Any movement away from this equilibrium combination will

result in a loss of surplus benefit to someone within the community: in this way the Pareto criterion is being satisfied and welfare, therefore, is being maximized.

The work in Chapters 2 and 4 allows an alternative explanation of how the price mechanism leads to an optimum allocation of resources. This approach is based upon **marginal analysis** and is given in an appendix on p.138.

4 Conclusion

Given the assumptions necessary for perfect competition and for our definition of welfare, the price mechanism has been shown to result in an efficient allocation of resources. This is the traditional case for the market economy.

In the real world, however, things are not so simple. Markets are not always perfect. Broader definitions of welfare may be more applicable. The many assumptions cannot be taken for granted. In some situations, even with the major assumptions intact, the price mechanism will result in the production of too much or too little, that is a non-efficient allocation of resources. Situations such as these are examples of market failure.

Part 2 *New theories of market failure*

Whenever the price mechanism fails to produce an optimum allocation of resources **market failure** can be said to exist. Looking around the world we live in, examples of market failure are not hard to find: food mountains, poverty, congestion, and pollution are but a few. In general terms market failure can be seen as overproduction in some markets and underproduction in others.

Where the market system fails there would seem to be a case for the state to step in. However, there are many questions to be asked about the form and extent of state intervention. It too has to be assessed in terms of efficiency. Intervention can take the form of **state provision**. A whole industry can be taken over by the state (e.g. coal mining in the UK) or only a part of an industry which then exists alongside private enterprise (e.g. British Leyland in the UK).

A further type of state intervention is through the use of **subsidies** and **taxation**. If the theatre is subsidized, more scarce resources will be allocated to its provision than there would have been under a pure market system. Alcohol can be heavily taxed, thereby reducing the resources allocated to its production.

Several forms of state intervention could come under the general heading of **state regulation**. Where imperfections in the market system have resulted in underproduction, the state might enforce a system of rationing or queueing. Where overproduction is the problem, production ceilings may be imposed. If the prices generated by the market system are considered unacceptable, maximum and minimum prices can be set.

The rest of this chapter will look at some of the main causes of market failure and at how government intervention tries to take account of them.

1 Monopoly and monopsony

The market system only results in an efficient allocation of resources as long as all the markets are perfect. The assumptions necessary for the existence of a perfect market mean that all of the many firms are price-takers and that this price is given by the intersection of the supply and the demand curves for the industry. However, in some markets varying degrees of monopoly will develop. Instead of many firms there will only be a few or, in the extreme case, only one.

The first point to notice is that such firms are no longer price-takers. Given certain assumptions price can be set higher and output lower under monopoly conditions than under perfect competition. This will be explained in detail in Chapter 4, p.84.

Consider Fig 1.18. It represents the supply and demand conditions in a given market. Under conditions of perfect competition the equilibrium price would be P, while the quantity would be Q. The outcome is an efficient allocation of resources and welfare is maximized. The total surplus to the community as a whole is at its maximum level and equal to the triangle *ade*.

However, if the total supply is controlled by one firm (the monopolist) rather than the many firms necessary for a perfect market, this single

Fig. 1.18   *Monopoly as a market failure: overpricing*

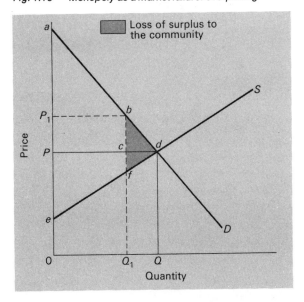

producer has the power to choose a different price/quantity combination, given the constraint of existing demand conditions. What if he were to choose P_1/Q_1?

Under perfect market conditions the producer surplus or profit was the triangle Pde. With the new price/quantity combination the producer surplus has increased by the rectangle P_1bcP, while decreasing by the triangle cdf. This is a net increase in profit. As a profit maximizer the monopolist would choose this price/quantity combination rather than that dictated by the price mechanism.

By following this line of action, the monopolist has reduced the consumer surplus by P_1bdP. As this reduction in consumer surplus is greater than the increase in producer surplus, there has clearly been a loss to the community as a whole. The new total surplus is equal to $abfe$, so that the loss of surplus is equal to the triangle bdf. (See Chapter 4, Fig. 4.14, p.85 to discover exactly which price/quantity combination the monopolist would choose.)

The outcome of all this is that the monopolist's behaviour has resulted in a misallocation of resources, despite the fact that the monopolist is better off. From the point of view of economic efficiency, too few resources are being devoted to the production of this good, and hence too many are being devoted to other products. The existence of monopoly has resulted in a situation where it would be possible to make at least one person better off without someone else becoming worse off. The Pareto criterion is no longer satisfied.

Another related practice adopted by monopolists is **price discrimination** (see Chapter 4, Fig. 4.15, p.86). Here the monopolist can, under certain conditions, use his power within the market in order to sell the same good to different consumers at different prices. The monopolist may differentiate between consumers in different parts of the country, consumers of different ages, consumers with different incomes, those who consume at different times of the day, and so on.

Monopoly power can also be found in the markets for factors of production and such a monopolist could differentiate between users by charging different prices for the same factor.

For example, British Gas has been known to charge large industrial contract users a lower price than other gas users such as smaller industrial and commercial customers or households. Any form of price discrimination will break the conditions necessary for perfect competition and once again resources will be misallocated within the economy.

Monopoly does not only occur on the sellers' side of the market. Just as perfect competition assumes many sellers, it also assumes many buyers. Where a single buyer is no longer a price-taker but powerful enough to influence the price he pays, **monopsony** is said to exist. The monopsonist may use his market power to lower the price below that which would be established by the market forces under conditions of perfect competition. Again, this would cause a misallocation of resources with a loss of welfare to the community as a whole, despite any gains made by the monopsonist.

Consider Fig. 1.19. Under perfect market conditions the price would be P, while the quantity would be Q. The total surplus to the community (i.e. consumer surplus + producer surplus) is being maximized at a level equal to the triangle adg. Now assume that the consumer uses his monopsony power to lower the price to P_1. Consumer surplus has then increased by $PceP_1$, while falling by bcd. This

Fig. 1.19   *Monopsony as a market failure: underpricing*

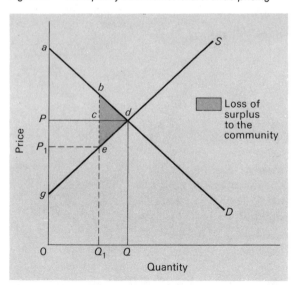

is a net gain. The producer surplus has fallen by $PdeP_1$. As this reduction in producer surplus is greater than the increase in consumer surplus, there has clearly been a loss to the community as a whole. The new total surplus is *abeg*, so that the loss of surplus is equal to the triangle *bde*. This analysis is of course the same as the one applied to the monopolist.

Examples of monopsony can be found where firms are selling a specific car component to a single car manufacturer or where producers of North Sea gas are faced with one buyer in the form of British Gas. The best examples, however, are often found in the labour market. The government is often the major buyer or employer of a particular type of labour. In this way the markets for teachers and doctors display monopsony characteristics (see Chapter 5, p.118).

Whilst considering monopoly as an example of market failure, it is worth mentioning the concept of **natural monopoly**. A natural monopoly is an industry where costs are minimized only if one firm satisfies the whole market. Public utilities such as gas, electricity, and water are typical examples. The most common feature of such industries is large fixed costs or overheads that result from the technical characteristics of production. More exactly, it is the size of these costs relative to the size of the potential market that is important. Where fixed costs are high relative to market size, the market cannot sustain more than one firm as only a single firm could cover its costs.

For example, to set up the basic network of lines necessary for a telephone service is a great expense. Extra users can 'plug' themselves into the system quite easily, but it would be an inefficient and wasteful use of resources if separate companies each had their own network taking in every town and running down every street. For this type of reason it is considered desirable to allow one firm to have the entire market to itself. A similar argument can be made for allowing a small village to have just one launderette (a local monopoly).

Taking the natural monopoly argument to the extreme, what if even the single firm's output fails to reduce costs to a point where a profit can be made? If no profits are being made, the firm will be unable to remain in business and the market system will fail to produce the good at all. The country would find itself without a telephone service and the village would be without a launderette.

Market intervention

It is in the case of natural monopoly that the most extreme form of state intervention—state provision through nationalization—is usually found. Examples in the UK are British Gas, the Central Electricity Generating Board, and the Water Board. However, the government can adopt other approaches in an attempt to minimize the misallocation of resources due to the existence of monopoly. Monopolies can be forcibly broken up, mergers that could create a monopoly can be declared illegal, and the behaviour of monopolies in terms of their pricing policies, etc. can be regulated. The British government tries to monitor monopoly behaviour in this way through institutions such as the Monopolies and Mergers Commission and the Restrictive Practices Court.

We have already established that a social cost is associated with monopoly. Government legislation in this area has encouraged institutions such as these to compare this loss of welfare with any benefits that might accrue from a particular monopoly. In the light of this comparison it must be decided whether or not the monopoly or proposed monopoly is in the public interest. The Monopolies and Mergers Commission prevented the proposed merger between Sealink UK and European Ferries in 1981 as it was felt it would not be in the public interest. The Commission felt that the resulting market domination could have led to higher prices and a reduction in services as well as making it increasingly difficult for other firms to enter the market.

An important potential benefit of a monopoly would be lower costs due to large-scale production. Others might be greater market stability, higher exports, and increased research and development.

Since the Fair Trading Act of 1973, the Director-General of Fair Trading has controlled the supervision and implementation of monopoly legislation as part of his general responsibility of protecting consumers' interests.

2 Advertising

The sort of power that monopoly producers enjoy may also be used to induce changes in demand. The price mechanism sees the consumer as 'king'. The concept of **consumer sovereignty** implies that through the price mechanism resources are allocated in line with consumer preferences.

However, through advertising producers may have the power to control the direction and speed of change in consumers' taste. The sellers become very good at selling and consumers find themselves buying things they do not really want. This has been described as **producer sovereignty** and it may result in a distortion of the market. As well as increasing the demand for a product, it is possible through advertising to make the demand for it more inelastic. Higher profits can be made by increasing sales and prices.

Demand is directed towards the goods that producers feel like producing and the resulting allocation of resources fails to reflect the 'true' wants and needs of consumers. Rather it reflects the 'false' wants and needs created by producers. How often are heavily advertised toys discarded by the end of Christmas week. Taken to its extreme this type of market failure is seen by some as one of the evils of modern capitalism. Others are less convinced and doubt that there is any such thing as 'true' or naturally innate consumer preferences. There are clearly many normative issues surrounding the role of advertising.

3 Distribution of income

The traditional argument that concludes with the price mechanism resulting in a socially desirable outcome, seen in terms of the maximization of welfare, involves an assumption that we have not yet highlighted. There is an implicit assumption that the existing distribution of income and wealth is 'fair' or 'equit-

able'. Given the existing distribution, the market mechanism will result in an economically efficient outcome, that is costs will be minimized while satisfaction will be maximized. However, the mechanism can provide as many technically efficient outcomes as there are possible distributions of income and wealth. It has been suggested that a fundamental weakness of welfare economics is its apparent inability to choose between these possible outcomes.

The normative problem of what constitutes a 'fair' distribution rests upon what is meant by 'fairness'. Is there such a thing as an objectively fair or equitable distribution of income and wealth?

Markets respond to 'votes' cast by consumers in the form of their everyday decisions regarding what to buy. Therefore, the more money you have, the more votes you have, and as a result you have a bigger say in how resources are allocated. This, of course, can result in scarce resources being used to produce luxuries for the rich, while the poor go without necessities. The market mechanism, whilst being economically efficient, is capable of producing extreme poverty. The market mechanism treats different people differently. Can such inequality be thought of as a further example of market failure?

It might be helpful to ask how a given distribution of income has come about. The market system operates through providing incentives, and this results in the system itself distributing income and wealth. Those who possess abilities or own resources which are both scarce and in great demand earn high incomes. International sportsmen earn high wages, and owners of property in Oxford Street earn high rent. People whose abilities and resources are less valued will earn low incomes. The redundant textile worker will have little hope of high future rewards, and the owner of obsolete equipment will earn little from its employment. Similarly, entrepreneurs who make the right decisions will earn large incomes in the form of profit, while those who make the wrong decisions will make losses.

Supporters of the market mechanism, or *laissez-faire*, argue that in this way income is distributed according to the contribution individuals make to production. Such 'market justice' may be interpreted as 'fair'.

Others, however, would not see such a distributive process as inherently fair. Abilities and the ownership of resources are not shared out equally and this generates the problem of poverty. Imperfections in the market system such as discrimination are also identified. Economic discrimination occurs when equivalent factors of production earn different incomes for equal contributions to output. Although difficult to quantify, there is evidence to suggest that discrimination exists in terms of sex, colour, and social background. Discrimination is not simply related to employment opportunities but also to educational opportunities which in turn influence ultimate employment. Nor is discrimination only a matter of paying unequal wages for the same work; women might simply never be promoted to high income jobs.

Critics of the market system's role in the distribution of income and wealth might also point to the part played by inherited wealth and luck. They would question whether there is anything inherently fair about the influence of these two factors. The majority of the very rich acquired their initial wealth as a result of the activities of others. Some achieved their wealth through good luck, e.g. the farmer who finds oil on his land. And some can blame bad luck for their present situation, e.g. the student who trains to be a teacher only to find that a fall in the birth-rate results in no job opportunities.

There are two interrelated problems regarding the whole area of income distribution. Firstly, is there any such thing as the optimum distribution? Is it possible to determine an ideal amount of inequality in order to provide incentives? Secondly, if there is an ideal distribution, does the price mechanism go any way towards achieving it? Economic analysis has something to offer in trying to answer these questions and some work has been done. However, the issues involved are so loaded with value judgements that no precise answers have emerged.

Market intervention

To the extent that market failure of this type does exist, state intervention would take the form of the **redistribution** of income and wealth. In general terms this can be done in two ways.

The first involves taking from some people in order to give to others. Clearly this would involve **taxation** and government expenditure decisions. This approach alters the relative incentives that the market mechanism would provide. If you are to be deprived of part of what you earn, your incentive to earn, so the argument goes, will decrease. Although doubts have been expressed about the extent of this effect, any tendency towards such an outcome will distort the incentives thrown up by the market system.

The second approach involves the manipulation of prices so that some earn more, while others earn less, than they would have done. Where governments impose minimum wage rates on employers or maximum rent charges on landlords, they are indulging in this type of behaviour. Again the working of the price mechanism is being distorted. Figs. 1.20 and 1.21 highlight some of the possible outcomes.

Assume that Fig. 1.20 represents the market conditions for a particular type of labour. In the absence of government intervention the equilibrium wage would be W with Q workers being

Fig. 1.20   Fixing a minimum price, e.g. minimum wage legislation

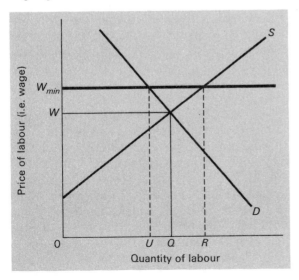

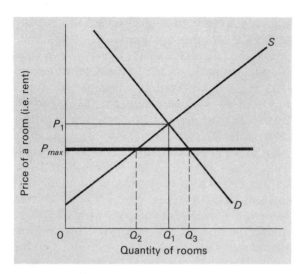

Fig. 1.21   Fixing a maximum price, e.g. in the market for rented accommodation

employed. If this wage is considered 'unacceptably low', the government may set a minimum wage of W_{min}. Unfortunately, this increase in real income may be at the expense of the number of workers employed. In Fig. 1.20 the number employed falls to U with perhaps as many as UR unemployed (R being the number of workers attracted to the market at the higher wage rate).

Assume that Fig. 1.21 represents the market for rented rooms. In the absence of controls, the equilibrium price would be P_1 with Q_1 rooms being occupied. If the government felt that such a price was beyond the means of many people, it might impose a price ceiling at P_{max}. However, only Q_2 rooms will now be made available, leaving an unsatisfied demand of Q_2Q_3. An accommodation shortage has been created.

If you accept that market failure exists in the first place, then state intervention could have potential benefits. If you feel that market forces should be allowed to determine distribution or that there is no guarantee that state intervention will improve the situation, then interference with the market mechanism will have potential costs. The potential benefits will have to be weighed against the potential costs.

4 Externalities

The market system operates so as to ensure that the consumers and producers directly involved receive the maximum benefit at the minimum cost. However, the activities of consumption and production can result in benefits other than those enjoyed by the consumer and costs other than those faced by the producer.

Imagine a toll bridge across a river mouth which saves a long detour through several villages. The users, that is the motorists, will happily pay the toll as using the bridge will save them a great deal of time and petrol. However, the users are not the only people to benefit. The residents of the villages will also benefit from the bridge as it will lead to less congestion, less air pollution, less noise, fewer accidents, and so on. These are **external benefits** which are not paid for by those who receive them.

The classic example of an **external cost** takes the form of pollution. A firm may be disposing of its waste by dumping it into a river at very little cost to itself. However, by polluting the river, it is imposing further costs on others. Those who used to fish and swim in the river can no longer do so, while those living by the river have to live with the smell. Indeed, should the pollution become a health hazard, resources would have to be used to fence off the river or even to carry out purification. These external costs are not borne by the firm whose productive activity has caused them.

Such externalities exist when the economic activity of consumers and producers causes benefits or costs to third parties without any equivalent compensation.

The price mechanism fails to take into account any external costs and benefits that might exist. The price mechanism only reacts to internal (or private) costs and benefits. The costs of production actually met by the firm in paying for the necessary factors of production are called **internal costs**. The benefits enjoyed by those actually consuming the firm's product are called **internal benefits** and they are reflected in the price paid. These internal costs and benefits manifest themselves as flows of money and it is to these that the price mechanism responds. External costs, as experienced by families living by polluted rivers, and external benefits, as experienced by families living in a bypassed village, fail to manifest themselves as flows of money. As a result they are ignored by the price mechanism.

The criticism of the market system that results from the above distinctions is that in order to maximize welfare through efficient resource allocation the full **social costs** and **social benefits** to society as a whole should be taken into account. These can be thought of as follows:

Social costs = all internal costs + all external costs
Social benefits = all internal benefits + all external benefits

The market system fails in so far as it only takes the internal costs and benefits into account.

What will be the outcome of this type of market failure? In broad terms, when a firm creates an external cost it is in effect getting something for nothing, for example free waste disposal. Not surprisingly, the firm will not be disposed to minimize such an external cost. On the other hand, if a firm provides an external benefit but receives no payment for it, it will not be disposed to devote many resources to the activity even if it is very socially desirable. For example, ramblers will benefit from the existence of pathways in the countryside, but farmers will spend little on their up-keep. The

outcome of this behaviour is illustrated in Figs. 1.22 and 1.23.

Consider Fig. 1.22. The normal working of the price mechanism would result in an output of Q. Now assume that there is an external cost to society as a whole which the producers do not have to pay. If the producers were forced to cover the full social cost of their activity, this extra cost would shift their supply curve from SS to S_1S_1 (we saw on page 15 that any increase in cost will shift the supply curve to the left). Always assuming that other things remain equal, this will reduce output to the lower level of Q_1. The general conclusion is that where firms cause external costs, and do not pay for them, they produce more than is socially desirable. There is then a misallocation of resources that can be seen in terms of overproduction. Indeed, if the firms produced less, not only could the reduced output in itself reduce the external cost, it would also release resources which could be used to reduce further the external cost.

A similar analysis can be applied to external benefits (Fig. 1.23). The normal working of the price mechanism would result in an output of Q. Now assume that there is an external benefit to society as a whole for which producers receive no payment. If consumers were forced to pay for the full social benefit they receive, this would shift the demand curve to the right from D to D_1. Consumers would have to pay a

Fig. 1.22   External costs as a market failure: overproduction

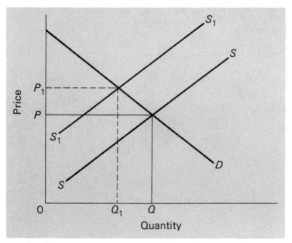

Fig. 1.23   External benefits as a market failure: underproduction

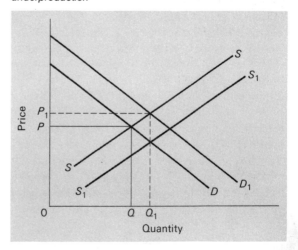

higher price for each possible quantity of output. This will have the effect of increasing output to the higher level of Q_1. This time the general conclusion is that where firms cause external benefits, they produce less than is socially desirable. There is a misallocation of resources that can be seen in terms of underproduction.

Market intervention

How might state intervention attempt to minimize the effect of this flaw? The basic approach of the government is to encourage activities that result in external benefits while discouraging those which result in external costs.

Assume that Fig. 1.22 applies to the market for cars. At a price of P a quantity equal to Q is sold. However, cars create an external cost in the form of exhaust fumes. What if the government passes legislation forcing car manufacturers to equip all cars with expensive anti-pollution exhaust systems? The producers' costs would rise, shifting the supply curve to the left (SS to S_1S_1). Fewer cars would be sold (Q_1), but pollution would be reduced. It is interesting to note that the higher price means that some of the extra cost has been passed on to the consumer. In fact, this is not an unreasonable outcome as they will benefit from lower levels of air pollution.

Rather than trying to control behaviour through legislation, the government might use subsidies or grants and taxation. Housing insulation has an external benefit to the community in terms of fuel conservation. As a result the government may give a grant to any householder who is willing to insulate his home. In terms of Fig. 1.23 the grant would have the effect of shifting the demand curve to the right (D to D_1). This will result in the socially optimum amount of insulation (Q_1). The same output could have been achieved by subsidizing the producers of home insulation. The subsidy would shift the supply curve in Fig. 1.23 from SS to S_1S_1, with the amount of insulation again reaching the socially optimum level of Q_1.

Some of the external costs generated by pollution have already been identified. One solution that has been put forward involves the government imposing a tax on firms which cause pollution. The more pollution they cause, the more tax they pay. The imposition of such a tax would shift the firms' supply curve to the left. In the case of Fig. 1.22 the supply curve would shift from SS to S_1S_1. This would result in the socially optimum output of Q_1. Once again the price will have increased, showing that some of the tax will have been passed on to the consumer. One advantage associated with this approach to the control of pollution is that it creates a continuing incentive to firms to try and reduce pollution. This is the only way in which they can reduce the tax.

In practice there are many problems associated with these attempts at government intervention. Ideally, the size of the grant, subsidy, or tax should be exactly equal to the external cost or benefit. The nature of such externalities makes them difficult to identify and even more difficult to measure in monetary terms. An approach called **cost benefit analysis** attempts to identify and place monetary values on time, health, noise, happiness, and so on. More will be said about this approach when looking at the next example of market failure.

5 Public goods

If goods are not profitable, the market system will fail to produce them. Any private business that fails to make a profit will soon go bankrupt. If such goods are considered necessary by a community despite their inability to be produced on a profitable basis, then production must be undertaken despite the negative signals of the price mechanism. Under these circumstances it is usually the government who will undertake such productive activity. Public goods fall into this category for they display two basic properties that together make their provision on a profitable basis very difficult.

The first property of a public good is that it cannot be supplied to one consumer without simultaneously being supplied to others. It is in this sense that the public good is an extreme example of externality theory. When the good is provided for one individual, it will bring external benefits to many others. This property is called **non-excludability**.

The second property is that once the good has been supplied to a single consumer there is no additional cost in supplying it to others. The supply of benefits generated by the good are in no way depleted no matter how many people use it. This property is called **non-rivalry**.

To bring out the significance of these two properties it may be useful first to contrast them with those properties displayed by the opposite type of commodity—the **private good**.

Imagine that you have bought a ticket for a football match. This is a private good. The fact that you have bought a ticket will not allow your friends to enjoy the game. They will be excluded from any benefits unless they too buy a ticket. Private goods display the property of **excludability**.

Your friends now decide that they would also like to watch the game. However, as there is a limited number of tickets, the fact that you have bought one means that there is one less available for your friends. As a result of buying a ticket you have depleted the supply. Some of your friends may find that there are no tickets left. All those who would like to watch the game are rivals for the limited number of tickets. Private goods display the property of **rivalry**.

A good example of a public good is street lighting. Imagine a street at night. On any given evening many people may walk or drive along the street. They will all benefit from the street lighting regardless of who pays for it. Consider the difficulties a private firm would have in getting people to pay a price. Each individual knows that as long as the street is lit he cannot be excluded from the benefit whether he pays or not. With this in mind individuals would tend to hide their preference and say that they do not really need the lighting in the hope that others will pay for it. This inability to exclude non-payers or 'free riders' from the benefits is the characteristic of a public good that we have called non-excludability.

Non-rivalry, the second characteristic of a public good, also applies to street lighting. Once a street has been lit, the improved visibility is available to all who use the street, be it two people or 2000 people. One person's consumption of the light provided will not reduce the amount of light available for others. The cost of providing the light for two people is the same as providing it for 2000 people.

Pure public goods need to display both total non-excludability and total non-rivalry. In practice this is not always the case. Roads are often given as an example of a public good even though tunnels, bridges and some stretches of motorway (which are suitably well-defined with limited entrances and exits) operate in such a way that people who use them can be charged and those unwilling to pay excluded. However, the practical difficulties that would be involved make the major part of any road network in essence non-excludable. The characteristic of non-rivalry may break down when a road becomes congested. Charging motorists a price if they wish to enter a city centre may reduce the congestion problem, but once again the practical problems mitigate against such schemes.

In reality public goods have a sizeable degree of non-excludability or non-rivalry rather than total amounts of both. Consider the following examples in terms of the extent to which they display either or both of these two qualities: defence, lighthouses, police, fire protection, and a reduction in air pollution.

In the light of the discussion so far we are now in a position to offer the following as a definition of a **public good**: it is any economic good which finds it difficult, if not impossible, to exclude non-payers from its benefits and whose benefits are not reduced by extra users. The two aspects of this definition provide the two reasons why the market mechanism fails to operate satisfactorily in the case of such goods.

The first aspect, non-excludability, results in the problem of 'free-riders'. People will not pay for goods which they think can be acquired free. Private firms cannot provide goods free of charge. One solution is for such goods to be provided by private collective action in the form of non-profit-making institutions. The more common solution is through public collective action where government authorities are left to supply the goods.

The second aspect, non-rivalry, in effect means that the cost of supplying an extra user with the good is zero. If five people walk down a street on a particular evening rather than four, the benefit enjoyed by the fifth from the street lighting has not resulted in an increase in costs, nor has it reduced the amount of light available. In terms of the Pareto criterion it would be inefficient to charge a price. Indeed, when you think that any extra user can benefit from the good at no extra cost to society, charging a price would clearly discourage some potential users and result in a loss of total benefit to society.

Market intervention

The aspect of non-excludability makes it impossible to charge a price, while that of non-rivalry makes it undesirably inefficient. A good for which there is no price will not be supplied by private enterprise. If such a good is considered necessary, the obvious solution is for the government to provide it. In many cases this is exactly what happens, even though some goods only conform to a very diluted definition of a public good (e.g. health and education).

Having got this far there is still a further problem. In the absence of the price mechanism the government needs to decide what amount of a given public good to provide. Who is to say that the decision reached by the state will be any more efficient than that which would have been given by an imperfect price mechanism? One approach to this problem is called **cost benefit analysis**. This approach attempts to reach a decision about resource use by calculating the full economic costs and comparing them with the full economic benefits. In other words, it will compare the total opportunity cost to society as a whole with the total benefits. To enable such a comparison to take place all costs and benefits have to be expressed in monetary terms. Herein lies one of the great practical difficulties associated with this approach.

The following example illustrates the basic ideas involved. Consider a city faced with the problem of air pollution. No anti-pollution legislation exists and the price system is clearly failing to provide any control. This is hardly

surprising as the activity of reducing such pollution fits our definition of a public good very closely. Any reduction in air pollution will simultaneously benefit all residents whether they pay anything towards it or not. Hence it displays the property of non-excludability. The benefits provided by less air pollution will not be diminished by the number of people who experience them. Hence it displays the property of non-rivalry.

For the reasons given these two characteristics would make the activity of reducing pollution 'uneconomic' as far as any private firms are concerned. Faced with this situation the local authority might decide to devote some of its resources to the reduction of air pollution. At the same time it might pass legislation forcing those polluting the air to take steps to reduce the extent to which they do so. We now have to ask how many of the community's scarce resources should be devoted to the reduction of air pollution. It is to this question that cost benefit analysis might help provide an answer.

A comparison would be made between all the costs involved and all the benefits resulting from increasingly large degrees of control. Attempts would be made to quantify all the costs and benefits to the community as a whole. These would include social and financial costs and benefits whether direct or indirect.

The costs would take the form of higher taxes together with higher prices for consumers and lower profits for firms (assuming that the costs were shared out between the two). All this would be necessary in order to finance industrial devices and production techniques that would reduce pollution. Householders may face direct costs in the form of expensive smokeless fuels.

The benefits are perhaps even more difficult to quantify. They would include improved health and the resulting reduction in expenditure on health services. Damage to crops and animals would be reduced, and clothing and materials would last longer and need cleaning less often. The quality of life would generally be improved. One of the biggest problems facing cost benefit analysis is trying to place monetary values on benefits such as these.

However, if these problems can be overcome, this approach can help to determine how many resources should be devoted to the reduction of air pollution. The degree of control should be expanded for as long as the total benefits exceed the total costs. The optimum degree of control is reached as soon as the total cost is equal to the total benefit.

Fig. 1.24 expresses this same idea in a slightly different way. The optimum degree of control is shown as that which minimizes the total costs of control and damage. Curve *A* shows how the total cost of damage due to pollution decreases as the degree of control increases. Curve *B* shows how a greater degree of control will cost the community more. By adding the two curves together we arrive at curve *C*. The optimum balance between costs and benefits is said to be achieved by a degree of control that will minimize the total cost to the community. This optimum degree of control (*Q*) does not eliminate all pollution; there is such a thing as an optimum amount of pollution.

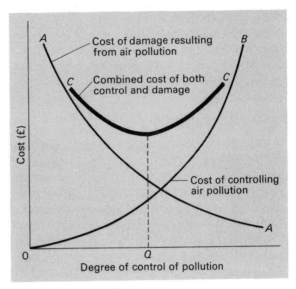

Fig. 1.24   *The optimum control of pollution*

6 Merit goods

At best the concept of merit goods is simply an example of other types of market failure. At worst some argue that there is no such thing.

Those who believe in the existence of **merit goods** define them as goods that 'society' knows to have greater benefits for individuals than the individuals themselves realize. The implication is that as individuals we do not know what is good for us. If left to our own devices, we would undervalue the benefits to be enjoyed from the consumption of certain goods. As a result our demand, and therefore the price we are willing to pay, is lower than it ought to be. The outcome of this is the price mechanism under producing. Education and health are often given as examples.

Those who see the merit good as no more than a specific example of other types of market failure suggest that individuals fail to appreciate the full benefits of such goods because of a lack of information. Where consumer ignorance regarding all the potential internal and external benefits is the problem, merit goods can be seen in terms of a failure to provide enough information (see transaction costs, p.34). A similar view stems from the fact that a common characteristic of so-called merit goods is that they provide more external than internal benefits. In this way market failure in the form of underproduction can be attributed to the existence of externalities (see p.28). These points emphasize the overlapping nature of concepts such as merit goods, public goods, externalities, and transaction costs. Many goods show varying degrees of more than one of these market failures.

Those who believe in the concept argue that even when fully informed with regard to all internal and external benefits, consumers may still make wrong or inefficient decisions. The implication is not only that the majority of consumers do not know what is good for them, but that someone else (presumably a government 'expert') does. Even with all the appropriate information, the argument goes, people may, for example, undereducate themselves if left to their own devices.

Those who doubt that any one group (scientists, politicians, etc.) can be an absolute authority on such issues doubt the existence of merit goods. However, at this point we are moving away from economic theory towards political theory and philosophy, both of which are outside the scope of this book. The following examples show the normative nature of this type of issue: seat belts, preventive medicine, nuclear defence, etc.

Market intervention

To the extent that merit goods do exist, the market system will fail to produce enough of them. One obvious solution to this under-production would be through the use of subsidies. A government subsidy will clearly lower the price of a seat at the ballet. As a result the demand for seats will be higher and more people would go to the ballet than would have done otherwise. In subsidizing the ballet, someone has decided that consumer demand operating through the price mechanism will result in an inefficiently low supply. Someone has decided that the mass of consumers under-estimate the benefit to be gained from watching the ballet. Of course, it may be that the ballet is not 'objectively' good for us, and all that is happening is the decision-makers are imposing their interests on the rest of us. In making this last point we are once again moving away from economic theory.

Fig. 1.25 helps to identify the effects of subsidizing a good, for example the market for ballet. A subsidy is the opposite of a tax. By

Fig. 1.25   Subsidizing a merit good

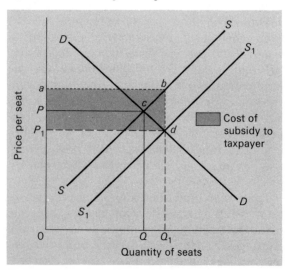

subsidizing this artistic activity, the supply curve will shift from SS to S_1S_1. The resulting increase in seats from Q to Q_1 may lead to the opening of a new theatre. The quantity of resources employed by this industry will have increased, thereby reducing the number of resources available for other industries. The total amount spent by consumers on the ballet will also be affected. In Fig. 1.25 $PcQO$ was spent before the subsidy, while P_1dQ_1O was spent after the subsidy. The size and direction of the change in consumer expenditure will vary with the size of the subsidy and the elasticity of demand for the ballet. A final point to remember is that the government must finance the subsidy. In this case the subsidy is equal to the area $abdP_1$. The government's taxation policy will determine who actually meets the cost of the subsidy.

It would seem that any assessment of the effects of the subsidy would involve political and ethical views as well as economic theory.

7 Transaction costs

Transaction costs involve all the costs of en-suring that a transaction between buyers and sellers will take place under ideal conditions. Ensuring ideal conditions for the transaction involves costs in the form of finding the most suitable buyer or seller to deal with, negotiating a contract, covering oneself against fraud or default, and so on. One of the most interesting examples of a transaction cost is the cost of gathering the information necessary to allow the transaction to take place under perfect conditions.

One of the assumptions of the traditional theory is that such costs are equal to zero. For example, the traditional theory assumes that conditions of perfect knowledge already exist. By failing to take transaction costs into account, the price mechanism will develop imperfections. The market system will fail whenever the transaction costs exceed the benefits to be gained from the elimination of imperfections. When the cost of creating per-fect conditions for a transaction is too great, imperfect conditions will be allowed to prevail.

Everyday examples of market failure stemming from transaction costs are plentiful. For example, on some evenings a theatre will have empty seats; people have stayed away because the price is too high. On other evenings people will arrive at the theatre only to discover that the tickets have all been sold. To avoid market failure of this type, the ticket prices would have to be set for each performance so as to equate exactly supply and demand. This would involve collecting accurate information regarding consumer demand, setting a price in accordance with this information, printing tickets, informing customers of the price changes, and so on. As well as posing many practical difficulties such a procedure would clearly be very costly. The transaction costs involved would far exceed the benefits.

The transaction of business would be much cheaper to administer if the same price was charged for each performance. However, this would result in a misallocation of resources as it would involve the use of non-market methods of allocation. In the case of excess demand these would take the form of queueing and rationing; first come first served, one ticket per head, and too bad for those who go without.

We have already suggested that an important and very common transaction cost relates to being informed. While the market mechanism assumes perfect knowledge, it is possible to identify both producer and consumer ignorance in the real world. Attempts are made to rectify this, and there is indeed a market for information just as for any scarce economic good. However, the market for information is far from perfect.

Producers are not always aware of the most efficient productive and distributive methods. The publication of trade journals and the general encouragement of more research and development would improve the situation. However, such activities are often not undertaken. Firstly, the initial costs involved may be prohibitive. Secondly, the firms involved would often create external benefits for those who are not involved. Those who consider undertaking expensive research will be discouraged by the thought of competitors benefiting from their discoveries free of charge.

Market intervention

Under these circumstances the government may feel it necessary to intervene. Intervention may take the form of subsidies or grants to firms and universities willing to undertake research. Alternatively, the government could undertake research itself. In the UK the government's Central Office of Information provides industry with a great deal of detailed information.

Consumers also suffer from a lack of relevant information. If you wish to buy a car, you can first buy various magazines in an attempt to make a more informed decision about the type of car to buy. Informative advertising may help you decide from which dealer you should buy the car. However, the consumer will rarely be perfectly informed. Imperfections in the market for information will result in a less than optimum supply. Insufficient information will result in wrong decisions being made and a misallocation of resources will follow. The consumer may spend an important part of his savings on a car that does not satisfy his needs.

In the face of a less than optimum supply of information the government can either attempt to supplement the supply or transfer decision-making from the consumer in the market to a minority group of 'experts'. For example, decision-making with regard to allocation in the National Health Service is left more to 'experts' than consumers.

Before leaving the market for information, it is worth mentioning recent developments in information-processing. The advent of the computer has done much to reduce transaction costs generally and those relating to a lack of information in particular. An increasing number of institutions such as banks, schools, and firms of all sizes are equipping themselves with computers which enable them to collect, store, and refer to vast amounts of information. In this way information can be made available at a relatively low cost in a very short period of time. Consumers also benefit from it through the use of computerized credit cards, Teletext systems such as Ceefax or the Oracle, computerized second-hand car markets, library microfiles, and so on.

8 Immobility of resources

The market system produces maximum welfare for the community as long as conditions of perfect competition exist. One such condition is that resources are perfectly mobile. This means that factors of production or resources can move from the production of one good to another or from one geographical location to another quickly and smoothly. Factors must be both occupationally and geographically mobile. Disequilibrium in the form of excess demand or excess supply must be immediately rectified by the movement of resources in or out of industries.

In reality resources are not perfectly mobile. Disequilibrium may exist within markets for some time. This constitutes a market failure, with prolonged disequilibrium preventing the maximization of welfare.

Imagine a sudden increase in demand for cars. According to the theory of the price mechanism, the market would adapt as shown in Fig. 1.26. The increase in demand results in the demand curve shifting from DD to D_1D_1. The new price of P_1 will be higher than before (P) and the quantity produced will increase from Q to Q_1. In theory this increase in output will take place, if not instantaneously, at least very quickly.

In practice, if the car industry is already working at full capacity, this increase in output cannot be satisfied by the existing capital equipment, materials, and labour. Rather than increasing immediately, the output will at best increase 'eventually'. Unfortunately, this may take a long time. New factories will have to be financed and built. Plant and equipment will have to be installed. The supply of materials and components will have to be increased. New labour will have to be attracted to the industry and trained. The immobility of all these resources may result in 'eventually' being years rather than a few weeks. For as long as it takes to reach the new equilibrium position, disequilibrium will remain. In practice the adjustment process can be irregular and slow, whereas in theory it is supposed to be smooth and quick.

In this context it is worth identifying three basic time-periods. In the very short or momentary run, supply will be very inelastic. With time elasticity will increase. Fig. 1.27 shows how this will affect the outcome of a sudden increase in demand from DD to D_1D_1.

1 The momentary supply curve (S_m): During this time-period supply is fixed to what is already on the market. As the quantity supplied stays the same at Q, the increase in demand causes a considerable price rise to P_1.

Fig. 1.26   An increase in demand in theory

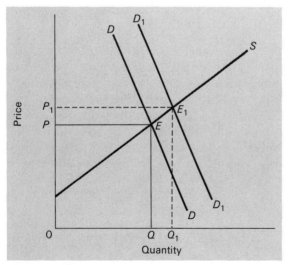

Fig. 1.27   An increase in demand in practice: immobile resources

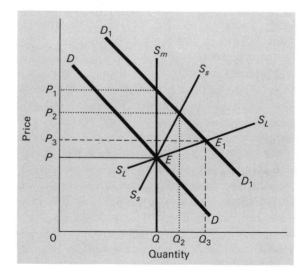

2 The short-run supply curve (S_s): During this time-period more can be supplied as a result of more intensive use of existing capacity. As the quantity supplied increases to Q_2, the price will fall to P_2.

3 The long-run supply curve (S_L): During this time-period capacity can be expanded and new firms may enter the industry. As a result the quantity supplied can increase even further, thus causing the price to fall even further. The new equilibrium position gives a price of P_3 and a quantity of Q_3.

Under perfect market conditions the movement from equilibrium point E to E_1 would take place immediately and smoothly. In practice the transition may be slow and jerky.

Similar problems are created when the demand for a product falls. Consider a situation where the development of new materials has occasioned a fall in the demand for steel. The theory assumes that output will fall quickly. Plants will be closed, thereby releasing capital, materials, and labour to be employed in growing industries.

However, social and political factors may slow down the rate at which closures take place. The resources which are released may not be suitable for employment in the industries that happen to be growing. The labour skills required by the microelectronics industry may be very different from those possessed by steel workers. Even assuming workers are willing, lengthy retraining programmes may be necessary. Much of the capital equipment released by the steel industry might be so specialized that no other use will be found for it, whatever the time-period. Growing industries will not necessarily be located in the same areas as declining industries. The need for labour as well as other factors to move geographically will be a further limitation on mobility.

The general outcome of the existence of immobility will be a shortage of resources in some industries and geographical locations, while unemployed resources exist in other industries and areas. The existence of such imbalances is clearly an example of market failure.

Market intervention

Once again government intervention may try both to improve and replace the working of the market system. The provision of financial incentives and retraining facilities can help increase occupational mobility. Through their regional policies governments try to reduce the need for geographical mobility by attracting firms to areas with unemployed resources.

9 Allocation: present versus future

So far we have considered the efficiency of the market mechanism in terms of its ability to allocate resources between different uses at any particular point in time. This type of market failure looks at the ability of the price mechanism to allocate resources between the present and the future. In effect this involves analysing the allocation of resources between consumer goods and capital goods.

Consumer goods are bought by households for use in final consumption, e.g. food, beds, radios, televisions, clothing, etc. Capital goods are man-made goods that are used in the production of consumer goods, e.g. tractors, factories, machines, etc. The quantity and type of resources allocated to capital goods today will determine the quantity and type of consumer goods available tomorrow.

The choice between consumer and capital goods can be shown in the form of a **production possibility curve**. Fig. 1.28 shows the possible combinations of consumer and capital goods that an economy is capable of producing given its fixed resources. If all the existing resources were devoted to the production of consumer goods, A would be produced. If they were devoted to capital goods, B would be produced. The points on the curve between A and B represent all the possible combinations of consumer and capital goods that could be produced with the resources available in a given year. For example, point C represents an output of E consumer goods and G capital goods, while point D represents F consumer goods and H capital goods.

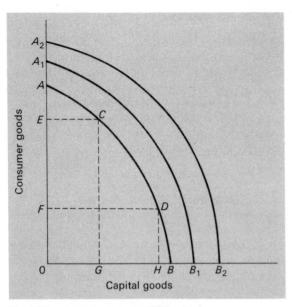

Fig. 1.28   A production possibility curve

The shape of the curve implies not only that more resources are devoted to consumer goods when less are devoted to capital goods, but also that the increases in consumer goods get smaller and smaller as the production of capital goods decreases by constant amounts. This is referred to as the **diminishing marginal rate of transformation** and it can be explained by the fact that some resources are better suited to the production of capital goods, while others are better suited to consumer goods.

To begin with the resources released from the production of capital goods will be those which are best suited to the production of consumer goods. The corresponding increases in the output of consumer goods will therefore be large. As the output of capital goods is reduced still further, it will become increasingly necessary to transfer resources that are best suited to the production of capital goods. Under these circumstances the corresponding increases in the output of consumer goods will become smaller.

Consider now the implications of choosing point C on the curve rather than D. During the given year consumers would enjoy a higher standard of living with more consumer goods being produced ($E > F$). However, the fact that fewer capital goods have been added to the economy's stock of capital ($G < H$) will mean

that the economy's future capacity will be lower than if point D had been chosen. In terms of Fig. 1.28, choosing point C will result in the following year's production possibility curve being A_1B_1, whereas if point D had been chosen it would have been A_2B_2. By choosing C, present consumption has been given priority over future potential consumption, i.e. economic growth.

Various factors might lead one to doubt just how effective the market mechanism is at allocating resources between the present and the future. In allocating resources to satisfy future demand an element of **uncertainty** is introduced. The expected demand may never materialize. This undermines the assumption of perfect certainty which is necessary if the price mechanism is to operate efficiently. Individuals may not be willing to take the amount of risks that would be optimal from society's point of view. This would result in a less than optimum amount of investment for the future.

In order to eliminate this form of market failure all risk would have to be removed. A step towards this would involve the creation of **future markets** for all goods. Such markets already exist for currencies and some commodities, e.g. wool, cotton, and wheat. These markets allow contracts to be made today concerning the buying and selling of goods at a fixed price on a fixed date in the future. In this way the risk involved in trading can be reduced. In addition to this, more comprehensive insurance markets would be needed. For example, firms would have to insure themselves against all possible production failures. It can be argued that without such a network of future markets and insurance markets the market system will inevitably fail.

It has also been suggested that consumers are biased towards present consumption at the expense of the future. This attitude is well illustrated by the adage: 'Eat, drink, and be merry for tomorrow you may die'. This is of course purely a value judgement. However, if the state feels that its value judgement is a valid one, it may impose low levels of present consumption so as to make resources available for investment in the future. In the UK company taxation is used to this effect. Profits which are distributed to shareholders are taxed more heavily than those which are retained for reinvestment in the firm. Rather than shareholders enjoying higher present standards of living, firms might opt for human or capital investment that would lead to future benefits.

A final factor that might result in the price system misallocating resources between the present and the future is the rate of interest. Low interest rates mean that investment is cheap to finance. As a result people invest more, and thus more resources are devoted to the future. The opposite is true for high interest rates. As long as the rate of interest is determined by market forces operating under perfect conditions it should not result in a misallocation of resources.

However, interest rates are increasingly manipulated by governments to try and achieve a variety of macroeconomic ends relating to prices, unemployment, growth, and the balance of payments. It is doubtful whether governments bear in mind the effects of such interest-rate changes on the allocation of resources between the present and the future.

10   The cobweb theory

In this case the market failure manifests itself in the form of instability. The process that we are about to describe incorporates elements of the previous three types of market failure: lack of information, inflexibility of resources, and the problem of relating one time-period with the next.

The basic theory is built upon very restrictive assumptions. It assumes that the producers will behave in an unco-ordinated and naïve way and that they never learn from their mistakes. However, the theory shows how instability can result whenever there is a time-lag between the making of a production decision and the final delivery of the product to the market place. This is best seen in the markets for livestock and agricultural products although there is evidence to suggest that to a degree the theory has wider implications.

Consider Fig. 1.29 which represents the fixed supply and demand conditions in the Christ-

Table 1.5   An explanation of the cobweb theory

Year	Price and output fluctuations
1	Assume that due to a widespread disease amongst poultry the supply of Christmas turkeys drops to Q_1. This will mean a higher price of P_1. This higher price will encourage the producers to supply more the following Christmas.
2	The farmers will now bring Q_2 turkeys to the market and find that they can sell their production at a price of only P_2. At this low price they will plan to reduce their supply the following year.
3	When brought to the market, this lower quantity (Q_3) will sell at the higher price of P_3. Again, this will result in an increase in supply the following year, and so it goes on.

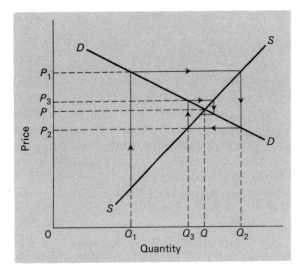

Fig. 1.29   The cobweb theory

mas market for turkeys. In a given year farmers bring Q turkeys to the Christmas market and sell them at a price of P.

Assume that the turkey farmers look at this year's price to determine the quantity that they will bring to the market the following year. This assumption means that the supply curve SS incorporates a **time-lag**: the next market's quantity will be connected with the present market price. The initial price P and quantity Q would represent an unchanging equilibrium as long as market conditions remained unchanged.

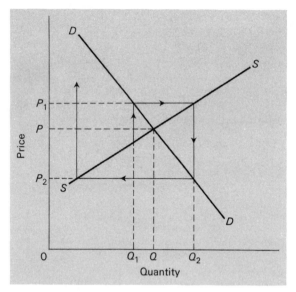

Fig. 1.30   Diverging cobweb

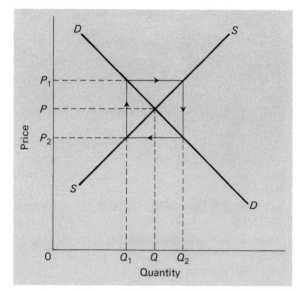

Fig. 1.31   Perfect cobweb

Now suppose that in one particular year the market conditions are altered. Fig. 1.29 and Table 1.5 show the price fluctuations that would result from such a change. In this case the outcome of the initial movement away from equilibrium is a series of fluctuations, as over several time-periods the price returns to its original equilibrium level. This is called a **converging cobweb** (Fig. 1.29), the reason being that the supply curve is steeper than the demand curve.

Where the supply curve is flatter than the demand curve, the price fluctuations will get greater and greater in each subsequent period, moving further away from the original equilibrium. This is a **diverging cobweb** (Fig. 1.30).

If the supply and demand curves have the same slope, the price will oscillate between two levels indefinitely without ever returning to the original equilibrium. This is called a **perfect cobweb** (Fig. 1.31).

This simplified analysis provides at least some insight into the fluctuations which can be identified in many markets.

Market intervention

More flexible resources would reduce the time-lags in some markets, while more efficient

information or future markets could eliminate some of the uncertainty regarding prices. However, in the absence of the above, price fluctuations can be diminished by a more direct intervention in the form of a **buffer stock** policy.

A buffer stock involves some form of central agency setting minimum and maximum price levels. If the market equilibrium price is between the two, the buffer stock does not operate (Fig. 1.32).

If the equilibrium price is below the minimum, the minimum price is enforced and all excess supply is bought by the agency and stockpiled (Fig. 1.33). If the equilibrium price is above the maximum, the maximum price is enforced and the agency satisfies the excess demand by selling from the stockpile at this price (Fig. 1.34).

Many practical difficulties are associated with the setting up and operating of a buffer stock. Storage and the fixing and readjustment of minimum and maximum prices are two problem areas. Many controversies surround the question of who should run and finance the agency. Should it be run, for example, by producers, consumers, or the government? Examples of buffer stock schemes would include the International Tin Council and the common agricultural policy of the EEC.

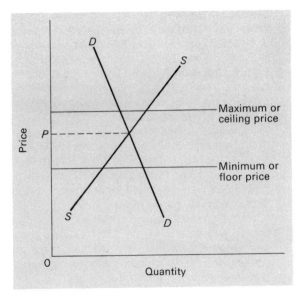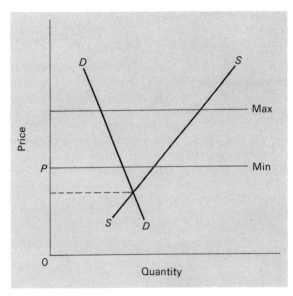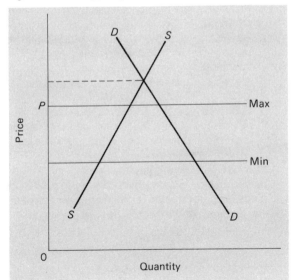

Fig. 1.32   Neutral policy

Fig. 1.33   Buying policy

Fig. 1.34   Selling policy

11 Conclusion

Market failure can provide an economic case for state intervention. The state can redistribute income when faced with inequity, and control the behaviour of firms when faced with monopoly. Through state provision, taxation, and subsidies resources can be directed towards public necessities and the general enhancement of the quality of life. By increasing the availability of information and the mobility of resources, governments can reduce some of the deficiencies found in the market system.

However, it must be remembered that state intervention, like the market system, is not immune from imperfections. A comparison has to be made between the imperfections of the two.

State provision can become too bureaucratic. It can lack incentive for efficiency and inventiveness. Its administrators can be dominated by self-interest. State attempts to regulate prices and other aspects of the behaviour of private enterprise can also result in undesirable effects. Black markets and elaborate systems of evasion can develop. Subsidies can encourage inefficiency.

More fundamentally the state, despite its 'expert' advice, may simply get things wrong. The case for state intervention is a strong one, but such intervention is far from perfect and must always be assessed in terms of its costs.

Examination questions

Data response question

'Efficient market co-ordination of economic activity depends on competition and on consumers exercising free and well-informed choices. If, on the other hand, there is market power or consumers have poor information, the "invisible hand", which is supposed to reconcile individually self-interested behaviour with the communal good, falters or is overruled. Public policies in this area therefore seek to monitor market competitiveness and consumer interests, and apply remedies where these are infringed.'
(A. R. Prest and D. J. Coppock, *The UK Economy*, Weidenfeld & Nicolson)

In the light of the above passage, discuss the ways and means by which the efficiency of market co-ordination can be safeguarded or improved.
(*London S, 1984*)

Essay questions

1 Why is it considered that perfect competition provides the optimum allocation of resources? (*Oxford and Cambridge A, 1981*)
2 Will maximizing consumer's surplus maximize economic welfare? (*Cambridge S, 1982*)
3 'Market failure can arise from two general sources, namely, externalities and imperfection.' (K. Hartley). Discuss.
(*Associated Examining Board S, 1980*)
4 'In a free market system, consumption depends on the willingness and ability of the consumer to pay. For this reason, it is necessary to lower the price of some goods by subsidy.' Discuss.
(*London A, 1980*)
5 Discuss what is usually meant by 'market failure'. Consider, giving examples, what forms of corrective action government can take to remedy this.
(*Joint Matriculation Board S, 1982*)

6 Distinguish between private and public goods. What do you consider to be the best way to ensure an adequate provision of public goods in a market economy? (*Oxford and Cambridge A, 1980*)
7 Discuss the case for and against cost benefit analysis. (*London A, 1983*)
8 a) Giving examples from the UK economy, explain how economic activities may lead to social costs as well as to private benefits.
  b) Discuss ways in which those responsible for the existence of social costs might be made to help to pay for them. (*Scottish H, 1982*)
9 How should the government restrict the activities of firms that create pollution?
(*Oxford Colleges Entrance, 1982*)
10 Explain, with examples, the terms 'external costs' and 'external benefits'. Why and how might the government discourage activities involving excessive external costs? (*London A, 1984*)
11 Use demand and supply curves to predict the effects of the following alternative government policies designed to increase the incomes of producers of certain agricultural commodities.
  a) The imposition of quotas on domestic producers with the intention of restricting the quantities produced.
  b) Advertising campaigns stressing the nutritional value of certain products.
  c) Intervention purchasing to ensure that producers receive minimum prices above free market levels.
  d) Subsidies paid to producers whenever freely established market prices fall below a certain guaranteed price (set above free market levels). (*Welsh A, 1982*)
12 'Anything of benefit to the community will be carried out by private entrepreneurs in search of profit. Most government expenditures are therefore wasteful in ignoring the view of the market.' Discuss. (*Oxford S, 1982*)

Chapter 2 *Consumer behaviour: price*

Microeconomics is concerned with the behaviour of individual decision-making units. Individuals or individual households are such units and **consumption** is an important aspect of their behaviour. Consumption can be defined as expenditure devoted to the satisfaction of wants through the acquisition of goods and services. When faced with scarcity in the form of a limited income or budget, consumption choices have to be made and these will be the subject matter of this chapter and the next. Taken together, these two chapters will help explain consumer behaviour and thereby further our understanding of the theory of demand as introduced in Chapter 1.

This chapter will consider two related choices. Firstly, given fixed incomes and current market prices, how will consumers choose between the variety of possible combinations of goods and services that confront them? Secondly, how will their consumption of goods and services vary as the prices of these goods and services vary?

Our earlier look at demand theory introduced certain aspects of consumer behaviour. The law of demand identified the relationship between a good's price and the quantity consumed over a given time-period. Everyday experience and common sense led us to accept that as the price of a good falls so the quantity consumers demand goes up. However, accepting that such a relationship exists is not the same as understanding why it exists. The aim here is to provide such an understanding.

To begin with we shall outline the oldest of the theories that tries to answer the question 'why do consumers buy more of a good at a lower price than at a higher price?' This theory is based on the concept of **marginal utility**. Dissatisfaction with some of this theory's assumptions will lead us to an analysis of alternative theories — **indifference curve theory** and **revealed preference theory**.

Two basic assumptions are necessary before any meaningful analysis can take place. Firstly, consumer behaviour is assumed to be **consistent**. If behaviour is totally haphazard so that today's behaviour bears no relation to yesterday's or tomorrow's, the formulation of any theory would be impossible. Secondly, consumer behaviour is assumed to be **rational**. Consumers will allocate their expenditure so as to maximize the satisfaction or welfare derived from consumption.

Part 1 *Traditional marginal utility theory*

The concept of **utility** can help us understand two related aspects of consumer behaviour. On the one hand, it enables us to predict how an individual will allocate his expenditure, given a fixed income, between the goods and services available for consumption. On the other hand, it enables us to predict the effect of a price change on the quantity demanded of a good and so confirm the law of demand.

It will first be necessary to clarify the meaning of utility as well as the crucial distinction between total and marginal utility.

1 Total and marginal utility

Utility is the term used by economists to convey the pleasure and satisfaction derived from the consumption of goods and services. Utility represents the fulfilment of a need or desire through the activity of consumption.

At this point an important assumption must be introduced. We must assume that it is possible to quantify and measure changes in satisfaction or utility. For this purpose a 'util' will represent 1 unit of satisfaction. In reality, utility is a psychological concept and its subjective nature makes it unmeasurable. Nevertheless, we shall ignore this and proceed as if utility can be measured in utils in just the same way as distance can be measured in metres or temperature in degrees. The standard util is totally imaginary.

Total utility represents the satisfaction gained by a consumer as a result of his overall consumption of a good. **Marginal utility** represents the change in satisfaction resulting from the consumption of a further unit of a good.

Assuming that utility can be measured, we can say, for instance, that a given individual enjoys 37 units of satisfaction (utils) from drinking 3 pints of beer during an evening. This is a measure of his total utility. If one more pint increases his total utility to 42 utils, the marginal utility of the fourth pint would be equal to 5 units of satisfaction. The marginal utility of the fourth pint equals the total utility derived from 4 pints minus the total utility derived from 3 pints. Marginal utility is the increase in total utility that results from the consumption of one more unit.

Table 2.1 gives a possible utility schedule for a given individual spending his evening in the local pub. The figures clearly display a crucial element of utility theory: the **law of diminishing marginal utility**. The law states that the satisfaction derived from the consumption of an additional unit of a good will decrease as more of the good is consumed, assuming that the consumption of all other goods is held constant.

Table 2.1 satisfies this law in that although each pint consumed until the ninth pint adds to total satisfaction, it does so by decreasing amounts. While the third pint adds 8 units of satisfaction, the fourth pint adds only 5 units. Neither of these can compare with the first pint that resulted in 17 units of satisfaction.

Had the beer been free, the individual would have drunk up to 8 pints. There is no incentive to go beyond this point as further drinks would bring him no extra satisfaction. It is also interesting to note that marginal utility can be negative. If the individual were forced to drink a ninth pint, his total utility would actually be reduced. This is sometimes called **disutility**. If the figures in Table 2.1 were represented graphically, the total and marginal utility curves would look like those in Fig. 2.1.

It is important to appreciate fully the implications of the distinction between total and marginal utility. If you were given the choice of giving up totally your consumption of either water or petrol, you would choose to give up petrol. The implication is that water provides you with more total utility than petrol.

Table 2.1   An individual's utility schedule

Pints drunk in an evening	Total utility (units of satisfaction)	Marginal utility (units of satisfaction)
0	0	—
1	17	17
2	29	12
3	37	8
4	42	5
5	45	3
6	47	2
7	48	1
8	48	0
9	47	−1

Fig. 2.1   Total and marginal utility curves

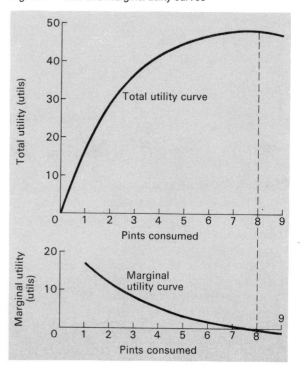

You place greater value on water than on petrol. However, if you were offered the choice of a free gallon of water or a free gallon of petrol, you might well take the petrol. At first sight, this seems to suggest that you place greater value on petrol than on water. Indeed, you would normally expect to pay more for petrol than for water. The explanation of this apparent paradox is to be found in the distinction between total and marginal utility.

There is a world of difference between comparisons based on total utility and those based on marginal utility. Given the value that we place on our lives, the total utility of water is clearly greater than that of petrol. However, as water is plentiful we can consume so much of it that we reach a point where its marginal utility is very low. If petrol is not so plentiful, we can only consume it to a point where its marginal utility is still quite high and certainly not as low as that of water. Thus under these conditions an extra gallon of petrol is worth more to us than an extra gallon of water.

A man dying of thirst in the desert is faced with different conditions and therefore different marginal utilities. He would clearly place more value on an extra gallon of water.

From these examples we can see that when a consumer makes a decision, he is concerned with the relative utilities of different goods. But given the availability of resources, economic behaviour will be determined by relative marginal utilities rather than total utilities: 'Shall I consume a few extra units of good A at the expense of good B?'

2 An explanation of consumer equilibrium

It will first be necessary to make the following assumptions about an individual's situation:

1 There must be so many consumers that the demand of no single consumer will be able to affect prices, and price alone will determine the quantity demanded. Taste, preferences, etc. will be constant.
2 The individual must know what he wants as well as to what extent the many goods available will go towards satisfying these wants.

3 He must pay known prices for the available goods.
4 His income is fixed and limited.
5 And finally, he will distribute his total expenditure so as to achieve the greatest possible amount of satisfaction from his limited budget, that is **maximize** his total utility.

This consumer is faced with the classic economic problem. In the face of **scarcity** he is having to make **choices**. His limited budget has to be distributed between a variety of different goods. Each choice he makes involves an **opportunity cost** (see p.6): to spend more on one good he must spend less on another.

Having set the scene we are still faced with the same question. How will an individual allocate his expenditure given that his aim is to maximize his satisfaction?

Imagine that you are trying to decide how to split part of your limited budget between salt and pepper. What if the last penny spent on salt generates 4 utils, while the last penny spent on pepper generates only 1 util. Here total utility could be increased by switching a penny of expenditure from pepper to salt. You will have sacrificed a small amount of utility in order to gain a larger amount.

What if you were allocating part of your monthly budget between food and drink so that the last pound spent on food brought you 400 utils, while the last pound spent on drink brought you 150 utils? You would be spending too much on drink and not enough on food. In terms of total utility you would gain by switching expenditure from drink to food.

In general, we can conclude that as long as the aim is to maximize total utility, expenditure switching between goods will take place until the marginal utility of a pound's worth of each good consumed is equal to the marginal utility of a pound's worth of any other good consumed. If this condition is not satisfied, then with the same fixed budget total utility can be increased by altering the pattern of expenditure.

Consider the following numerical example. An individual has £4 a day to spend. Only two goods are available for consumption: good A and good B. Given the utility schedules in

Table 2.2   Utility schedules for good A and good B

Number of £ per day	Total utility (utils)		Marginal utility (utils)	
	Good A	Good B	Good A	Good B
1	40	· 100	40	100
2	76	160	36	60
3	108	200	32	40
4	136	230	28	30

Table 2.2 and the fact that his aim is to maximize total utility, how will he allocate his expenditure? For simplicity, assume that the goods can only be bought in multiples of £1.

Given his fixed budget, the individual could choose any of the patterns of expenditure shown in Table 2.3. The total utility that each possibility would bring him has been calculated from Table 2.2. Choice 4 clearly results in the highest level of total utility, and as a result the consumer will choose this pattern of expenditure: £1 on good A and £3 on good B.

Now look at the marginal utility schedules in Table 2.2. The marginal utility of £1 spent on good A is equal to the marginal utility of £3 spent on good B at 40 utils. This is the utility maximizing condition that we have already highlighted. The last unit of expenditure spent on each commodity consumed will buy amounts of them that will yield identical amounts of utility. When this condition is satisfied, no shifting of expenditure between goods can serve to increase total utility and **consumer equilibrium** is said to exist.

Table 2.3   Possible patterns of consumption of good A and good B

Choice	How budget is spent	Total utility (utils)
1	£4 on A	136
2	£4 on B	230
3	£2 on A and £2 on B	236
4	£1 on A and £3 on B	**240**
5	£3 on A and £1 on B	208

In our two-good example equilibrium will occur when:

$$MU_a = MU_b$$

where MU_a represents the marginal utility of £1's worth of good A and MU_b represents the marginal utility of £1's worth of good B. The same can be said for any number of goods so that:

$$MU_a = MU_b = MU_c = \ldots MU_n$$

would represent consumer equilibrium in a multi-good situation.

3 An explanation of the law of demand

The above statement of consumer equilibrium can be used in conjunction with the law of diminishing marginal utility to provide an explanation of the law of demand. The law of demand states that as the price of a good goes up so the quantity demanded will fall, and vice versa.

It will first be necessary to rewrite the above consumer equilibrium equation so that the same principle is expressed in terms of physical units rather than pounds' worth of goods. If MU_A equals the marginal utility of a physical unit of good A, while P_A equals the price of a physical unit of good A in pounds, then:

$$MU_A = MU_a \times P_A$$

or

$$MU_a = \frac{MU_A}{P_A}$$

This enables us to re-write the equation for the multi-good situation:

$$MU_a = MU_b = MU_c = \ldots MU_n$$

in the following form:

$$\frac{MU_A}{P_A} = \frac{MU_B}{P_B} = \frac{MU_C}{P_C} = \ldots \frac{MU_N}{P_N}$$

Of the many goods that this consumer buys, assume that two are apples and oranges. If the consumer is maximizing his total utility, the following equality must hold:

$$\frac{MU \text{ of oranges}}{\text{Price per orange}} = \frac{MU \text{ of apples}}{\text{Price per apple}}$$

Given his fixed income, the consumer cannot gain by altering his present distribution of expenditure between the two goods. What would happen if the price of oranges were to drop, while his income and the price of apples remained fixed? The above equality will no longer hold, which means in effect that the consumer is no longer maximizing his total utility. To restore equality between the two ratios the marginal utility of oranges will have to fall. The extent to which it would have to fall would be reduced if the marginal utility of apples could be increased.

The law of diminishing marginal utility tells us that *more* oranges must be *consumed* if their marginal utility is to fall. By doing this, the individual is behaving in accordance with the law of demand. The fall in the price of oranges has resulted in the individual consuming more oranges in order to reduce their marginal utility, and so restore equality to the equation. As long as the two ratios are unequal, the individual is failing to maximize his satisfaction and such behaviour would be irrational.

We have already hinted at the fact that the effects of a fall in the price of oranges need not be confined to the demand for oranges. Increasing the marginal utilities of other goods would move the ratios in the equation towards equality. As oranges are substitutes for apples, it may well be that a fall in the price of oranges would result not only in a rise in the consumption of oranges but also a cutting back in the consumption of apples. Any fall in the consumption of apples will increase their marginal utility in accordance with the law of diminishing marginal utility. This illustrates the fact that a relationship can exist between the demand for a commodity and the price of other commodities.

Before moving on, it should be mentioned that the utility maximizing consumer equilibrium position can usefully be thought of in more than one way. So far we have said that for any individual to maximize his total utility the following must hold good for any two goods consumed:

$$\frac{MU_A}{P_A} = \frac{MU_B}{P_B}$$

This equation can also be expressed as:

$$\frac{MU_A}{MU_B} = \frac{P_A}{P_B}$$

In this way the utility maximizing allocation of expenditure occurs when the ratio of the marginal utilities of any two goods equals the ratio of their prices. As far as the individual is concerned, the ratio of prices is given while the ratio of marginal utilities can be altered through his own consumption decisions. When confronted with a change in price the individual can only regain a utility maximizing equilibrium by altering his expenditure pattern.

4 Marginal utility and the demand curve

The above analysis has led us to the conclusion that if the price of a good rises, assuming that income and all other prices remain constant, the quantity demanded by each individual will fall. Each individual's demand curve for every good will slope downwards. It is possible to go a step further and show that an individual's marginal utility schedule will give us his demand schedule for the same good.

In order to do this we need to assume that the utility derived from a particular good can be identified with the consumer's willingness to pay for the good. In other words, the utility of a

Table 2.4   Utility schedule for cartridges

Packets of cartridges bought per month	Total utility (£'s worth)	Marginal utility (£'s worth)
1	20·00	20·00
2	35·00	15·00
3	47·00	12·00
4	57·00	10·00
5	65·00	8·00
6	71·00	6·00
7	75·00	4·00
8	77·25	2·25
9	78·75	1·50
10	79·75	1·00

Table 2.5   Demand schedule for cartridges

Price of cartridges (£ per packet)	Packets demanded per month
20·00	1
15·00	2
12·00	3
10·00	4
8·00	5
6·00	6
4·00	7
2·25	8
1·50	9
1·00	10

good to a consumer will be measured by the maximum amount of money this consumer is willing to pay for it. This will enable us to place a monetary value on satisfaction and talk in terms of pounds' worth of utility rather than utils.

Consider an individual who decides to take up clay-pigeon shooting. He buys a gun and the appropriate clothing, and joins the local club. To enjoy his new hobby he now needs to buy cartridges. The question is how many should he buy each month, assuming that they can only be bought in packets of ten? To answer this question, we need to look at the individual's utility schedule for cartridges (Table 2.4).

In accordance with the law of diminishing marginal utility, his first packet of 10 cartridges

brings him more utility than any subsequent packet. In fact, his first packet will bring him £20 worth of utility, while the tenth packet will only bring him £1's worth of utility. If he had no cartridges for a given month, he would be willing to pay up to £20 for a packet, while if he had 9 packets, he would only be willing to pay up to £1 for an extra one.

In fact, he will have to pay the existing market price for however many packets he decides to buy. If the market price were £4 a packet, how many would he buy each month? To find the answer to this question, consider Fig. 2.2 which shows the individual's marginal utility curve and the current market price.

The rational consumer would buy 7 packets of cartridges. The fifth packet would bring £8 worth of utility at a cost of only £4—the rational consumer would buy it. Similarly, the sixth packet would also be bought, as £6 worth of satisfaction will be gained for a price of £4. The seventh packet would just be value for money with £4 worth of utility costing £4. The rational consumer will not go beyond this point: he would only be willing to pay £2.25 for the eighth packet which at a price of £4 does not represent value for money.

In effect, we are now saying that the price an individual will be willing to pay for a given quantity of a good is that which is equal to the marginal utility of that quantity. The individual's demand schedule for cartridges is shown in Table 2.5. If the demand schedule were plotted graphically, this individual's

Fig. 2.2   The marginal utility curve for cartridges representing the demand curve

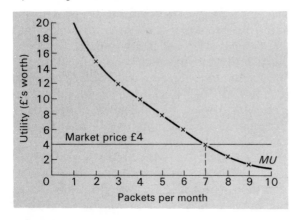

demand curve would be exactly the same as the marginal utility curve in Fig. 2.2. It will slope downwards from left to right in accordance with the law of demand.

5 Marginal utility and elasticity of demand

So far we have used marginal utility theory to confirm the direction in which the quantity demanded will change in response to a given price change. **Elasticity** is a measure of the extent to which the quantity demanded will change as a result of a given price change. The concept has already been introduced in Chapter 1, p.12.

We are now in a position to throw some light on the concept of elasticity. If the price of good X increases by 50 per cent, individuals will have to reduce their consumption of it up to the point where its marginal utility has increased by 50 per cent, always assuming that the consumption of other goods remains constant along with everything else.

Whether it will take a large or small change in consumption to bring about such a change in marginal utility will depend upon the slope of the marginal utility curve over the appropriate range (Fig. 2.3). For this marginal utility curve both the large percentage fall in quantity (Q_1 to Q_2) and the small percentage change in quantity (Q_3 to Q_4) have resulted in 50 per cent increases in marginal utility. The conclusion is that the elasticity of demand depends on the nature of marginal utility over the relevant price range.

It is important to notice that there is no link between the total utility of a good and its elasticity over a particular price range. It is for this reason that attempts to explain elasticity in terms of the distinction between necessities and luxuries are of little value. A necessity may have a high total utility, but its marginal utility and, therefore, its elasticity will vary greatly depending on the price range under consideration.

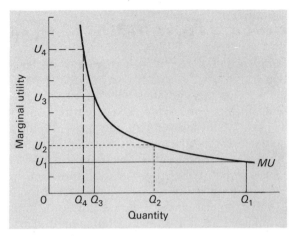

Fig. 2.3   Price elasticity of demand and the slope of the marginal utility curve

6 Conclusion

The best defence of marginal utility theory is the fact that its predictions about consumer behaviour closely reflect what actually happens in the real world. There may be exceptions, such as the increasing marginal utility experienced by the alcoholic who finds that successive glasses of whisky bring increasing amounts of satisfaction. However, these can be thought of as abnormalities. For most people marginal utility does decline as consumption increases.

Given the basic assumptions the theory is a sound one. However, many economists have become increasingly dissatisfied with some of the necessary assumptions and no longer consider marginal utility theory to be the best way of explaining demand. We shall now look at some more theories that try to explain consumer behaviour. Having outlined these theories, we shall conclude the chapter by using them to help explain possible exceptions to the law of demand.

Part 2   *New theories of consumer behaviour*

Many economists are unhappy with at least two of the basic assumptions implicit in marginal utility theory. The two newer approaches that follow try to overcome these difficulties.

1 The first difficulty surrounds the assumption that satisfaction and, therefore, marginal utility is measurable. Our earlier analysis used what is called a **cardinal approach** in order to measure utility. This enabled us to place precise and absolute figures on marginal and total utilities and to make comparisons by saying exactly how much utility is derived from different combinations of goods.

  The indifference curve theory which follows overcomes this unacceptable assumption by adopting an **ordinal approach** to the measurement of utility. This is based on a ranking procedure, and as a result avoids the need for the precise measurement of how much utility is derived from a good. Any given combination of goods needs to be ranked, relative to any other combination, only in terms of total satisfaction. The individual needs to decide only whether a given combination of good A and good B will bring him more, less, or the same level of satisfaction than any other possible combination.

2 The second criticism of marginal utility theory relates to the assumption that income remains fixed. While money income may be limited and fixed, real income will undoubtedly vary. If the price of any good rises, even assuming that all other prices remain the same, the individual will find that he can buy only a smaller volume of goods and services with the same money income. Therefore, his real income must have fallen. Revealed preference theory tries to incorporate this effect.

1 Indifference curve theory

In order to explain consumer equilibrium, two geometrical tools of analysis will first have to be introduced: the **indifference curve** and the **budget line**.

1.1 The indifference curve

In order to draw an indifference curve a consumer has to answer the following types of related questions. Assume that you have a basket containing 16 eggs and 6 bags of crisps.

If someone comes along with a basket containing 20 eggs and 5 bags of crisps and offers to change baskets, would you accept, refuse or find it impossible to decide as you would be 'indifferent' between the two baskets?

Alternatively, what would be the minimum number of eggs you would require in order to compensate exactly for the loss of one of your 6 bags of crisps? If your answer to this second question is 3 eggs, you are in effect saying that you are indifferent between a basket containing 16 eggs and 6 bags of crisps and one containing 19 eggs and 5 bags of crisps: each would give you the same total utility. This being the case, the original offer would certainly have been accepted as 20 eggs and 5 bags of crisps clearly represent a more attractive combination.

In this way it is possible to build up a set of combinations of any two goods between which the consumer is indifferent. Each combination will provide the same total utility. This whole operation can be carried out without ever having to put a precise figure on the amount of utility involved. For example, for a given individual over a given time-period, Table 2.6 might represent a set of baskets between which he is indifferent.

The information in Table 2.6 can be repre-

Table 2.6   *An indifference schedule*

Basket	Eggs	Bags of crisps
A	23	4
B	19	5
C	16	6
D	12	8
E	10	10
F	8	14

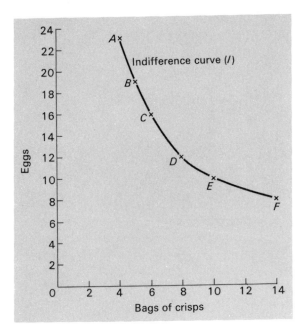

Fig. 2.4   An indifference curve

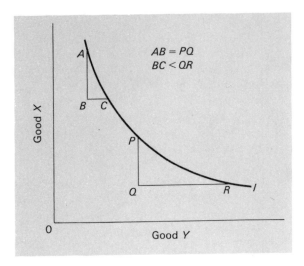

Fig. 2.5   The marginal rate of substitution

sented graphically by plotting eggs on the vertical axis and bags of crisps on the horizontal axis (Fig. 2.4). This curve is called an **indifference curve**, and each point on the curve represents a combination of eggs and bags of crisps between which this particular individual is indifferent.

The nature of the curve reveals various aspects of consumer behaviour. Consider the following indifference curve in Fig. 2.5. The slope of the curve between A and C is given by the ratio $AB \div BC$. BC represents the amount of good Y necessary to make up for the loss of AB of good X that would result if the individual moved from combination A to combination C. The rate at which one good can be substituted for another without any change in total utility is called the **marginal rate of substitution**.

Looking at Fig. 2.5, we notice that the marginal rate of substitution between P and R (i.e. $PQ \div QR$) is lower than that between A and C. Not surprisingly, the higher the quantity of good X the consumer has to begin with, the smaller will be the quantity of good Y necessary to compensate for the loss of a unit of good X, and vice versa. The fact that this ratio decreases as one moves down the curve from

left to right is known as the **diminishing marginal rate of substitution**.

Another point to notice is that an indifference curve slopes downwards from left to right. Assuming that both goods are desirable, the rational consumer could not be indifferent to a basket containing more of both goods. Therefore, as we move from one point to the other on the indifference curve, while the quantity of one good increases, the quantity of the other good has to decrease if total utility is to remain unchanged. This is why the slope of an indifference curve is normally negative. When both

Table 2.7   What the indifference curves in Fig. 2.6 tell us

Indifference curve	
A	Good X and good Y are not close substitutes
B	Good X and good Y are closer substitutes
C	Good X and good Y are perfect substitutes
D	The individual does not like good X; its consumption generates zero satisfaction
E	The individual does not like good Y; its consumption generates zero satisfaction
F	The individual is not very fond of good Y and will eventually be saturated. A point is reached where the consumption of good Y starts to bring negative satisfaction
G	Good X and good Y are perfect complements

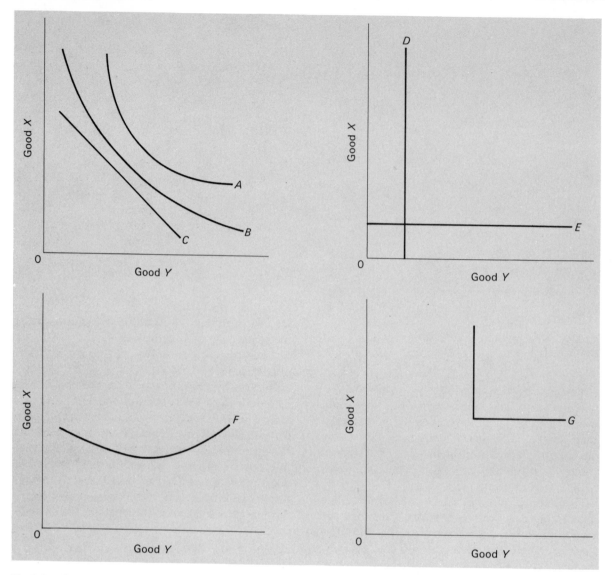

Fig. 2.6   Some unusual indifference curves

goods are desirable, an upward sloping curve would be quite unrealistic as it would imply that more of both goods leaves the consumer indifferent and does not increase total utility.

Consider the indifference curves shown in Fig. 2.6. Without consulting Table 2.7, try to draw your own conclusions about the consumer's tastes and the nature of the relationship between goods X and Y in each case.

No attempt is made in Table 2.7 to provide a full explanation of the shape of each indifference curve in Fig. 2.6. You will have grasped

fully the concept of the indifference curve once you have established the explanations for yourself.

The indifference map

A single indifference curve represents but one possible level of total utility. In Fig. 2.7 combinations A, B, C and D all represent identical levels of total utility (I).

If point E was taken at random, then together with all other points which provide an ident-

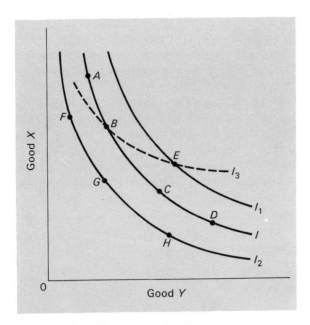

Fig. 2.7   *An indifference map: indifference curves never cross*

1.2 The budget line

While an indifference curve describes a consumer's preferences, a **budget line** shows the various combinations of two goods that can be bought at current prices with a fixed budget or income. Assume that an individual has £3 a week to spend on eggs and bags of crisps, and that eggs cost 10p each while crisps cost 15p a bag. If the individual spends all of his budget on eggs, he can afford 30. If he spends it all on crisps, he can afford 20 bags. Between these two extremes there is a variety of other possibilities, e.g. 15 eggs + 10 bags of crisps. Each point on the budget line (Fig. 2.8) represents one of the several possible combinations that will cost exactly £3.

If x represents the number of bags of crisps and y the number of eggs consumed per time-period, we can write the equation of the budget line as:

$$(15 \times x) + (10 \times y) = 300$$

x bags of crisps at 15p each and y eggs at 10p each must come to a total of 300p or £3.

In the light of market prices, the slope of the budget line is the amount of one good that has to be sacrificed in order to buy an additional unit of the other good. This will be the same for any point on the budget line (Fig. 2.9). If this consumer reduces his consumption of eggs by *AB*, he will save just enough to buy *BC* bags of

ical amount of total utility, it would form a second indifference curve (I_1). Clearly, all the combinations given by points on I_1 would provide a higher level of total utility than any given by I.

Point F would represent a lower level of total utility than any point on either I or I_1, but an equal level of utility when compared to any other point on I_2, e.g. G or H.

There is an infinity of indifference curves, each representing a different level of total utility. A representative sample of a consumer's many indifference curves, over a given time-period, is called an **indifference map**.

A final point concerning indifference curves at this stage is that they never cross. If they did the consumer would be showing contradictory preferences and this would not be consistent behaviour. In Fig. 2.7, I_3 would not constitute a possible indifference curve. I_3 would imply that the consumer is indifferent between B and E, while I tells us that the consumer is indifferent between B and C. To be consistent, therefore, the consumer would have to be indifferent between E and C. This is not possible as combination E is made up of more of both good X and good Y than is combination C.

Fig. 2.8   *A budget line*

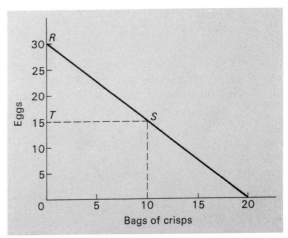

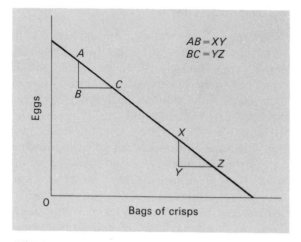

Fig. 2.9   The slope of a budget line

crisps. While the slope of the indifference curve tells us the rate at which the consumer is willing to trade one good for the other, given his preferences, the budget line tells us the current market rate of exchange, given existing prices.

In Fig. 2.9 the slope of the budget line is $AB \div BC$ or $XY \div YZ$. In Fig. 2.8 the slope of the budget line could similarly be thought of as $RT \div TS$. In terms of physical units this would be 15 (eggs) $\div$ 10 (bags), giving us a slope of $1\frac{1}{2}$. Moving from point R to point S on the

budget line has meant sacrificing 15 eggs in order to be able to buy 10 bags of crisps. From here we can go on to conclude that the slope of the budget line is equal to the ratio of the prices of the two goods.

If 15 eggs can be exchanged for 10 bags of crisps, the price of an egg must be two-thirds of the price of a bag of crisps. The ratio of their prices is therefore $1 \div \frac{2}{3}$, i.e. $1\frac{1}{2}$. We were, in fact, told earlier that crisps cost 15p a bag, while eggs were 10p each. From this we could have calculated that the price ratio and, therefore, the slope is $15 \div 10$ or $1\frac{1}{2}$.

Shifts in the budget line

The budget line will shift its position as a result of any change in the consumer's budget or changes in the prices of either of the two goods under consideration.

If the consumer's budget is doubled, he could now buy 60 eggs if no crisps are consumed, or 40 bags of crisps if no eggs are consumed. An increase in income will shift the budget line away from the origin (Fig. 2.10a), while a fall in income will shift it towards the origin. Unless the relative prices change, the new budget lines will be parallel to the original one.

If income and the price of eggs remain constant while the price of crisps doubles, the

Fig. 2.10   Shifting budget lines

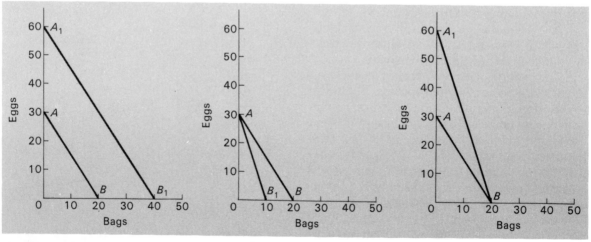

a) An increase in income

b) An increase in the price of crisps

c) An increase in income and in the price of crisps

new budget line will be as shown in Fig. 2.10b. The total budget of £3 can now only buy a maximum of 10 bags of crisps at the new price of 30p a bag. Changes in relative prices will always alter the slopes of the budget lines.

Fig. 2.10c shows what the outcome will be if both these changes occur simultaneously.

1.3 Consumer equilibrium

Having explained both indifference curves and budget lines, we are now in a position to represent consumer equilibrium graphically. By drawing an individual's budget line and indifference map on the same graph, consumption possibilities and preferences can be compared (Fig. 2.11).

Given the constraint of his budget line the individual's aim is to maximize his total utility. Each point on the budget line represents a combination of eggs and bags of crisps that he can afford. He is looking for the point which lies on the indifference curve that is as far away as possible from the origin. The further the indifference curve is from the origin, the higher is the level of total utility it represents. In this way point B is preferable to point A, as it lies on I_2 which is farther from the origin than I_1. This consumer would be indifferent between point B and C as they both lie on I_2. Out of all the points on the budget line point E will bring the greatest amount of satisfaction, as all other points on the budget line lie on indifference curves which are nearer to the origin.

In Fig. 2.11 the consumer is in equilibrium (i.e. maximizing his total utility, given his fixed budget) when he is consuming 15 eggs and 10 bags of crisps per time-period. This is given by point E on the budget line, the point where the budget line is just tangential to one of the consumer's indifference curves.

Point D is clearly preferable to point E, but given current market prices and a fixed budget, this combination lies outside the consumer's range of consumption possibilities. **Consumer equilibrium** is represented graphically by the point of tangency of the budget line with an indifference curve. At such a point of tangency, the slope of the budget line is equal to the slope of the indifference curve. It follows that con-

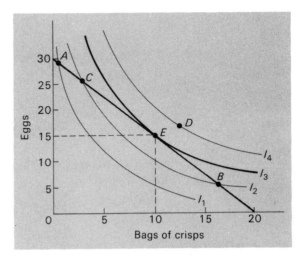

Fig. 2.11   Consumer equilibrium

sumer equilibrium is reached when the ratio of the prices of the two goods is equal to the consumer's marginal rate of substitution.

1.4 An explanation of the law of demand

Consider an individual with a fixed weekly budget of £12 to be spent on good X and good Y. The price of good X is £1 per unit, while that of good Y is £4 per unit, so that the individual's budget line would be X_1Y_1. The consumer's equilibrium point is marked A in Fig. 2.12a. The individual will consume 8 units of good X and 1 unit of good Y per week. Fig. 2.12a can be used to show how the quantity of good Y consumed will change as its price falls. The individual's budget and the price of good X will remain constant throughout.

If the price of good Y was to fall from £4 per unit to £2, the individual's fixed budget of £12 could now buy 6 units of good Y. The individual's new budget line would be X_1Y_2, and his new equilibrium point would be B. This tells us that the individual would now buy 3 units of good Y.

What if the price of good Y falls again, this time to £1 per unit? The individual's fixed budget of £12 could now buy 12 units of good Y and his new budget line would be X_1Y_3. The equilibrium point would now be C and he would be consuming 7 units of good Y.

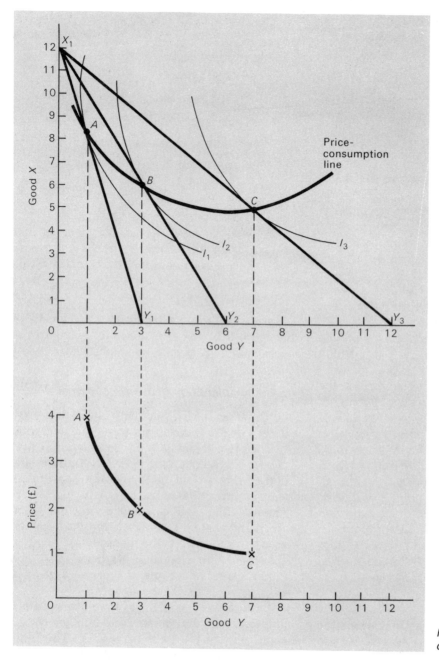

Fig. 2.12a An individual's equilibrium points

Fig. 2.12b An individual's demand curve for good Y

If the points *A*, *B* and *C* in Fig. 2.12a are joined together, they trace out what is called a **price-consumption line**. This shows how the consumption of the two goods varies as the price of one good, and nothing else, varies.

This information enables us to draw the individual's demand curve for good *Y* as shown in Fig. 2.12b. When good *Y*'s price was £4, only 1 unit was demanded. A price of £2 resulted in 3 units being demanded and 7 units were demanded at a price of £1. The consumer's demand curve is clearly downward sloping in accordance with the law of demand.

1.5 *Cardinal and ordinal approaches compared*

In the first part of this chapter it was established through the marginal utility theory that a consumer would choose a pattern of expenditure that would equate the marginal utility derived from the last unit of expenditure on all goods consumed. For any two goods this was expressed in the following way:

$$\frac{\text{MU of good } A}{\text{Price of good } A} = \frac{\text{MU of good } B}{\text{Price of good } B}$$

and was rewritten as:

$$\frac{\text{MU of good } A}{\text{MU of good } B} = \frac{\text{Price of good } A}{\text{Price of good } B}$$

or

$$\frac{MU_A}{MU_B} = \frac{P_A}{P_B}$$

To arrive at this conclusion, it was assumed that the cardinal measurement of utility was possible.

Through an ordinal approach to the measurement of utility, indifference curve theory has shown that the consumer will choose a pattern of expenditure that leaves his budget line tangental to one of his indifference curves. At such a point of tangency, the slopes of the two curves must be equal. As was shown on p.51 the slope of the indifference curve is the consumer's subjective marginal rate of substitution.

In looking at budget lines, we saw that their slope is equal to the ratio of the prices of the two goods, which can also be thought of as the market's objective marginal rate of substitution. It follows that at the point of tangency:

$$\frac{\text{Marginal rate of substitution}}{\text{of good } B \text{ for good } A} = \frac{\text{Price of good } A}{\text{Price of good } B}$$

or

$$MRS \ (B/A) = \frac{P_A}{P_B}$$

Now, if we bring together the conclusions of both theories, we can write:

$$MRS \ (B/A) = \frac{P_A}{P_B} = \frac{MU_A}{MU_B}$$

In other words, the marginal rate of substitution between the two goods is equal to the ratio of their marginal utilities, i.e.

$$MRS \ (B/A) = \frac{MU_A}{MU_B}$$

In this way the marginal rate of substitution at any point on the indifference curve will represent the ratio of the marginal utilities of the two goods. This is not surprising as whatever arbitrary figures are given for the marginal utilities, they must always reflect the consumer's order of preference.

If for a given combination the consumer only accepts to change 1 unit of good A for 3 units of good B, it is fairly obvious that the satisfaction he derives from the last unit of good A is three times greater than that derived from the last unit of good B. Here,

$$\frac{MU_A}{MU_B} = 3 = MRS \ (B/A)$$

In the same way the diminishing marginal rate of substitution is analogous to the law of diminishing marginal utility: the greater the quantity of a good consumed, the smaller its marginal utility and the smaller the compensation needed for the loss of one unit.

This last section has shown that despite their different approaches, marginal utility theory and indifference curve theory arrive at the same conclusion. Consumer equilibrium is represented by the same equation. The difference is conceptual and lies in the fact that indifference curve theory only involves the ratio of the marginal utilities of the goods (marginal rate of substitution), thereby avoiding the cardinal measurement of utility.

2 Revealed preference theory

This approach tries to explain the law of demand without making any assumptions about marginal utility. In this way it avoids the whole debate concerning the cardinal and ordinal measurements of utility. The only necessary assumption for this theory is that consumers will be rational and that their behaviour will be consistent.

Revealed preference theory highlights the fact that changes in the quantity demanded of a good will depend upon changes in **real income** and in the **relative prices** of the goods. The theory shows that, while money income and all other prices remain constant, a change in the price of one good will in fact alter both the consumer's real income and the relative prices of the goods involved.

The change in demand that results from a change in a good's price can be broken into two separate components:

1 The **income effect** is the change in demand brought about by a change in the consumer's real income.

2 The **substitution effect** is the change in demand brought about by a change in the good's relative price.

It is for theoretical purposes and for the sake of a clear explanation that we shall study these components separately. In practice both the income effect and the substitution effect take place simultaneously. By analysing these effects a further explanation of the law of demand can be found.

2.1 Income effect

Before explaining the income effect of a price change, it will be helpful to consider the effects of a change in real income that has resulted from an increase in money income, assuming that prices remain unchanged throughout.

In Fig. 2.13 an individual has a fixed money income represented by the budget line AB. He could afford any combination of good X and good Y, represented by a point on the budget line AB or within the triangle OAB. By choosing a point within the triangle rather than on the budget line, he would be failing to spend all

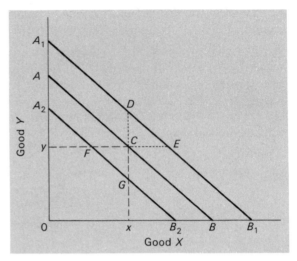

Fig. 2.13   Changes in real income resulting from changes in money income

his income. We shall assume throughout the following discussion that he will spend all of his given money income. Further assume that he chooses point C, and thereby consumes x units of good X and y units of good Y.

An increase in the consumer's money income, remembering our assumption of constant prices, will result in a parallel shift in the budget line from AB to A_1B_1. Given that he will spend all his income, he will now choose a point on his new budget line A_1B_1. It would seem reasonable, and observable behaviour supports this, to expect a consumer to react to an increase in income by consuming more of both good X and good Y. This would involve choosing a point on A_1B_1 between the points marked D and E.

Similarly, a fall in income will shift the budget line from AB to A_2B_2 and we would expect this to result in a reduction in the quantities consumed of both goods. The new combination of good X and good Y consumed would be represented by a point between F and G.

At this stage we can introduce the concept of an **inferior** good. Examples might be remoulded tyres, margarine, or clothing made of synthetic materials. These goods are usually thought of as second best and are cheaper than the real thing. It is assumed that the consumption of such goods decreases as income increases. Why indeed should one continue to consume margarine when one prefers and can now afford butter? In the case of inferior goods a change in income will have the opposite effect on the quantity demanded from that predicted so far. As your real income increases, so the quantity of inferior goods consumed will fall.

If in Fig. 2.13 good X had been an inferior good, the increase in income would have resulted in the consumer demanding less of it, and as a result he would choose a point between A_1 and D on the budget line A_1B_1. A decrease in income might result in him having to consume more of the inferior good. This would involve choosing a combination of good X and good Y represented by a point between G and B_2 on the budget line A_2B_2.

Our analysis of the effect of a change in real income would lead us to conclude that:

1 If good X and good Y are **normal** goods, an increase in real income has a positive effect on consumption (more of both goods is consumed), while a decrease in real income has a negative effect on consumption (less of both goods is consumed).

2 If good X is an **inferior** good and good Y a **normal** good, an increase in real income has a negative effect on the consumption of good X (less of good X is consumed), while the effect on good Y remains positive. A decrease in real income has a positive effect on the consumption of good X (more of good X is consumed), while the effect on good Y remains negative.

So far we have been looking at changes in real income brought about by changes in money income during a period of constant prices. However, changes in real income can also be brought about by changes in prices, where money income remains unchanged. For example, if the prices of good X and good Y were to change simultaneously by the same percentage amount while money income remained constant, the budget lines would shift while remaining parallel just as in Fig. 2.13. This would also represent a change in real income.

Of more interest to us here is the fact that a change in the price of *one* good only can also result in a change in real income. Fig. 2.14

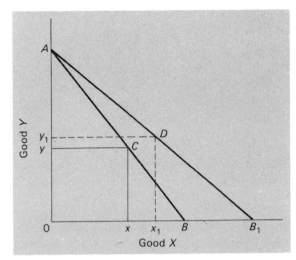

Fig. 2.14   A fall in the price of good X

shows a fall in the price of good X, assuming that both money income and the price of good Y remain constant.

As Fig. 2.14 shows, the budget line would shift from AB to AB_1. The consumer can now buy x units of good X and y units of good Y for less money than before. He can buy his original combination of good X and good Y given by point C and still have money left to spend. There is no reason why our earlier analysis of a change in real income should not apply to an increase in real income brought about by a price change. Assuming that neither good X nor good Y are inferior goods, it would seem reasonable to expect the consumer to buy more of both. This would involve choosing a point such as D on the new budget line AB_1.

However, point D will not necessarily be the outcome as so far we have considered only one of two effects that will result from a fall in the price of good X.

2.2 Substitution effect

Consumers prefer to achieve their satisfaction at the lowest possible cost. As a result, if a good becomes relatively cheap, there is a tendency to substitute the cheaper good for relatively expensive goods. If the price of holidays abroad fell due to cheaper air travel, you might well substitute holidays abroad for holidays at

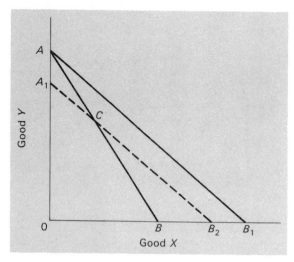

Fig. 2.15   *Isolating the substitution effect*

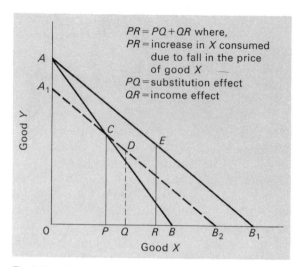

Fig. 2.16   *Income and substitution effects*

home. Indeed, a holiday abroad might be chosen in preference to a music centre you had considered buying.

In this way a fall in the price of good X would make it relatively more attractive than good Y. This would result in the consumer buying more of good X and less of good Y. An increase in the price of good X or a decrease in the price of good Y would obviously have the opposite effect.

The **substitution effect** is the change in the quantity demanded of a good which results solely from a change in the relative prices of the goods. This substitution effect is shown in Fig. 2.15. AB is the consumer's original budget line and out of all the possible combinations of good X and good Y the consumer has chosen that represented by point C. The price of good X now falls and the new budget line is AB_1. Assuming that good X is not an inferior good, we know that the fall in price will have increased real income and that as a result more of both goods will be consumed.

In order to isolate the substitution effect it is necessary to eliminate the income effect. In order to do this we shall artificially reduce the consumer's income by moving AB_1 inwards to the origin 0 until the consumer can once again just afford to buy the original combination. The budget line will be redrawn through C but parallel to AB_1. This is shown on the diagram by

A_1B_2. The shift from the original budget line AB to A_1B_2 reflects only the change in relative prices that has resulted from the fall in the price of good X. Any income effect has been eliminated.

It is now that the assumption of consistent behaviour becomes crucial. Before any price change the consumer **revealed his preference** by choosing point C rather than any other point within the triangle OAB. In doing this the consumer rejected all the points that now lie between A_1 and C. Having rejected them once, we can assume that he will reject them again now that he is faced with choosing a point of consumption along A_1B_2. This means that any movement away from C due to the substitution effect must be to a point between C and B_2. Any such point will represent an increase in the consumption of good X. Such an increase would represent the quantity of good X that the consumer would substitute for good Y as good X is more attractive now that it is cheaper.

The general conclusion is that the substitution effect will never cause a fall in consumption of the good whose price has been reduced.

2.3 An explanation of the law of demand

Fig. 2.16 can be used to show the simultaneous income and substitution effects of a given price change. With a fixed money income and current market prices an individual has chosen point C on his budget line AB. The price of good X now falls, giving a new budget line of AB_1.

The substitution effect of this price change will result in more of good X being consumed at the expense of good Y. Demand for good X might rise from P to Q. Assuming that good X is not an inferior good, there will be, in addition to this positive substitution effect, a positive income effect. This might further increase the demand for good X by QR, leaving point E as the consumption point on the new budget line AB_1.

This means that a fall in the price of good X has been shown to result in an increase in the quantity of good X demanded. This is in accordance with the law of demand.

What would happen if good X had been an inferior good? In this case the income effect of a fall in the good's price would have been negative, i.e. less of it would be consumed. However, this would not necessarily result in a contradiction of the law of demand.

If the negative income effect is not large enough to cancel out any increase in consumption resulting from a positive substitution effect, the quantity demanded would still have gone up as a result of the fall in price. Point E_1 in Fig. 2.17 would represent such an outcome.

If the negative income effect was larger than the positive substitution effect, the law of demand would be contradicted. Point E_2 in Fig. 2.18 would represent this possibility. More will be said about such an outcome when considering exceptions to the law of demand (p.62).

In practice it would seem that where negative effects do exist they are rarely large enough to cancel out the positive substitution effects. Inferior goods are not unusual, but goods with upward sloping demand curves are.

2.4 An explanation of elasticity

Through analysing these effects, we have been able to explain the direction of a change in demand in response to a price change. These effects can also be used to help explain the extent of any such change.

Where an individual is spending a high

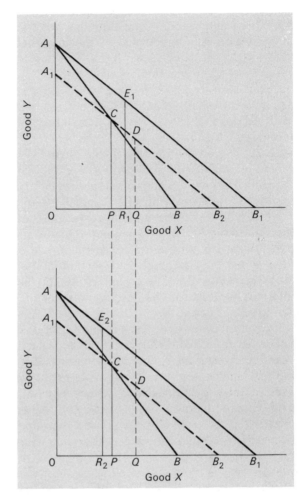

Fig. 2.17   *The positive substitution effect is greater than the negative income effect*

Fig. 2.18   *The negative income effect is greater than the positive substitution effect*

percentage of his budget on a good, the income effect of a price change on the quantity demanded will be large so that demand will tend to be elastic.

Where a good has few close substitutes, the substitution effect of a price change on the quantity demanded will be small so that demand will tend to be inelastic (see Chapter 1, p.13).

3 Exceptions to the law of demand

A further way in which these new theories can be seen as an improvement on the marginal utility theory is in terms of their ability to explain exceptions to the law of demand.

The classic example of an upward sloping demand curve is that of the **Giffen good**. An explanation of this can best be illustrated by presenting income and substitution effects with the help of indifference curve theory.

Sir Robert Giffen is said to have shown that English peasants in the nineteenth century increased their consumption of bread as the price of wheat increased. The explanation of this contradiction of the law of demand is based on two assumptions: firstly, that bread is seen as an inferior good, and secondly, that bread accounted for a large percentage of the total expenditure of the average nineteenth-century English peasant.

With an inferior good the income effect of a fall in its price would be negative. Any such negative income effect would be large due to the fact that expenditure on bread constituted such a large percentage of a poor person's expenditure. It now only needs this large negative income effect to be greater than any positive substitution effect and the contradiction has been explained.

Consider the more contemporary example of a peasant farmer in a Third World country whose diet is made up mainly of rice. His budget line can be drawn in a slightly different way from those used so far. Along the horizontal axis the quantity of rice consumed is measured while on the vertical axis the value of all other goods consumed is measured (Fig. 2.19). His fixed money income leaves him with a budget line AB and consumer equilibrium will exist at the point where it is tangential to one of his indifference curves, i.e. point C. This tells us that his consumption of rice is equal to R.

The price of rice now falls, leaving him with a new budget line of AB_1. He can now buy the same amount of rice for less money, meaning that he has experienced an increase in real income. As a result of this higher income he

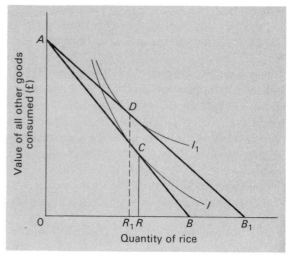

Fig. 2.19   A Giffen good

feels able to consume less rice and more of other foodstuffs such as meat or fish. This negative income effect may turn out to be so large that his consumption of rice actually falls.

In Fig. 2.19 this is just what has happened as his new budget line AB_1 is tangental to one of his indifference curves at point D, showing a fall in the consumption of rice to the lower level of R_1. This new indifference curve I_1 represents a higher level of satisfaction, which the consumer is now in a position to enjoy following the increase in real income. Its position also reflects the fact that this consumer sees rice as an inferior good and that under certain circumstances a fall in the price of such a good can result in a negative income effect that is in excess of any positive substitution effect. In other words, combination D contains less rice but provides more satisfaction than combination C.

Other examples of exceptions to the law of demand can be explained in terms of negative substitution effects outweighing any positive income effects that result from a fall in price. One example of this is sometimes referred to as **conspicuous consumption**. Here the consumer is buying something because it is expensive, wanting it to act as some kind of status symbol. Such a consumer might buy more of a particular artist's work as it becomes more expensive and less of the work of other artists as theirs is relatively less expensive.

Where price is seen as an indication of quality, negative substitution effects can be found as a consequence of a fall in price. If the lower price is felt to signify a fall in quality, consumers may buy less of the product and more of substitute products, despite the fact that they are now relatively more expensive.

As we can see it is certainly possible to find hypothetical examples of upward sloping demand curves. However, in the real world they are rare and the predictions of our theories of consumer behaviour hold in the vast majority of cases.

4 Conclusion

Broad doubts can be expressed about any attempt to develop a general theory of consumer behaviour. Do people have definite consumption goals? To what extent is the satisfying of future wants more important than the satisfaction of present wants? How efficient are people as consumers: do they make informed decisions or are they misled by advertisers? Is consumption more habitual than rational?

Despite these doubts and the many assumptions necessary for the analysis of consumer behaviour, each of the basic theories outlined provides useful insights. Concepts such as diminishing marginal utility, diminishing marginal rate of substitution, income effect and substitution effect all help to explain the behaviour of consumers.

It is also reassuring to find each theory leading to the same prediction that an inverse relationship exists between price and the quantity demanded, particularly as this prediction seems to fit observable behaviour in the real world.

Note: Questions on consumer behaviour can be found at the end of Chapter 3, p.74.

Chapter 3   *Consumer behaviour: income*

This chapter will explore the relationship between the consumer's income and his consumption, a relationship that has already been mentioned. In Chapter 1 a change in income was seen as a factor that would cause increases or decreases in the quantity demanded, and the extent of such changes was quantified in terms of the income elasticity of demand. In Chapter 2 the income effect of a price change was analysed.

Despite this the emphasis so far has been very much on the price-consumption relationship. It can be argued that such an emphasis is misplaced, and this is a common criticism of demand theory. There is evidence to suggest that changes in income produce more significant changes in consumption than do changes in prices. The aim of this chapter is to redress this apparent imbalance.

In this context we are talking about changes in **real income**. As money income increases, prices must either be constant or increase at a slower rate for a real change to have taken place. Changes in real income will have implications for two broad aspects of consumption. Firstly, they will affect the **level of total expenditure**. As real income changes so the proportion of income spent on consumption will tend to change. Here we are interested in the choice between consumption expenditure and saving, where saving is defined as any income not spent on consumption. Secondly, they will affect the **pattern of expenditure**. As total expenditure changes with changes in real income so will the proportion of total expenditure devoted to different goods. Hence the quantity consumed of different goods by a given household may vary accordingly.

The bulk of what follows in this chapter will analyse the first of these aspects of consumer behaviour in some detail. This is normally explored at an aggregate level and as a result it is usually seen as an aspect of macroeconomics. Our intention is to look at this relationship in terms of the household. As a single decision-making unit the behaviour of the household can be viewed in terms of microeconomics. We are interested in seeing to what extent income is the single most important determinant of the household's total consumption. By consumption we mean the **level** of expenditure rather than the pattern of expenditure. The aggregate implications of such behaviour will not concern us.

Several theories have been put forward in an attempt to explain the exact nature of the relationship between income and total expenditure on consumption. The oldest of the theories will be outlined first and is called the **absolute income hypothesis**. This will be followed by a look at some newer theories: the **relative income hypothesis** and the **normal income hypothesis**.

Before leaving the income-consumption relationship we shall conclude by taking a brief look at the second aspect of the relationship — the effect of income changes on the **pattern** of expenditure.

Part 1   *The traditional absolute income hypothesis*

The basic hypothesis is a very simple one. It argues that the single most important determinant of consumption is income. As our interest is in total consumption we need not concern ourselves with relative prices. By **absolute income** we mean the present disposable real income of the household. **Disposable income** is that which remains after the deduction of taxation. That part of disposable income not spent on **consumption**—that is expenditure on goods and services—will be classified as **savings**. Consumption in excess of disposable income must be financed by **dis-saving** or borrowing. The spending of savings (dis-saving) implies that consumption must have been less than disposable income during an earlier time-period. In order to repay debts households must spend less than their disposable income during some future time-period.

This approach to the analysis of consumption was first undertaken by J. M. Keynes. In order to describe the relationship between real disposable income and consumption, he introduced two useful concepts:

1 The **average propensity to consume** (*APC*): this relates total consumption (*C*) to total disposable income (*Y*) in the following way:

$$APC = C \div Y$$

It represents the proportion of total disposable income devoted to consumption. From this we can see that if consumption is equal to income, the household's *APC* will be one. If saving is taking place, the amount of money devoted to consumption will be smaller than total disposable income and the *APC* will be less than one. Dis-saving or borrowing in order to finance consumption will result in the household's *APC* being greater than one.

Keynes argued that a household's *APC* would tend to decrease as real income increases. In other words, this means that when its income rises, the household will tend to devote a relatively smaller part of it to consumption.

2 The **marginal propensity to consume** (*MPC*): this shows the extent to which consumption will change ($\triangle C$) as a result of a given change in real disposable income ($\triangle Y$) in the following way:

$$MPC = \triangle C \div \triangle Y$$

The *MPC* represents the proportion of the change in income by which consumption would be altered.

Keynes argued that a household's *MPC* would tend to fall as real income increases and that it would be less than the house-

hold's *APC*. The higher a household's income, the smaller the proportion of an increase in income which would be spent on consumption.

Having identified these aspects of the consumption-income relationship, Keynes went on to represent them diagrammatically.

1 *The consumption function*

By measuring the household's total consumption up the vertical axis and the household's disposable income along the horizontal axis, the **consumption function** shows the expenditure on goods and services at each possible level of income (Fig. 3.1).

The consumption function tells us that this household will spend C_1 when income is equal to Y_1 and C_2 when income is equal to Y_2. The consumption function illustrates the basic proposition that consumption depends upon income and this can be expressed as follows:

$$C = f(Y)$$

where *f* means that consumption is 'a function of' or 'depends upon' income,

   C represents total consumption,

   Y represents total disposable income.

A first point to notice is that the consumption function intersects with the vertical axis at point C_0. This means that even when the household's income is zero, expenditure on consumption will at least be equal to C_0. Rather than starve, the household will dis-save, borrow, or sell assets. We can conclude that consumption *C* is always at least equal to C_0.

A second point to notice is that the consumption function in Fig. 3.1 is a straight line. This means that its slope is constant. The slope at point A_2 is given by $c \div y$ and this is equal to $C_2 C_1 \div Y_2 Y_1$. This, in turn, is equal to $\triangle C \div \triangle Y$ which is our equation for *MPC*.

The slope of the consumption function is equal to the marginal propensity to consume and it is constant. In other words, whatever the original income level was, the same proportion of any increase in income will always be spent on consumption.

We can now bring these two points together

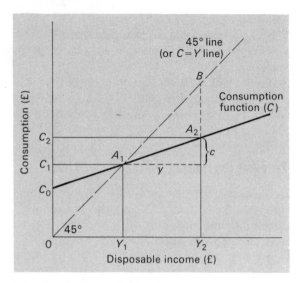

Fig. 3.1   A consumption function

and write the equation of the consumption function as:

$$C = f(Y)$$
$$C = C_0 + (s \times Y)$$

where C represents total consumption,

Y represents total disposable income,

C_0 represents expenditure on consumption when income is zero,

s represents the slope. The fraction of any disposable income received that is spent on consumption in addition to C_0, i.e. $s = MPC$.

This equation tells us that a minimum expenditure on consumption will always take place (level C_0) and that it will increase by amounts which always represent the same proportion (or fraction) of the corresponding increase in disposable income.

We may now consider some further points. Look at the broken line on Fig. 3.1 that intersects the origin at 45°. (Note: it is only 45° if the vertical and horizontal scales are the same.) If the household were to spend on consumption their entire disposable income, whatever that income might be, then this would be their consumption function (i.e. $C = Y$). The consumption function shown tells us that the household will only behave this way at an income level of Y_1. Any income level

above this will result in saving. For example, at point A_2 when income is Y_2, saving will be equal to A_2B with C_2 having been spent on consumption. Income levels lower than Y_1 will result in consumption in excess of income, so that some consumption will take place even when income is zero.

Another feature of the consumption function in Fig. 3.1 is that its slope is less than that of the 45° line. This implies that the APC will fall as income rises. Up to an income level of Y_1 the APC will be greater than one, at an income level of Y_1 it will equal one, and beyond an income level of Y_1 it will be less than one.

A further implication follows on from the fact that the consumption function intersects the vertical axis at a value greater than zero. This means that the APC will always be greater than the MPC. This can be confirmed mathematically. If we rewrite our earlier equation for the APC in terms of the equation given for the consumption function we get:

$$APC = \frac{C}{Y}$$

$$= \frac{C_0 + (s \times Y)}{Y}$$

$$= \frac{C_0}{Y} + s$$

This confirms our assertion that APC will fall as income rises.

We can also use this to show that the APC is always greater than the MPC:

$$\frac{C_0}{Y} + s > s$$

that is, $APC > MPC$

These are the relationships implied by the shape of the consumption function in Fig. 3.1. Whether or not this is an accurate representation of consumer behaviour needs to be confirmed by empirical evidence.

2 The shape of the consumption function

If consumption functions were found to display alternative shapes, then different conclusions would have to be drawn. Consider Fig. 3.2. Any straight-line consumption function that passes through the origin (C_1) will have a constant MPC that is equal to the APC. The fact that C_1 is less steep than the 45° line means that the percentage of income devoted to consumption will always be less than 100 per cent.

The consumption function C_2 is similar to that in Fig. 3.1. The APC falls as income rises while remaining in excess of a constant MPC. In comparison to the consumption function in Fig. 3.1 C_2 is steeper (i.e. the MPC is greater), the level of consumption when income is zero is lower (i.e. the constant C_0 in the function's equation will be smaller), and finally, saving begins at a lower level of income (i.e. C_2 cuts the 45° line at a lower level of disposable income).

By now it should be clear that the shape and position of the consumption function reflect the nature of the relationship between income and consumption.

The relationship suggested by C_2 differs from that described by Keynes in one main respect. Keynes felt that the MPC would tend to decline as disposable income increases. In order to incorporate this characteristic the consumption function would have to be non-linear, such as that labelled C_3. The MPC at any point on C_3 will be given by the slope of the tangent at that point. The slope, and therefore the MPC, is clearly greater at point A than at point B.

Non-linear consumption functions complicate the analysis without adding much to the basic predictions of the absolute income hypothesis. The basic hypothesis is illustrated by consumption functions such as the one in Fig. 3.1 and C_2 in Fig. 3.2. It is also worth stressing that the very act of drawing a consumption function implies that income is the most important determinant of consumption. Other factors that might influence consumption are held constant so that changes in income will alter consumption by moving the household to different points along the consumption func-

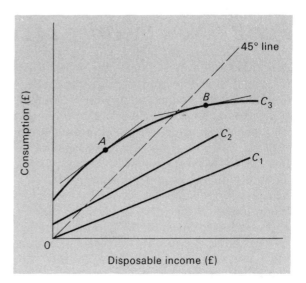

Fig. 3.2   *Alternative shapes for consumption functions*

tion. If these other factors were to change, the whole consumption function would shift to a higher or lower position. Such factors would include the household's expectations regarding future changes in prices and income, interest rates, the availability of credit, and the household's wealth.

3 Conclusion

To what extent does empirical evidence support the absolute income hypothesis? Evidence can be collected in two ways:
1 Cross-section data involve the analysis of a cross-section of households with different income levels at the same point in time.
2 Time-series data involve the analysis of households over a period of years as their incomes are changing.

Cross-section data display a good 'fit' with the predictions of the absolute income hypothesis. Average and marginal propensities to consume tend to fall as income increases and households with low incomes tend to dis-save. However, some of the evidence based on time-series data fails to support the absolute income hypothesis. The newer theories that follow can help explain this.

Part 2   *New theories of consumption*

According to the absolute income hypothesis, a household's level of consumption expenditure is primarily determined by its **present income**. Whenever income increases, consumption will also increase. It can be observed, however, that consumption does not increase as fast as income, so that if we consider consumption as a proportion of income, this proportion will decrease as income increases. In Keynesian terminology these characteristics can be expressed as follows: the *MPC* is smaller than the *APC* and, as income increases, both the *MPC* and the *APC* will tend to fall. The empirical evidence provided by cross-section studies suggests that at any given point in time households will behave in accordance with the absolute income hypothesis.

The new theories that follow try and explain why in the long run a household's behaviour might be somewhat different. Before outlining these new theories, we shall highlight the empirical evidence that fails to satisfy the absolute income hypothesis. Such evidence is provided by time-series studies which reflect the household's consumption behaviour over a given time-period.

Where time-series studies are based on changes in income and consumption from one year to the next, their results are not dissimilar from those of cross-section studies. However, they do seem to suggest that in the short run households are more responsive to an increase in income. The proportion of income spent on consumption will be higher. It will still tend to decrease as income increases, but at a slower rate. The consumption function still broadly conforms to the absolute income hypothesis, but it tends to be steeper and more linear. Here the *MPC* is higher and more consistent though it remains smaller than the *APC*.

It is where time-series studies are based on longer time-periods that the results begin to be significantly different from those predicted by the absolute income hypothesis. In the long run, responses to changes in income are greater and more consistent, and consumption increases proportionally with income. The proportion of income spent on consumption is no longer decreasing but constant. In other words, the *MPC* is not only higher, but it is constant and equal to the *APC*. The consumption function will be both linear and steeper as well as passing through the origin (Fig. 3.3).

In Fig. 3.3 C_1 represents the evidence provided by cross-section data, and this resembles household behaviour according to the absolute income hypothesis. How then can we explain the way in which the findings based on time-series data result in consumption functions such as C_2 in the short run and C_3 in the long run?

The new theories suggest that the answer is to be found by taking a closer look at exactly what we mean by 'income'. The absolute income hypothesis relates consumption to **current** disposable income. The newer theories use broader measures of income. As well as current absolute income they include in their analysis relative, past, and expected future incomes.

Fig. 3.3   Consumption functions based on different empirical evidence

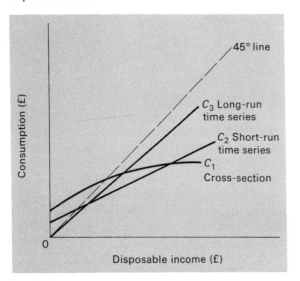

1 The relative income hypothesis

This approach to the explanation of consumption behaviour has been developed by J. S. Duesenberry. At the heart of the theory is the view that a household's consumption will not depend so much on the absolute size of its income as on its **relative** size. Two aspects of relativity can be distinguished. Firstly, a household can compare its income to the income levels of other households. Secondly, a household can compare its present income to its previous incomes.

This first aspect of relativity emphasizes the importance of a household's position on the income-scale. People do not only derive satisfaction from consumption itself, but also from how their consumption compares with that of others. A certain standard of consumption will impart a certain status on a household. 'Trying to keep up with the Joneses' can become an important objective and thus an important factor in explaining consumer behaviour. For this reason it is essential to know whether an increase in income will improve a household's position on the income-scale or simply maintain it as all other households have experienced a similar increase.

The argument is that the APC does not simply fall with higher incomes, but that it falls as one moves up the income-scale. If a household improves its relative position its APC will tend to fall, as other households' incomes have not increased the household will not need to increase its consumption by much to maintain or improve its social image. However, if all incomes increase by a similar amount, leaving each household in the same relative position, then each household's APC will remain unchanged. The household will have to increase consumption proportionally with income in order to maintain its social standing. This can be shown graphically in Fig. 3.4.

In Fig. 3.4 a household's income has increased from Y to Y_1. If this increase moved the household to a higher position on the community's income-scale, consumption expenditure will increase from c to c_1. In other words, the household's APC will have fallen as shown by

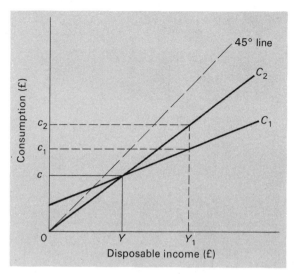

Fig. 3.4   *The household's consumption function when its income level is relative to that of other households*

the consumption function C_1. However, if the increase in income has not improved the household's relative position, as everyone else has experienced similar increases, then the APC will remain unaltered. This would imply a consumption function such as C_2 and a new level of consumption of c_2.

A consumption function such as C_1 is of the type given by cross-section data. The shape and position of C_2 displays a closer fit with the results of long-run time-series data where the APC is constant.

The second aspect of relativity emphasizes the way in which households become accustomed to previous levels of consumption. Present income levels must be seen in terms of how they compare with previoius peak levels of income. Having become accustomed to a certain standard of living, a household will increase its APC when faced with a falling income in an attempt to maintain it. On the other hand, each time a previous peak income is exceeded, the entire consumption function will shift upwards as expectations are increased. Taken together these two aspects of behaviour can be used to explain the behaviour represented by Fig. 3.5.

Assume that the household in Fig. 3.5 has an income level of Y and that it has never known a higher one. If its income was now to fall, the

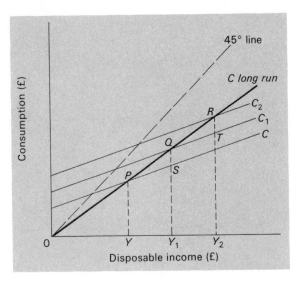

Fig. 3.5   The household's consumption function when its present income level is relative to previous income levels

household would move down the consumption function C. Such a movement away from point P would signify falls in consumption. However, each step down C represents an increase in APC. This can be explained in terms of the household attempting to maintain its previous standard of consumption. If the trend were reversed and income began to grow again, the household would move up consumption function C.

What if the household's income rose above its previous peak of Y to a level equal to Y_1? At first consumption might be given by point S. However, Y_1 now represents a new peak income level. In the light of this, the argument goes, the household will shift its consumption function upwards to C_1. This will result in a new level of consumption given by point Q. A subsequent increase in income to a new peak of Y_2 would eventually shift the consumption function upwards to C_2, resulting in a new consumption level as given by point R. Long-run increases in income would in this way move the household along the long-run consumption function ($C_{long-run}$).

An explanation of consumer behaviour built upon the above arguments can help explain the conflicting findings of short-run and long-run empirical studies.

2 The normal income hypothesis

There are two alternative versions of the normal income hypothesis. In both cases the concept of 'normal' income involves viewing income as a long-term flow rather than as the household's current disposable income. What is thought of as normal in this context will depend upon both past experience and future expectations. Households may use past experience to estimate the next round of income, and this may have implications for present consumption. Any anticipated promotion may also affect present consumption. If income should suddenly increase beyond what is seen as its normal level, the household may first be reluctant to increase consumption as the increase may only be temporary. Similarly, should income fall below its normal level, consumption may not be reduced if it is felt that a return to normal will soon follow.

By stressing the importance of normal income, the following theories display significant similarities.

2.1 The permanent income hypothesis

This theory was developed by Milton Friedman. Normal income is referred to as permanent income and it is seen as the household's expected flow of income over a long planning period. More specifically, **permanent income** is defined as that amount which, given future expected earnings, can be made available for consumption during each time-period, without altering the present wealth of the household. Expected rates of interest will clearly play a role in this calculation.

Friedman argues that consumption will be largely determined by the size of the household's permanent income. The extent to which the household's actual income varies from what is seen as its permanent income is referred to as **transitory income**. An injury at work could result in a period's transitory income being negative, while unexpected overtime could make it positive. The theory suggests that variations in transitory income will have little effect on consumption. Negative transitory income will lower actual income below its expected permanent level. However, consumption will be maintained at its planned level by an increasing *APC*. Positive transitory income will increase actual income above the expected permanent income. Despite this, consumption will fail to increase significantly, making *APC* unusually low.

Transitory changes will only affect consumption either when they are very large or when it is felt that they will persist in the future. Where the change is seen as a lasting one, the household will revise its conception of permanent income, and this in turn will bring about a change in consumption.

Consider a household who hears of the death of a distant relative. What if in the will it is left a sum of £1000? This would represent a positive transitory income for that year. However, as a one-off increase in income it would have a negligible effect on the household's perceived permanent annual income over the rest of its expected lifespan.

Now assume that rather than a sum of £1000 they were left some stocks and shares that would earn them £1000 a year indefinitely. During the first year the change in actual income would be identical in both cases. However, the circumstances outlined in the second case would result in an increase in permanent income.

What would be the implications of all this for the household's consumption during the year of the relative's death? The absolute income hypothesis would predict the same increase in consumption in both cases. The permanent income hypothesis would predict a very small increase in consumption in the first case, but a significant increase in the second case. This significant change would be seen as a permanent one.

The major implication of the permanent income hypothesis is that present consumption is a function of permanent income rather than present actual income. Changes in present income will only affect actual consumption in so far as they affect permanent income. Purely transitory changes in income will have very little effect on consumption.

2.2 The life-cycle hypothesis

This theory was developed by F. Modigliani and R. Brumberg. They argue that a household will plan expenditure in terms of its expected lifetime income. This assumes that a household is certain about future income and life expectancy. A further simplifying assumption is that each household intends to leave no legacies to its heirs. By the end of its lifetime it will pass on no accumulated assets or debts.

This last assumption implies that saving will only be undertaken in order to rearrange consumption during its lifetime. A typical household may experience relatively low income levels during its early earning years, high income levels during middle and late earning years, and low income during retirement. Being aware of this likely income stream in advance the household may plan to borrow in the early years in order to finance consumption, repay these loans and save during high income years, and run down savings in order to supplement low income during later years.

Different households will anticipate different **income profiles**. Occupations with long training-periods such as accountancy will expect low incomes to begin with. Manual workers may expect to reach their peak income quite early. In some professions incomes will go on increasing up until retirement, while others will reach a plateau. Some workers will experience declining incomes towards the end of their working lives and pension entitlements will vary from one occupation to another.

A possible income profile is given by Fig. 3.6. The breadwinner in this household expects to begin work at 16 years of age and reach a peak income at around 50 years of age. Between then and retirement at 65 income will fall slightly, and during retirement a pension of about a third of his final earned income is anticipated.

Normal or permanent annual income is calculated by dividing total expected income (the shaded area *ABCDEF*) by the life expectancy in years from the time work is started (i.e. 59 years). This normal income reflects a steady rate of consumption made possible by borrowing early on, repaying loans and saving during higher income years, and dis-saving during

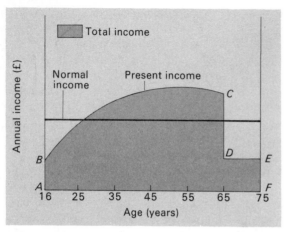

Fig. 3.6   An income profile

retirement. Normal income represents the maximum level of annual consumption that a household could undertake during its lifetime without accumulating any debts or assets.

The analysis so far has implicitly assumed a zero rate of interest. With a positive rate of interest normal income can no longer be determined simply by dividing the sum total of all future incomes by life expectancy measured in years. When borrowing, a household will incur interest payments. When saving, earned income will be supplemented by unearned income in the form of interest. These outflows and inflows will cause normal income to differ from that given by the simple dividing calculation.

While linking consumption to expected future income as well as current income, the life-cycle hypothesis also stresses the importance of the household's wealth at any given point in time. Holdings of financial and real assets can have a significant effect on the percentage of disposable income devoted to consumption. It seems reasonable to assert that where such holdings are high greater percentages of a given income will be spent on consumption if only because the need to accumulate further assets is that much less important.

Bringing together the threads of the life-cycle hypothesis we can see that in attempting to explain consumption it emphasizes the household's age, expected future income and wealth in addition to its current level of income.

3 Conclusion

Chapter 2 brought out the importance of prices in determining certain aspects of consumer behaviour. This chapter has shown that the household's income is also an important factor. The emphasis so far has been on how income can determine the level of expenditure. At the beginning of the chapter we pointed to the fact that income also helps to determine patterns of expenditure as households seek to maximize their total utility. The **income-consumption line** highlights the impact of income changes on expenditure patterns.

In considering the relationship between a household's level of income and its consumption of different goods, indifference curves and budget lines once again prove to be useful analytical tools. Their employment in Fig. 3.7 differs slightly from earlier diagrams. Units of the good under analysis are measured along the horizontal axis while the household's money income is measured on the vertical axis. A budget line shows how consuming a greater quantity of the good will leave less money available for the consumption of other goods. Each indifference curve gives a series of combinations of the good in question and money to be spent on other goods between which the household is indifferent. An increase in money income, assuming constant prices (i.e. an increase in real income), will shift the consumer's budget line further out from the origin while remaining parallel to its original position.

In Fig. 3.7a the good in question is petrol and AB represents the original budget line. A_1B_1 and A_2B_2 are subsequent budget lines following two increases in income. E is the original equilibrium point with E_1 and E_2 being the equilibrium points that result from the increases in income, each given by the point of tangency between an indifference curve and a budget line. The original level of income is A and this would enable the consumer to buy B units of petrol. In choosing equilibrium point E this individual has bought b units of petrol, leaving a of his income to be spent on other goods. From this we can deduce that b multiplied by the price of petrol per unit must equal

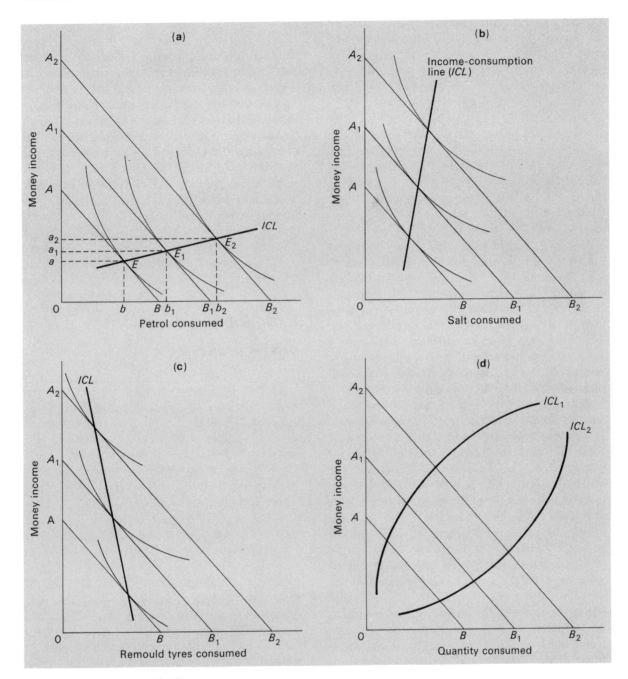

Fig. 3.7 Income-consumption lines

aA as this is the amount of income devoted to the consumption of petrol.

By joining together E, E_1, E_2 we arrive at the individual's income-consumption line (ICL). This shows how the consumer alters the quantity of a good consumed as his income changes. In the case of Fig. 3.7a the ICL is shallow. The implication of this is that the consumption of the good increases at a higher rate than income. This sort of behaviour is most common where luxury goods are concerned. As his income rises this individual may use his car more, buy a second car, or even change his car for a model with a higher petrol consumption.

73

In Fig. 3.7b we consider the case of salt. The ICL is steep, implying that the consumption of the good does not vary much with changes in income. It would be unusual for a consumer to react to an increase in income by greatly increasing his consumption of salt.

While Fig. 3.7a and Fig. 3.7b relate to what are called normal goods, Fig. 3.7c shows the ICL for an inferior good—remoulded tyres. This is a special case in that the ICL slopes backwards. In other words, the consumption of inferior goods falls as income increases. When people can afford it, they prefer to buy new tyres rather than remoulds for their cars.

Fig. 3.7d shows that income-consumption lines need not be straight lines. In the case of ICL_1, the quantity consumed of the good is increasing at an increasing rate with increases in income. If the ICL became horizontal, any further increases in income would all be devoted to the good in question. ICL_2 represents a consumer who increases his consumption of a good at a decreasing rate as income increases. If the ICL became vertical, any further increases in income would leave the consumption of the good in question unaltered.

Diagrams such as those in Fig. 3.7 can also show the income elasticity of demand. The demand for petrol is shown to be relatively income elastic while that of salt is relatively income inelastic. In both cases the coefficient of income elasticity will be positive. In the case of inferior goods such as remoulded tyres, the coefficient will be negative.

A knowledge of the income elasticities of goods is useful if changing future needs are to be planned for. The experience of industrial countries could well highlight future trends to be experienced by developing countries. Households with low incomes tend to have a high income elasticity of demand for food. A large proportion of any increase in income is spent on food. However, as incomes continue to rise, the income elasticity falls until only a very small proportion of any increase in income is spent on food with an increasing proportion being spent on consumer durables. As incomes continue to rise in industrial countries, a further trend is developing. The income elasticity of demand for consumer durables is falling while that of services is rising. Trends such as these have important implications for resource allocation and display the importance to macroeconomics of the aggregate behaviour of households.

Although the last two chapters have stressed the importance of prices and incomes, it would be an oversimplification to say that they are the only factors that influence how much we spend and how we spend it. Other factors would include advertising, the availability of credit, household expectations regarding inflation or unemployment, and so on.

Examination questions

Data response question

Price	Drink A £2	Drink B £4	Drink C £6
Quantity	Total utility	Total utility	Total utility
1	8	8	14
2	14	13¼	27
3	18	18¼	39
4	21	23	49
5	22	27½	55
6	24	31¾	60
7	25	35¾	62

Given in the table are the daily utility functions for three cold drinks for a man arriving at a desert oasis with a budget of £28.

Assuming that holding money has no utility for him and that he seeks to maximize his satisfaction, answer the following:
a) On his first visit the only drink for sale is B. How many drinks does he buy, and why?
b) In the circumstances of a), calculate the consumer's surplus.
c) On a return visit, with another £28, all the drinks are available. How will he now allocate his budget between the three drinks?
d) What is unlikely about the total utility figures for drink A? (London A, 1980)

Essay questions

1 'The demand for a commodity will usually be greater the lower the price, other things unchanged.' Explain why this is so and discuss the significance of 'other things unchanged'. (*Associated Examining Board A, 1981*).

2 a) How does a rational consumer, with given income and tastes, allocate his income among available goods and services?
   b) How may changes in income affect the demand for a good?
   c) How may changes in its price affect the demand for a good? (*Cambridge A, 1981*)

3 Show how individual and market demand curves are based on the concept of 'rational consumer behaviour'. (*Oxford and Cambridge A, 1980*)

4 Using either indifference curve analysis or marginal utility theory, explain carefully why an individual's demand for a product falls when the price rises. Analyse how the demand will be affected by an increase in income. (*Oxford A, 1982*)

5 'Indifference analysis demonstrates that when the price of a commodity falls, the quantity demanded may increase, remain constant or diminish.' What then is the value of this as a theory? (*Oxford and Cambridge S, 1981*)

6 a) Distinguish between the income and substitution effects of a change in a commodity's price.
   b) Explain why the consequences, for demand, of a price change are not always predictable. (*Cambridge A, 1982*)

7 How do we distinguish normal from inferior and Giffen goods? Why is the Giffen good a market rarity? (*Oxford and Cambridge A, 1982*)

8 '*Ceteris paribus* (or, other things remaining equal), consumers will buy more of a product if its price falls and will buy less of a product if its price rises.'
   a) Discuss the meaning and importance of the phrase 'other things remaining equal' in the above statement.
   b) Describe and account for exceptions which may exist to the normal responses of consumers to price changes. (*Scottish H, 1982*)

9 'The major criticism of demand theory is not that it is irrelevant but that the consumer is not rational.' How far do you think this statement is justified? (*Cambridge S, 1981*)

10 Compare and assess the relative merits of the various ways in which conventional economic analysis attempts to explain consumer's behaviour. (*Cambridge S, 1982*)

11 What are the main determinants of the rate of growth of real consumer's expenditure in the United Kingdom? For what reasons may the average and marginal propensities to consume change over time? (*Oxford S, 1981*)

12 'Unlike the Keynesian theory of consumption, the permanent and life-cycle hypothesis predict that actual consumption is not much affected by temporary changes in income.' Discuss and consider possible implications for the management of the economy of these alternative views of the consumption function. (*Joint Matriculation Board S, 1982*)

Chapter 4   *The theory of the firm*

We all come into daily contact with firms. The word 'firm' is familiar to us all. However, if you were asked to define exactly what a firm is, what would you say? In fact the answer is not too hard to find. A firm is any organization or business unit which employs scarce resources and combines them in order to produce and sell an economic good or service.

In this way the small corner shop is a firm, the local hairdresser is a firm, the average-sized manufacturer of a car component is a firm, and the huge multinational organization is a firm. Some will take the form of a one-man business or a partnership and be fairly small. Others will be owned by shareholders and take the form of a large company. Some will use predominantly labour (labour intensive), others predominantly machinery (capital intensive). All, however, can be thought of as firms.

The theory of the firm attempts to analyse certain aspects of the behaviour of individual firms. The theory focuses our attention on two basic and interrelated decisions facing the firm: what price to charge for its product and at what output level to produce.

Is such a theory necessary? The answer must be 'yes'. At an aggregate level the behaviour of firms has important implications for prices, employment, output, and international trade. In this way their behaviour has important implications for the issues that are of major concern to governments: inflation, unemployment, growth, and the balance of payments. For this reason alone an understanding of their behaviour is vitally important.

In this chapter our aim is to ask how comprehensive an understanding does the traditional theory provide. To begin with we shall outline briefly the traditional theory, discovering that it provides a great deal of insight into the pricing and output decisions of firms. However, this does not mean that it is above criticism. The traditional theory will be followed by a look at some alternative theories. The alternative theories take as their starting-point the dropping of some of the traditional assumptions. As a result they provide a more realistic analysis of certain aspects of firms' behaviour.

Part 1   *The traditional theory of the firm*

All firms exist within a market situation. A **market** is any situation where buyers and sellers exist and are in contact with each other. The behaviour of a particular firm will depend, to some extent, on the type of market in which it is operating. The basic possibilities in terms of market types will be outlined later in this chapter (p.79).

Whatever type of market a firm finds itself in, its decisions will be made in relation to its cost and revenue expectations. When talking of a firm's costs, we have in mind the money it pays for the factors of production it employs—wages for labour, rent for land, interest for capital, and profit for enterprise. A firm's revenue is the money it receives for the sale of its product. Before we can fully develop any theory of the firm it will be necessary to explain the basic elements of costs and revenue.

1 A firm's costs

There are two elements to a firm's costs:

1 Fixed costs are those costs that do not vary with output in the short run, although they may vary in the long run, e.g. machines, plant, buildings, etc.
2 Variable costs are those costs that do vary with output in both the short and the long run, e.g. labour and materials.

It is also possible to distinguish between total, average, and marginal costs:

1 Total costs are all fixed costs plus all variable costs.
2 Average costs are total costs divided by the number of units produced.
3 Marginal costs are the addition to total costs brought about when the production of a good is increased by one unit.

A firm's costs can be plotted graphically against changes in output so as to produce cost curves. In analysing a firm's behaviour its **average** and **marginal cost curves** are particularly important and we need to be familiar with their general shape.

1.1 Average cost curves

The traditional theory assumes that average cost curves will be U-shaped in both the short run and the long run. In other words, as output increases, average costs will fall up to a point.

Fig. 4.1   Short-run average total cost curve

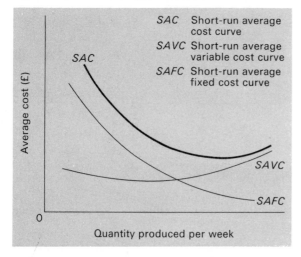

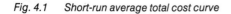

Quantity produced per week

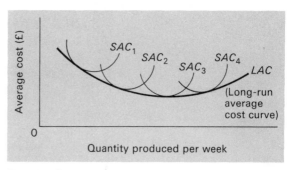

Fig. 4.2   Long-run average cost curve

Beyond this point (the **optimum size** of the firm) they will tend to rise. A detailed explanation of this need not concern us here. However, in the short run, average fixed costs will fall with output while average variable costs will eventually tend to rise in accordance with the **law of diminishing returns** (Note 2, p.140). The outcome of this will be a U-shaped short-run average cost curve (SAC) as in Fig. 4.1.

In the long run the employment of fixed factors can be increased, thus increasing the scale of production. This will result in the firm's short-run average cost curve moving outwards to the right. The envelope of these short-run average cost curves will give us the firm's long-run average cost curve. At first sight one might expect this to be a horizontal line. However, in expanding a firm will benefit from **economies of scale** (Note 3, p.140) which will tend to decrease average costs as output increases. Eventually the long-run average cost curve will turn upwards as the process runs out of economies of scale, and as diseconomies—perhaps in the form of less efficient management—set in. The result of this will be the short-run average cost curve moving upwards as it moves outwards. This will leave us with a long-run average cost curve that is also U-shaped but shallower than the short-run curves (Fig. 4.2).

1.2 Marginal cost curves

In what way would we expect marginal costs to vary as output is increased? To begin with they will fall. In other words the marginal cost curve will slope downwards from left to right. However, marginal costs will soon reach a minimum level, and from there onwards the curve

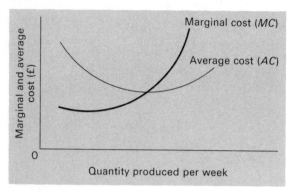

Fig. 4.3   Marginal cost curve

will slope upwards. The explanation of this is once again to be found in terms of the law of diminishing returns (Note 2, p.140).

A long-run marginal cost curve will include all costs while the short-run curve will relate only to variable costs. This will tend to make the long-run curve higher than the short-run curve. But increased efficiency due to economies of scale will tend to lower the long-run curve. The position of the final curve will depend on the relative strengths of these two forces.

If a firm's marginal cost curve is drawn on the same graph as its average cost curve, the marginal cost curve will always cut the average cost curve at its lowest point. The explanation of this is not too hard to find. When average costs are falling, marginal costs must be lower than average costs, i.e. the marginal cost curve must be below the average cost curve. When average costs are rising, then marginal costs must be higher than average costs, i.e. the marginal cost curve must be above the average cost curve. Taken together, these two statements must result in the marginal cost curve

cutting the average cost curve at its lowest point (Fig. 4.3).

A useful way of explaining this is through the example of a batsman's average in cricket. Take his average score as being average cost and his next score as marginal cost. If his next score is below his average, it will result in his average falling. If his next score is greater than his average, this will result in it increasing.

2 A firm's revenue

As with costs we can distinguish between total, average, and marginal revenue.
1 Total revenue is the price per unit multiplied by the quantity sold.
2 Average revenue is the total revenue divided by the quantity sold.
   Note: if total revenue = price × quantity

   and average revenue = $\dfrac{\text{total revenue}}{\text{quantity}}$

   then, average revenue = price
3 Marginal revenue is the addition to total revenue brought about when the quantity sold of a good is increased by one unit.

We know from our work on consumer behaviour (see Chapter 2) that as price falls the total quantity sold will increase. This enables us to give the revenue figures for a hypothetical firm producing a given good (Table 4.1).

Table 4.1 enables us to make two important points:
1 If average revenue is plotted against quantity, it will give us the same curve as if we had plotted price against quantity. The firm's average revenue curve is the same as the demand curve for the firm's product. In

Table 4.1   Revenue figures for a hypothetical firm

Price (£) (a)	Quantity sold per week (b)	Total revenue (£) (a × b)	Marginal revenue (£)	Average revenue (£) $\left(\dfrac{a \times b}{b} = a\right)$
12	1	12	12	12
10	2	20	8	10
9	3	27	7	9
8	4	32	5	8
6	5	30	−2	6
3	6	18	−12	3

effect we came across this when we noticed that average revenue equalled price.

The above tells us that we would expect average revenue curves to slope downwards from left to right by virtue of the fact that they are also demand curves.

2 This relates to the shape and position of the marginal revenue curve. In fact the marginal revenue curve will fall below the average revenue curve and at twice the rate. To explain how the figures in Table 4.1 lead us to this conclusion we need to refer to another idea introduced in Chapter 1 (p.12) — the **price elasticity of demand**.

Elasticity of demand is a measure of the responsiveness of the quantity demanded to a change in price. Demand is said to be elastic whenever a fall in price results in an increase in total revenue. Table 4.1 tells us that whenever total revenue is increasing, marginal revenue is positive, i.e. whenever marginal revenue is positive, elasticity of demand is elastic. Similarly, whenever total revenue is decreasing with a fall in price (i.e. when marginal revenue is negative), then elasticity is inelastic. When marginal revenue is zero, demand is said to be unitary, which in effect means that total revenue will remain unchanged following a change in price. When looking at the elasticity of a straight-line demand curve, it is also the case that the point half-way along its length is the point of unitary elasticity while all points

below it are inelastic and above it elastic (Note 4, p.140).

If all these facts are to be satisfied in a graphical representation of averge and marginal revenue curves, the outcome would be as shown in Fig. 4.4. From this we can see that the marginal revenue curve falls below the average revenue curve and that it falls at twice the rate.

Enough has now been said about a firm's costs and revenue to allow us to begin to develop the traditional theory of the firm. To summarize the important points, they are as follows:

1 The average cost curve is U-shaped while the marginal cost curve will slope upwards from left to right, intersecting the average cost curve at its lowest point.

2 The average revenue curve is in fact the demand curve facing the firm and as a result it will slope downwards from left to right. The marginal revenue curve will fall below the average revenue curve, at twice the rate.

3 Pricing and output decisions

We need to clarify exactly what the theory of the firm is trying to do. Given the following:

1 a set of possibilities about costs of production.

2 a set of possibilities about selling the product.

3 the basic and very important assumption that the aim of the firm is to **maximize its profits**.

We want to establish:

1 at what output the firm will decide to produce.

2 at what price that output will be sold.

The way in which a firm behaves in relation to the making of these two basic decisions will, to some extent, depend on the type of market in which it is operating—the market conditions that it is experiencing. The traditional theory identifies two extreme market types: the perfect market and the monopoly market. A brief outline will be given of how the theory explains behaviour in these two extreme situations. From here the traditional theory goes on

Fig. 4.4   Average and marginal revenue curves

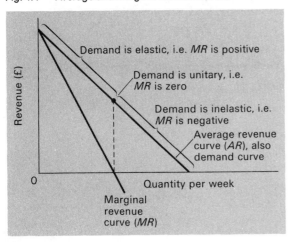

to look at behaviour in imperfect markets—the more realistic market types to be found between the two extremes. When the traditional theory tries to explain behaviour under market conditions more akin to the real world, its weaknesses are exposed. More recent theories may provide more convincing answers.

3.1 Perfect markets

Firstly, we must outline the conditions that are necessary for a perfectly competitive market to exist. Secondly, we must examine the implications for the individual firm operating under such conditions.

For a perfectly competitive market to exist the following conditions are necessary:

1 All units of the commodity must be homogeneous (i.e. identical) whichever firm produces them. In this way buyers will be indifferent as to the sellers they approach, and sellers indifferent as to the buyers they sell to.
2 There must be such a large number of buyers and sellers that no individual buyer or seller can affect the market price.
3 There must be perfect knowledge in the market amongst and between both buyers and sellers.
4 The firms must produce the product with common technology and perfectly mobile resources.
5 There must be freedom of entry and exit to the industry for firms wanting to get in and firms wanting to get out.
6 Firms must aim to maximize profits while consumers must aim to maximize utility.

When all these conditions exist there is one fundamental implication for all the individual firms in the industry: there will only be one price for the commodity which will be entirely due to the market forces of supply and demand and which cannot be influenced by individual buyers and sellers.

Now consider an individual firm producing good A under conditions of perfect competition. As the firm produces an infinitesimal part of the total supply of good A, there is no way that the firm can influence its price. Whether the firm sells one unit or 1000 units, the price per unit will be the same. The price confronting the firm will have been set in accordance with the demand and supply curves of the industry as a whole.

There is no reason to suppose that the shapes of the industry's demand and supply curves will be anything other than normal: the demand curve will slope downwards from left to right while the supply curve will slope upwards. However, as we have said, the price

Fig. 4.5a   *Aggregate supply and demand for the industry giving the market price*

Fig. 4.5b   *Demand curve for the individual firm: a price-taker*

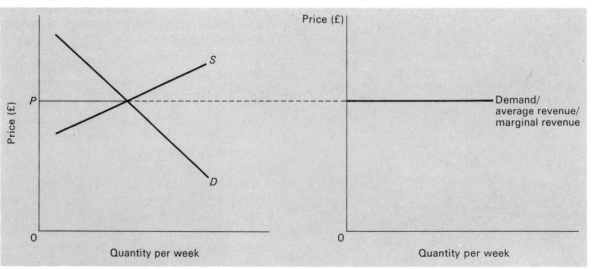

facing the individual firm will remain the same whatever their output level. This results in the demand curve facing the individual firm taking the form of a horizontal line.

During our earlier look at revenue we established that a firm's average revenue curve will be the same as its demand curve (p.78). A further point to notice is that under conditions of perfect competition, because the price is constant, a firm's total revenue will increase by the same amount (i.e. the price) with each additional unit sold. This, in turn, means that the marginal revenue curve will be the same as the average revenue and the demand curve (Fig. 4.5). From this we can see what is meant when the individual firm under conditions of perfect competition is described as a **price-taker**. The price is set by the overall market forces and the individual firm is unable to alter this price by its own activities.

How will the firm make a decision about output?

So far, we have considered the determination of price in a perfect market. The next point is very important. In terms of the traditional theory it applies not only to firms under perfect market conditions but to firms under any market conditions. Given the assumption that the firm is trying to maximize its profits, it will always produce at that level of output where:

marginal cost = marginal revenue

Why is this the case? If the marginal revenue (i.e. the extra revenue from the sale of one additional unit) is greater than the marginal cost (i.e. the extra cost of producing an additional unit), it must be to the firm's advantage to increase its output, as each extra unit will add to its total profit. At the same time, if output goes beyond where marginal cost equals marginal revenue, the cost of the extra unit is more than the revenue it will bring and therefore, additional units will not be produced as they would decrease the size of total profits (Fig. 4.6).

In Fig. 4.6 at output C the extra revenue to be earned by selling one more unit is CA while its cost would be CB. Therefore the extra unit

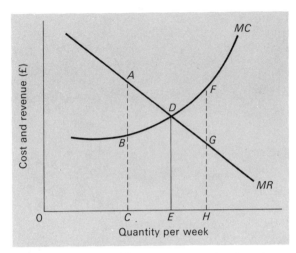

Fig. 4.6   Profit maximizing output

would be produced as it would increase total profit by BA. At output H, on the other hand, the extra revenue to be earned by selling one more unit is less than the cost of producing it. In fact, producing the extra unit would reduce total profit by GF and therefore, it would not be produced. In other words, as long as the aim is to maximize profit the firm would go on increasing output up to the level E in Fig. 4.6, but not beyond this point.

The cost and revenue curves of a firm in a perfect market

We are now in a position to represent certain cost and revenue conditions of the firm operating in a perfectly competitive market graphically and use them to analyse the firm's pricing and output decisions. Fig. 4.7 represents a long-run equilibrium situation. As long as the firm's costs and the aggregate market conditions remain constant, there will be no tendency to move away from the price and output condition shown.

For the firm in Fig. 4.7 the aggregate market conditions have resulted in a price of £4. Whatever quantity the firm produces it will have to sell at a price of £4 per unit. As we have already noted, the implication of this is that the demand curve facing the firm will be a horizontal line and will be equal to both the average and marginal revenue curves — the same curve will represent all three. The profit maximizing

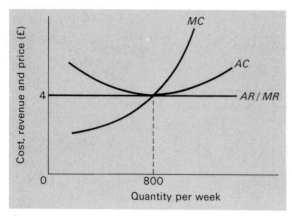

Fig. 4.7   Equilibrium in a perfect market

level of output will be that level of output that equates marginal cost with marginal revenue, in this case 800 units per week.

As you look at Fig. 4.7 it should become apparent that a further question needs to be answered. We know that the marginal cost curve will always cut the average cost curve at its lowest point. However, does the lowest point on the average cost curve always pass through the point of intersection between marginal cost and marginal revenue?

The answer is that it does in the long run, but in the short run it does not. While Fig. 4.7 represents long-run equilibrium, it represents only one of three possible short-run situations. The other two are shown in Figs. 4.8 and 4.9.

In Fig. 4.7 the firm is just covering all its costs, in Fig. 4.8 the firm is making profits in excess of all costs (**excess** or **abnormal profit**),

and in Fig. 4.9 the firm is making a loss. It is worth noting that in Fig. 4.9 the firm is minimizing its losses by producing at the level of output that equates marginal cost with marginal revenue.

Yet, in the long run, price must be equal to average cost as in Fig. 4.7. In the case of Fig. 4.8 the excess profit would attract new firms into the market. This would increase the overall supply in the market and so force down price until it equalled average cost at the point of production as it does in Fig. 4.7. In the case of Fig. 4.9, if firms continue to suffer such losses in the long run, they will be forced to go out of business. This would reduce the overall supply in the market, thus forcing the price up until the firms remaining were in a position such as the one shown in Fig. 4.7.

It may appear that in the long-run equilibrium position (Fig. 4.7) the entrepreneur is making no profit. This is not the case. His profit, or return for his enterprise, is one of the firm's costs and as such it is included in the average cost curve. Such profit is called **normal profit**, and it is defined as the amount of profit that is just sufficient to induce the entrepreneur to keep the firm in business. The crucial point about normal profit is that it is not a surplus over all costs, but the cost of the services which the entrepreneur provides. Enterprise is to be viewed as a factor of production, with normal profit being the cost of employing the factor. If you prefer, it is the income that must be earned by the factor if it is to remain in its present

Fig. 4.8   Excess profit (ABCD)

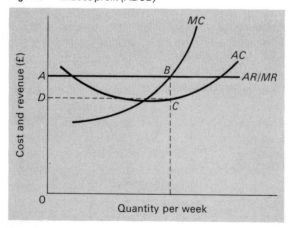

Fig. 4.9   Loss (EFGH)

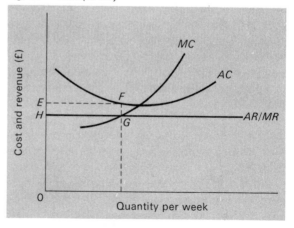

activity. The profit being made in Fig. 4.8 is abnormal profit, which is over and above normal profit. It is this abnormal profit that attracts new entrepreneurs into this line of business.

Further points about perfect markets

We have covered the fundamental points regarding pricing and output behaviour under perfect market conditions. Figs. 4.10, 4.11, and 4.12 expand on certain aspects of this. The amount of explanation given will be limited. Look carefully at the graphs and the comments relating to them. If you understand the graphs and follow the comments, you would seem to have grasped the essence of the traditional explanation of the perfect market.

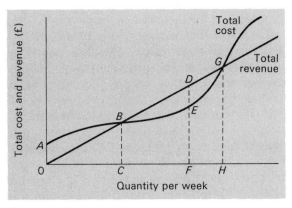

Fig. 4.10   *Total cost and revenue curves*

It is more common to analyse a firm's behaviour via average and marginal cost and revenue curves. However, as Fig. 4.10 shows, a similar analysis can be made using total cost and revenue curves. Consider the following seven questions and answers:

1 What type of market is this?

It is perfect because the total revenue curve is a straight line, i.e. it increases at a constant rate so that the average and marginal revenue curves will be the same horizontal line.

2 What output maximizes profit?

F maximizes profit because the tangent at E is parallel to the total revenue curve, i.e. marginal cost equals marginal revenue.

3 What is the excess profit at F?

ED is the excess profit because this is the

difference between total revenue and total cost. At no other output is the vertical distance between the revenue and cost curves greater, i.e. profits are maximized.

4 What is the price at output F?

The price is the total revenue (FD) divided by the quantity (F).

5 What are the firm's fixed costs?

The firm's fixed costs are A because these are the total costs when output is zero.

6 At what outputs would the firm make normal profits?

At outputs C and H because here total costs equal total revenue.

7 What does the shape of the total cost curve tell you?

It tells you that the average cost curve is U-shaped.

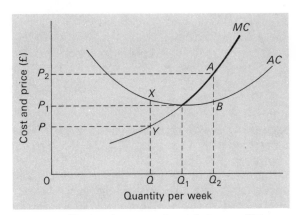

Fig. 4.11   *The supply curve under perfect competition*

Fig. 4.11 illustrates a point that might already have been noticed: under conditions of perfect competition a firm's marginal cost curve (MC) is its supply curve. The following steps provide the explanation why.

1 Profits are maximized when marginal cost equals marginal revenue.

2 Under conditions of perfect competition marginal revenue equals price.

3 From steps 1 and 2 we can conclude that the firm will produce at that output where marginal cost equals price. This means that the marginal cost curve is the supply curve.

Why has the average cost curve (AC) been included in Fig. 4.11?

1 All prices in excess of P_1 will result in excess

profit, e.g. at P_2 an excess profit of AB will be made on each unit.

2   At price P_1 normal profit will be made.

3   All prices below P_1 will result in a loss being made, e.g. at P a loss of XY will be made on each unit.

4   From steps 1, 2 and 3 we can conclude that in the long run the firm would only continue in production at a price of P_1 or above. In other words, the long-run supply curve is that part of the marginal cost curve which is above the average cost curve.

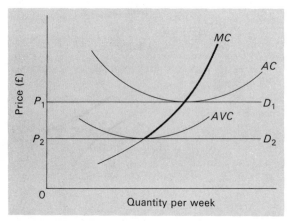

Fig. 4.12   *Shutdown and breakeven points under perfect competition*

Fig 4.12 includes not only an average cost curve (AC), but also an average variable cost curve (AVC). The variable cost curve simply does not include fixed costs and as a result falls below the average total cost curve. Consider the following prices:

1   P_1 equals the breakeven point where normal profits are being made.

2   Above P_1 equals a situation where excess profit is being made.

3   P_1 to P_2 equals a situation where average variable costs are being covered but average fixed costs are being only partially covered. Production will continue in the short run, but the firm could not continue in the long run under these circumstances.

4   P_2 equals the shutdown point, as any price below this would mean that the firm is failing to cover average variable costs and so produces zero output.

Note: all this leads us to the conclusion that

the short-run supply curve for a firm in perfect competition is that part of the marginal cost curve (MC) above the average variable cost curve.

3.2 Monopoly markets

Much of the groundwork has already been covered through our look at perfect markets, while the concept of monopoly was introduced in Chapter 1, p.23.

For a monopoly to exist, as defined in terms of a theoretical extreme, two conditions must be fulfilled. There must be:

1   A single producer, i.e. the supply to the market of a particular good or service must be controlled by one producer only.

2   No substitutes, i.e. there must be no adequate substitute for the good or service.

Therefore the market is dominated by one seller who, as a result, has the power to determine either the price at which he will market the product or the quantity he is prepared to sell.

It is worth noticing that even the monopolist does not have the power to determine both simultaneously as he cannot control demand. Clearly, the more effective a monopolist's restrictions on the emergence of new competitors and the fewer the close substitutes for his product, the nearer he will be to absolute monopoly power.

The essential point about monopoly is that there ceases to be a distinction between the firm and the industry. The total output of the industry is provided by one firm. For this reason the demand curve (average revenue curve) facing the firm will be the industry's demand curve, and as such it will slope downwards from left to right. In our look at revenue curves (Fig. 4.4, p.79) we established that the marginal revenue curve will fall below the average revenue curve at twice the rate. There is no reason why the average and marginal cost curves should be shaped any differently from those we have already come across, as the same basic reasoning applies. Therefore we can think of the monopoly market situation in terms of Fig. 4.13.

Consider Fig. 4.13. As under perfect compe-

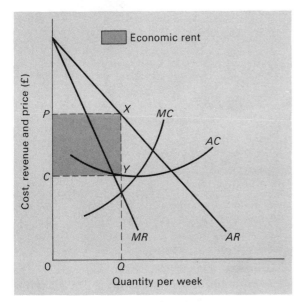

Fig. 4.13   Equilibrium in a monopoly market

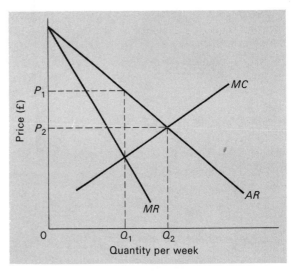

Fig. 4.14   The case against monopoly

tition, if the firm aims to maximize profit, it will fix its output at the level that equates marginal cost (MC) with marginal revenue (MR). This monopolist will supply Q, at an average cost of C, for a price of P. The difference between average cost and price will constitute the excess profit being made on each unit sold. In this way the total excess profit will be represented by the area PXYC.

The following is a vital point. Unlike excess profit earned under conditions of perfect competition, this excess profit (PXYC) can be earned in the long run. Fig. 4.13 represents a long-run equilibrium situation as the excess profit will not result in new firms being attracted into the market. The monopolist's excess profit is usually referred to as **economic rent** (see Chapter 5, p.127).

Further points about monopoly

We have covered the fundamental points regarding pricing and output behaviour under monopoly conditions. Figs. 4.14 and 4.15 expand on certain aspects of this. The amount of explanation given will be limited. Look carefully at the graphs and the comments relating to them. If you understand the graphs and follow the comments, you would seem to

have grasped the essence of the traditional explanation of the monopoly market.

Fig. 4.14 represents a particular market situation. Notice the following points:
1 If the market were satisfied by a monopolist, the monopolist would produce where marginal cost equalled marginal revenue. The price would be P_1, while the quantity consumed would be Q_1.
2 If the market were a perfectly competitive one, the market price would be given by the point of intersection between the supply curve (i.e. the marginal cost curve) and the demand curve (i.e. the average revenue curve) for the market as a whole. The price would be P_2, while the quantity consumed would be Q_2.
3 Therefore, under monopoly conditions the price is higher and the quantity lower than they would be under perfectly competitive conditions. (The resulting misallocation of resources and loss of welfare were displayed in Chapter 1, pp.23–4.)

The diagrams in Fig. 4.15 help to show how a monopolist has the power to charge different prices in different markets for the same good. This is known as price discrimination. To be able to do this, a firm must have a great deal of monopoly power. To be willing to do it, the firm must increase its profits, and greater profits will result if the elasticities of demand differ in the various markets.

Fig. 4.15   Price discrimination

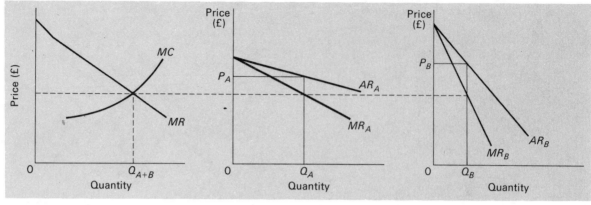

a) *Aggregate market*   b) *Market A*   c) *Market B*

Fig. 4.15a shows the firm's total production decision. The output chosen is that which equates marginal cost with marginal revenue. Figs. 4.15b and 4.15c show how much the firm should allocate, out of this total output, to the two markets in order to maximize profits. This will be achieved by equating the marginal revenues in the two markets. To begin with, if the revenue to be gained by selling one more unit in market A is greater than that to be lost by selling one unit less in market B, then the firm will transfer a unit from B to A.

This will continue until the situation in Fig. 4.15 is reached. Here the marginal revenues are equal and no further reallocation can affect total profit. The prices charged in the two markets would therefore be P_A and P_B.

3.3 Imperfect markets

Perfect competition and monopoly are rarely found in the real world. Reality presents us with a picture of imperfect markets. Imperfect markets are made up of a large number of firms, as in the perfect market, but the goods they produce are no longer homogeneous. Their products are different, and even if the real differences are small, the apparent differences due to such features as advertising, branding, wrapping and so on may be considerable. A degree of light can be thrown on the pricing and output decisions of such firms using diagrams similar to those we have already encountered (Fig. 4.16).

Compare Fig. 4.16a with Fig. 4.13. The short-run equilibrium diagram is similar to the monopolist's equilibrium diagram. However, under conditions of imperfect competition the excess profit will attract new firms into the market. As more firms enter, the total demand must be shared amongst this larger number so that each firm can expect a smaller share of the market. This will result in the individual firm's demand curve (average revenue curve) shifting to the left until it is tangential to the average cost curve. We now have the long-run equilibrium position (Fig. 4.16b) with the firm only making normal profit.

Two points are worth noting. Firstly, the price is still higher and the output still lower than they would be under perfect competition. Secondly, it may pay such a firm to engage in non-price competition, such as advertising, as it may shift its demand curve to the right and therefore result in short-run excess profits.

Perhaps the most important type of imperfect market is **oligopoly**. This is the name given to a market dominated by a small number of large firms. For example, banking in England is dominated by the 'Big Four' (Barclays, Midland, Lloyds, National Westminster) and the car and petrol markets are dominated by a handful of large producers.

In such a market the whole problem of price and output determination takes on a new dimension. The firm's policy now depends on how it thinks its competitors will react to its decisions. The outcome of the firm's policy

Fig. 4.16   Equilibrium in an imperfect market

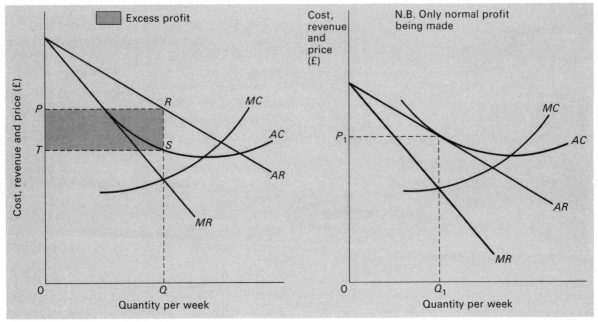

a) Short run

b) Long run

depends on how they do react. As we have seen, this problem did not exist for firms under perfect competition as they had too many rivals. Nor did this problem exist for the monopolist as he had no rivals at all.

In an oligopoly market, if one firm cuts its price, the others are often obliged to follow suit. If a firm increases its price, it must consider whether or not the others will follow suit. The danger of such price-warfare often results in price agreements between oligopolists where they accept the price leadership of some dominant firm. In such a situation competition takes the form of advertising, elaborate packaging, after-sales service, special offers, and so on rather than price competition.

This price stickiness can be at least partially explained in terms of the model shown in Fig. 4.17. The reluctance of oligopolists to change their price stems from a fear of how their rivals might react. Will their rivals match any price change? In Fig. 4.17 this uncertainty is reflected by drawing two demand curves. The demand curve DD represents the single oligopolist's demand curve, assuming that all the other firms in the industry will match exactly any price changes he makes. If, however, the

other firms refuse to match his price changes, D_1D_1 will represent the firm's demand conditions. This demand curve is clearly more elastic. If the firm lowers its price and the others do not follow it will greatly increase its sales, but if the others fail to match its price rises there will be a large decrease in its sales.

The model now assumes that the oligopolist in question will fear the worst. His competitors will match any price decrease while not matching any price increase.

Point E in Fig. 4.17 gives the equilibrium price and output levels. Any decrease in price will move the firm along the demand curve labelled DD as all other firms will decrease their prices. However, an increase in price will move the firm back along D_1D_1 in accordance with the assumption that other firms will not introduce similar price increases.

In this way the firm's demand curve is kinked at the existing price level, moving upwards from E along D_1D_1 and downwards along DD. Any price increase will move the firm along a relatively elastic demand curve, resulting in a large decrease in sales. Any price decrease will move it along a relatively inelastic demand curve so that the resulting increases

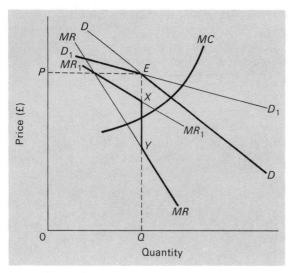

Fig. 4.17   The oligopolist's kinked demand curve

in sales will be small. Under these circumstances there is little incentive to change price.

A further insight into price rigidity can be shown by plotting the marginal revenue curve that corresponds with the kinked demand curve. For any output up to a level of Q the relevant marginal revenue curve is that labelled MR_1. Beyond the output level Q it will be that labelled MR. The resulting marginal revenue curve displays a vertical discontinuity from point X to point Y.

If price P and output Q are maximizing profit, the marginal cost curve must intersect this marginal revenue curve along its vertical

section. The implication of this is that while changing costs may shift the marginal cost curve, the price will not necessarily alter. As long as the marginal cost curve continues to intersect the marginal revenue curve between points X and Y, profits will continue to be maximized without any change in either the price or the quantity.

Although the model is useful, there is a danger of reading too much into models based on the kinked demand curve. They help explain price rigidity once a price has been set, but they fail to explain how the initial price is arrived at.

The outcome of all this is that there is no single set of rules for the equilibrium of either the firm or the industry. In the face of such uncertainty there is an incentive for oligopolists to **collude** in an attempt to maximize their **joint profit**. This can lead to collective pricing agreements that shift the market structure towards the monopoly model. However, uncertainty is still not eliminated. It may be in the interest of an individual firm to break the 'agreement' so as to gain at the expense of its rivals. This type of activity can trigger off a period of market warfare, the outcome of which cannot be predicted.

In other words, the traditional theory can no longer make meaningful predictions about pricing and output. Now that we are looking at a market situation that is commonly found in the real world, the traditional theory is failing to throw up many answers.

Part 2   New theories of the firm

The traditional theory undoubtedly has the advantage of simplicity. By assuming away many complexities it is able to make very clear-cut predictions about the firm's behaviour. However, it is one thing to make predictions, but another to say how realistic they are. If the answer is 'not very', then we must begin to question the usefulness of the theory. The traditional theory of the firm seems

to be at its best when analysing behaviour in perfect and monopoly markets. In the real world, however, these theoretical extremes hardly ever exist. In the real world imperfect markets, in particular oligopoly, represent the type of market conditions confronted by most firms. What we are now looking for in these new theories is the ability to analyse behaviour within an oligopolistic market situation.

The new theories that follow stem, in the main, from the dropping of one or both of the following assumptions that are at the heart of the traditional analysis:

1 Decisions are made under conditions of perfect knowledge.

2 The aim of the firm is to maximize its profits.

We shall consider these new theories under three basic headings: managerial theories, behavioural theories, and game theories. However, before doing this, we shall see what evidence exists to justify the dropping of the two assumptions above. In the same way we shall finish the chapter with a brief word about what evidence exists to support the new theories.

1 Why question the traditional theory?

1.1 The growth of oligopoly

The first and most obvious reason has already been mentioned: while oligopoly is the most common market structure in the real world, it is the one to which the traditional assumptions fit least well.

Empirical evidence of the growing importance of oligopoly can be found by measuring the degree of **concentration**. Industrial concentration is a measure of the degree to which a relatively small number of firms account for a significant proportion of output, employment, or some other criterion of size in an industry. Therefore, when an industry is concentrated, it displays the characteristics of oligopoly.

There are various concentration ratios that try to indicate the degree of concentration in an industry through a single number. The simplest approach takes the percentage of total industry sales, employment, or some other criterion of size held by the largest three or four firms. The greater this percentage, the greater is the degree of concentration. There are, needless to say, problems of definition and interpretation, but equations such as the following can be quite useful:

$$\text{Degree of concentration} = \frac{\text{Total employment in 3 largest firms}}{\text{Total employment in industry}} \times 100$$

Many industries have been analysed in terms of these concentration ratios and the general trend is towards a few large producers being dominant. A broad view of this trend can be seen by calculating the percentage share of the United Kingdom's total output of manufactured goods accounted for by the largest hundred firms in the United Kingdom. S.J. Prais (National Institute of Economic and Social Research) has compiled such figures and they suggest a considerable increase in concentration. In 1909 the largest hundred firms accounted for about 15 per cent of total output. This percentage share was found to increase substantially so that by the 1970s it was well over 40 per cent.

There are basically two aspects of the oligopoly situation that result in the traditional theory failing to provide a satisfactory explanation of market behaviour under these conditions. They are interdependence and uncertainty. In a sense the latter stems from the former. By mutual interdependence we are referring to the fact that each firm produces a sufficiently large proportion of the total output of the industry for its behaviour to affect the market share of the other firms in the industry. This results in uncertainty as the behaviour of one firm is conditioned not just by what its rivals are doing, but by what it thinks its rivals might do in response to any initiative of its own.

These two features of mutual interdependence and uncertainty make it impossible for the traditional theory to build up an acceptable model for oligopoly in the way that it does for the perfect market and monopoly. The new approaches that are to be outlined in the section on **game theories** (p. 97) will attempt to provide a more realistic framework within which to analyse decision-making under mutual interdependence and uncertainty.

1.2 The growth of managerial capitalism

The second reason for questioning the traditional assumptions follows on from the first and is particularly important when justifying the **managerial theories** that will follow shortly. It relates to a specific assumption that is central to the traditional theory, that of profit maximization, and it involves looking at forms of **ownership** and **control** in industry.

In their earliest form business units or firms were owned and managed by the same people. The people making the decisions and exercising effective control were also the ones who acquired any profit and carried any losses. Under these circumstances it would seem reasonable to assume that when making decisions the maximizing of profit was uppermost in their minds. Today the same situation may exist for the sole trader, the small partnership, and perhaps even some small private companies. However, as we have already said most production takes place in large firms where the circumstances can be very different indeed.

Most large firms take the form of public joint-stock companies. The organization of these companies is such that there is a separation of ownership from control. Ownership is in the hands of shareholders. Many will have no voting rights and many who do will never attend annual general meetings and exercise them. Control, then, is largely in the hands of directors and managers. Despite the fact that in theory they are ultimately responsible to the shareholders, they have in practice a great deal of independence when it comes to the running of the firm.

Most large firms are therefore controlled by managers and not owners. This is described as **managerial capitalism** rather than **entrepreneurial capitalism**. From here it is possible to question the assumption of profit maximization. The assumption seems acceptable under conditions of entrepreneurial capitalism, with the decision-makers benefiting directly from any profit made. However, is the assumption equally valid under conditions of managerial capitalism? Will managers, with at the most a very small financial interest in the firm itself, be motivated by forces other than profit maximization? Some of the new theories that follow will try to answer this question.

Before leaving this question of ownership and control, a further point is worth making. So far we have only considered the changing nature of ownership and control in the private sector. It is worth remembering the importance of the public sector, which includes all the firms and industries owned by the state. How useful is the traditional theory in explaining the behaviour of **nationalized industries**? Is profit maximization a relevant assumption in the context of nationalized industries? For the time being it will suffice to say that given the social and political backcloth to the activities of many of our nationalized industries, traditional assumptions such as this seem questionable.

1.3 Pricing policies in practice

The final two reasons for doubting the traditional assumptions identify shortcomings in the traditional theory that have led to the development of the **behavioural theories**.

The first is based largely on empirical evidence, and concerns pricing policies. In practice, the argument goes, businessmen do not have detailed information about the demand and cost conditions that exist. As a result they do not use the concepts of marginal cost and marginal revenue when making price and output decisions. Instead they will calculate the full cost of producing a certain level of output, work out the average cost of one unit, and then increase it by what they consider to be an acceptable profit margin. As much as possible will then be sold on the market at this price.

Certain aspects of the behavioural theories might help throw some light on the way in which an acceptable mark-up is determined, bearing in mind that it often appears to be little more than rule-of-thumb methods that are employed.

At this stage it might be worth considering the pricing policies of nationalized industries. After all, the sheer size of the public sector means that their behaviour will have a significant effect on resource allocation within the economy. Over the years two basic pricing guidelines for nationalized industries seem to have emerged.

1 The first is **marginal cost pricing**. Here prices need to be reasonably related to marginal costs so as to promote the efficient use of resources.

   The rationale behind marginal cost pricing

is as follows. Consider a situation where consumers are willing to pay more for some extra output than it would cost to produce. If under such circumstances an expansion of output and sales were to take place, the total welfare of the community would increase (see Appendix, p.138). The reverse case would be if consumers were unwilling to pay a price that covers the costs of producing marginal output. Under these circumstances a contraction of output and sales would increase welfare.

The new combination of goods available for consumption will provide the community with more satisfaction than the previous combination. It is in this sense that welfare will have increased. In terms of **resource allocation** the argument is that if any industry can use certain resources to produce output of greater value than another industry, those resources should be transferred from the latter to the former. The resulting pattern of output will increase the welfare within the economy.

2 The second is **average cost pricing**. Here prices should be set so as to result in revenues that would cover their accounting costs in full, i.e. try to break even or cover average costs while allowing for a surplus to cover future capital expenditure where possible.

However, there seems to be a conflict between the objectives of efficient resource allocation (i.e. marginal cost pricing) and breaking even (i.e. average cost pricing). Consider Fig. 4.18. Unless a nationalized industry is producing a level of output corresponding to the minimum point on its average cost curve, it is likely that losses (see P_1) or excess profit (see P_2) will appear as a result of marginal cost pricing.

If an industry were to set prices equal to aggregate average cost so that the industry as a whole would break even, this would result in cross-subsidization. This means that the losses made by some goods or services would be balanced by profits made on others. This can be criticized on the grounds that it causes a misallocation of resources, as prices may well be out of line with marginal cost. For example,

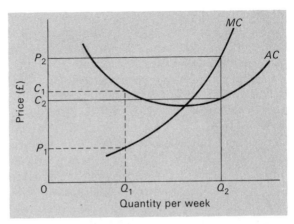

Fig. 4.18   Marginal cost pricing and average cost pricing

a coach network may choose fares equal to average costs and so break even. Profitable routes within the network will subsidize loss-making routes. Arguably, the resources used to provide a little-used route could well add more to the community's total welfare if employed elsewhere.

The above analysis overlooks many complications and what happens in practice with regard to nationalized industries is far from clear. What is clear is that while nationalized firms provide a large percentage of total output, the traditional theory of the firm does not provide a particularly useful framework within which to analyse their behaviour. Nor does it take into account the effects of a large public sector on the private sector of industry.

1.4 The organizational complexity of firms

The final point to be made regarding the casting of doubt on the traditional theory relates to the changing organizational structure of firms. This again stems from their increasing size. These days most industries are dominated by large firms and most large firms are very complex in terms of their organizational structure. For any firm there will be a number of interested parties such as owners, managers, workers, and consumers. It is increasingly the case that each will have a structured organization representing its views.

If the firm is a company, it will be owned by shareholders. Yet, we can distinguish between ordinary and preference shareholders and between speculators who are interested in the share prices over the short term and long-term shareholders who are interested in future dividend payments. Within management there will be various divisions and levels. Within the rest of the workforce there will be distinguishable groups such as white-collar and manual, skilled and unskilled. Each group of workers may be represented by a different union. Finally, there may even be sub-divisions within the ranks of the consumers — the regular consumer as opposed to the infrequent consumer, the industrial consumer as opposed to the individual consumer, and so on.

Given the complexity and number of groups and sub-groups, given the fact that each has its own interests and its own channels of power, its own aims and methods of trying to see them fulfilled, is it likely that any one theory will be able to predict the firm's behaviour? Is it likely that a single theory based on restrictive assumptions would be able to take account of so many forces, all of which, to some degree or another, will have a say in the formulation of the firm's policy? Once again we are in a position to question the traditional theory.

1.5 Summary

Before looking at the new theories we shall summarize the points that we have made in trying to justify our decision to question the traditional theory. Firstly, we have argued that the traditional theory copes least well with oligopoly, and yet it would seem that of all the market structures this is the most important in the real world. Secondly, we suggested that we have moved from an era of entrepreneurial capitalism to one of managerial capitalism, and as a result the assumption of profit maximization is no longer as appropriate as perhaps it once was. Thirdly, we pointed out that pricing policies in practice seem to bear little resemblance to those suggested by the theory. Finally, the sheer organizational complexity of many of today's firms seems to undermine some of the traditional theory's basic assumptions.

2 Managerial theories

We shall consider three variations on this particular theme. What they all have in common is that they reject the simple profit maximization assumption and then put forward alternative targets which firms aim to maximize. They identify these targets by concerning themselves with what motivates managers. We have already commented on the separation of the ownership/management functions. This often leaves managers, particularly when an acceptable level of profit is being made, with a great deal of freedom in the running of the firm — a freedom that permits them to pursue their own self-interest. The question now becomes what might the management group's self-interest depend upon?

2.1 Managerial utility maximization

This approach has been developed largely by the American economist Oliver Williamson. The theory is often referred to as the **managerial discretion theory**. This stems from the argument that managers in large firms have enough discretion to pursue those policies which give them personally most satisfaction. The theory develops by identifying what goals give managers most satisfaction. Together these goals will be the components of the **managerial utility function**. From then on we can see managers' behaviour in terms of their attempts to maximize their satisfaction or utility through the achievement of these goals.

Williamson argued that managers' self-interest could be seen in terms of the achievement of goals in four main areas:

1 Salaries: In addition to their salaries this includes all other forms of monetary income such as bonuses and stock options. Their desire for large salaries is not just to enable them to enjoy a high standard of living and a great deal of security. Their status level is also important to them and this is directly related to the size of their salary.

2 Staff under their control: This refers not only to the number but also to the quality of subordinate staff. The more highly qualified subordinates are, the better it is. This is

important as both a mark of status and a measure of power.

3 Power over new investment: By this Williamson does not mean investment that is essential for the firm to remain competitive and profitable, that is for its survival. He is referring to any investment over and above this, to any pet projects of the management that may affect the general development of the firm. Power over this type of investment may enable a manager to further his own personal interests. It is also important to the manager as it is an indication to others of the power he has over the firm's resources.

4 Availability of fringe-benefits or perquisites: Managers will strive for an expense account, a pretty secretary, a lavishly furnished office with a thick carpet, a chauffeur-driven car, and so on. Managers attach an importance to the extent to which they are able to carry out their job with style. Williamson regards such items as 'slack'—non-essentials that nevertheless become part of the firm's costs.

Williamson goes on to formalize his theory by the development of a model based on a series of equations. The basic equation is in the form of a utility function. Believing that there is a close link between factors 1 and 2, he combines them under the symbol S. The link can be seen in terms of the high correlation that often exists between salary level and the number of subordinates. Non-essential or discretionary investment is represented by I_d, while M represents expenditure on managerial perks. Using U to denote managerial utility, the maximization of this being the manager's aim, Williamson ends up with the following managerial utility function:

$$U = f(SI_d M)$$

Profit maximizing behaviour will not necessarily result in the maximization of a manager's income, power, or status. Price and output decisions will be made with a view to achieving values for S, I_d, and M that will result in U (utility), rather than profit, being maximized. In this way the Williamson theory goes about showing that values for price and output are likely to be very different from those predicted by the profit maximizing model.

At one stage, Williamson also builds a **minimum profit constraint** into his theory. He argues that managers will strive to increase their utility as long as this profit constraint is being satisfied.

2.2 Sales revenue maximization

This second model is based on another view of managerial motivation. Rather than maximizing profit or the value of a utility function, the assumption is that the firm attempts to maximize total sales revenues.

The theory is associated with William J Baumol. He justifies his hypothesis by a good deal of casual empiricism based upon his dealings with managers in his role as a consultant. He noticed the way in which a great importance was attached to sales. He explains that managers may see falling sales as a threat for the following reasons:

1 Consumers would view a firm with falling sales in a less favourable light, and thereby reduce sales even further—a sort of snowball effect.

2 Financial institutions may be less willing to deal with a firm suffering from declining sales, thus making the raising of capital more difficult and more expensive.

3 The distributive trade may be less co-operative when a firm's sales are declining.

4 Falling sales may result in reductions in staffing levels, including managerial staff.

5 Finally, executive salaries may well be closely linked to the level of sales—the greater the scale of production, the larger the salaries.

As with Williamson, Baumol's theory does not ignore profit altogether. He too imposes a **minimum profit constraint** on the firm. As long as this constraint is met, the firm will aim to maximize sales. All of this can be illustrated graphically in Figs. 4.19 and 4.20. These graphs allow comparisons to be made between the pricing and output decisions that would result from the traditional profit maximizing assumption, and those that result from sales revenue maximization. Fig. 4.19 ignores the probable existence of a minimum profit constraint while Fig. 4.20 tries to take it into account.

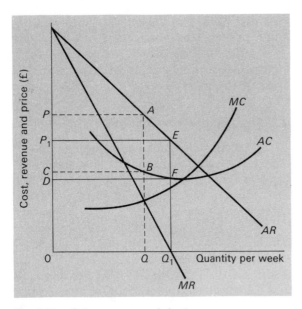

Fig. 4.19   *Sales revenue maximization*

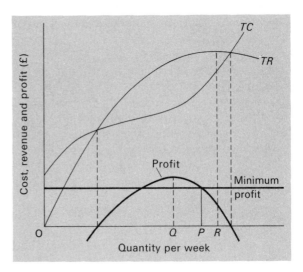

Fig. 4.20   *Sales revenue maximization with a profit constraint*

In Fig. 4.19 we show a firm confronted by normal demand and cost conditions. Think back to the beginning of this chapter where we defined marginal and total revenue (p. 78). Given those definitions, whenever marginal revenue is positive or negative, total revenue cannot be at its maximum. To maximize total revenue, marginal revenue must be equal to zero. In other words, the total revenue maximizing level of output must be Q_1, where the marginal revenue curve cuts the output axis. By taking a vertical line from Q_1 up to the demand curve (i.e. average revenue curve), the price under conditions of sales revenue maximization can be determined. The price will be set at P_1.

The profit maximizing output would be that which equates marginal cost with marginal revenue, i.e. Q in Fig. 4.19. This is lower than the revenue maximizing output. Drawing a vertical line from Q to the demand curve gives us the profit maximizing price P, which is higher than that for revenue maximization.

Now compare the profits earned as a result of the two possible pricing and output policies. Under profit maximization it would be greater than under sales revenue maximization, $PABC$ being greater than P_1EFD.

We now need to bring in the concept of a minimum profit constraint. Will P_1EFD be large enough to satisfy this constraint? If it is not output would have to be reduced, moving it away from Q_1 towards the profit maximizing output. This falling output would increase the profit area, and would continue until the minimum profit constraint was satisfied, thereby enabling the firm to pay shareholders the required level of dividend. The imposition of a specific profit constraint can, perhaps, be displayed more clearly on Fig. 4.20.

Fig. 4.20 shows total cost, total revenue, and a curve we have not used before that simply shows how profit varies with output. Superimposed on this we have the minimum profit constraint. If there was no profit constraint and the firm's aim was to maximize sales revenue, it would produce at output level R. However, if our profit constraint comes into effect, output must be reduced to P so that it is satisfied. This has in effect reduced the output level to a point nearer the profit maximizing output level of Q.

A final interesting implication of Baumol's model is that the firm produces at an output where its marginal revenue is less than its marginal cost.

2.3   Growth maximization

This final example of a managerial theory once again sees managerial motivation in terms of striving to maximize a target. This time the target is growth. This model has been developed by the Cambridge economist Robin Marris. His theory stems from his view of the institutional framework and organization of the modern corporation. He sees this in terms of bureaucratic tendencies. By modern corporation he means the large national or multinational firms that dominate industry. By bureaucracy he means the phenomenon of the large-scale administrative organization that involves the generation of an elaborate hierarchy of authority within which many secure managerial positions will develop.

From this standpoint he identifies several related justifications of his theory:

1 He emphasizes the strong link between growth and a desirable degree of security for the firm. For example, the larger the firm, the less likely the threat of takeover.

2 There is a close correlation between an executive's salary and status and the size of the firm generally, and more specifically, the size of the individual executive's department.

3 It would be nice to be able to judge an executive in terms of his contribution to profit. However, in practice this is difficult to assess. An alternative is to judge him in terms of his ability to increase the activities of the firm, particularly those for which he is directly responsible.

In this way Marris sees the firm as a typical bureaucratic organization—a self-perpetuating structure where growth and the security that it brings is seen as a desirable end in itself. The implications of this for pricing and output decisions can be shown in Fig. 4.21.

Marris argues that even under conditions of growth maximization there will be some constraints. Growth would not continue to the point of bankruptcy or to a point where being taken over would be made increasingly likely. Related to these dangers there would again probably be a minimum profit constraint.

In Fig 4.21 a growth maximizing management might choose to increase size up to the point where average cost equals average revenue. The output level would be Q and size will have been expanded up to the point where

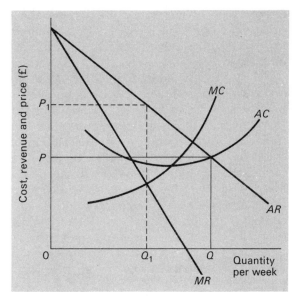

Fig. 4.21 Growth maximization

normal profits are being made. To increase size beyond this point would result in the making of losses. As with sales revenue maximization the level of output would be greater and the price lower than under profit maximization. Where profit maximization would result in a price/quantity combination of P_1Q_1, growth maximization would result in the combination PQ.

If the minimum profit constraint were in excess of normal profit, the level of output would have to be reduced. Indeed, if the minimum profit constraint were the same for both the revenue maximizer and the growth maximizer, the resulting output levels would be identical.

3 Behavioural theories

Unlike the managerial theories the behavioural theories do not see the aim of the firm as an attempt to maximize anything. In a sense, while the managerial theories might be seen as alternatives to the traditional theory, it might be fairer to consider the behavioural theories as a supplement to them. The behavioural theories focus our attention on the internal decision-making structure of the firm. The aim is to understand this decision-making process rather than try and make predictions about price and output. The theories, as a result, tend to address themselves to slightly different questions.

They not only address themselves to the organizational goals and objectives, but also to how targets are set for these goals and objectives. In the setting of these targets we are interested in not only what information is available but in how it passes through the organization, whether it is biased, and if the bias would affect the ultimate decisions? Having established a set of targets, we must finally consider the process by which they change over time. The behavioural approach is based upon psychology as much as economics and is typified by writers such as Simon, Gyert, and March.

The first step is to identify the various goals of the organization. This is not as simple as it sounds. The organization, that is the firm, can be thought of as a **coalition** of various groups: different departments, different levels of management, different groups of workers, different suppliers, different consumers, different shareholding groups, etc. A complex process of bargaining must take place between the groups within the coalition in order to determine their collective goals.

Here is a list of some possible goals without making any attempt to place them in an order of priority:

1 Production goal: output must fall within a satisfactory range.
2 Sales goal: there must be an acceptable level of sales effectiveness.
3 Market share goal: this is important as a measure of comparative success as well as growth.
4 Profit goal: for the traditional theory this is the only goal, whereas here it is one of at least four.

Having identified the variety of goals, the theory continues by arguing that the coalition of groups within the firm will have to set target objectives in terms of **acceptable levels of attainment** in relation to each of the identified goals. Here lies a crucial difference between the behavioural approach and those already discussed. The firm's aims are seen in terms of **satisficing** rather than maximizing. The aim will be to achieve a satisfactory performance regarding each goal.

What is to be considered a satisfactory performance will be related to the hopes and wishes of a coalition of decision-makers. In order to set these targets, forecasts will have to be made regarding variables such as the expected behaviour of competitors, expected levels of demand, and expected costs. There is some evidence to suggest that these estimated forecasts will be biased in the direction of the desired targets to be set for the various goals. Here we can see quite clearly the influence of psychologists. They argue that people's actions are, to a degree, a result of their aspirations, which in turn stem from their perception of how well they ought to be doing in the light of their experience.

Now that targets have been set in terms of collective goals, decisions will have to be made that hopefully will result in the targets being achieved. These decisions concern price, output, production methods, and so on.

The final stage in the process is to compare the outcomes with the targets. If the targets have not been reached, or have even overshot, then two interrelated activities will follow:

1 Search procedures: Estimates for costs, demand, etc. will be re-examined, as will the decisions that were made on the strength of these estimates, in an attempt to discover why the targets were not achieved. What would have happened, had different decisions been made, will be analysed with the benefit of hindsight, and this may result in new policies and decisions being made.
2 Re-examination of targets: In the light of experience the targets set for each identifiable goal may themselves be altered. In other words, target formation is constantly under review. This brings us back to our concept of managerial aspirations. They may change with experience. If the targets are exceeded, aspirations are raised and what is considered a satisfactory performance may be higher next time round. If the targets are not achieved, then they may be lower next time round. In this way the behavioural approach assumes that firms are an adaptive system.

In conclusion to this look at behavioural theories it is worth pointing out a fundamental difference between them and the traditional theory. The traditional theory assumes that market conditions dominate decisions concerning price and output. The behavioural theories argue that the internal decision-making structure of the firm can influence these decisions. Furthermore, in the case of oligopoly, the individual firm's internal decision-making can influence not only these decisions but the market itself. By focusing our attention on internal decision-making, this approach is typical of that employed by behavioural theorists.

Behaviourism studies the activities of human beings in terms of their relations with their environment. Within the complex environment of the firm, behaviour can usually be seen as a compromise between conflicting views and interests. In achieving this compromise it is unlikely that any one goal could ever be maximized.

4 Game theories

Game theory was first developed to help throw some light on decision-making in the context of international relations. However, the economists Von Neuman and Morgenstein have since applied the same principles in an attempt to produce a general theory of oligopoly. A 'game' situation is any situation, involving a number of participants, where there are conflicting interests and limited rewards to be shared out amongst them. Each participant, in the case of oligopoly each firm, when making a decision must be aware of the possible reactions of other participants in the game and the way in which they may affect the outcome of his own decision. This is an aspect of oligopoly that we have already mentioned (p.89). It is mutual interdependence and uncertainty that sets it apart from other market types.

This type of theoretical analysis distinguishes between two basic types of situation:

1 **Pure conflict**: this is where the gains made by one player (firm) are the losses of the other players (firms). This is a no cooperation situation.

2 A mixture of **conflict** and **co-operation**: in this situation the players (firms) may co-operate to increase their joint pay-off, but conflict may still arise over the sharing out of this increased pay-off between the players (firms).

Both of these situations can be found within the oligopoly market. Oligopolists want at least to maintain, and preferably increase, their market share for example, and this will result in pure conflict between them. However, in practice there is also an incentive to co-operate with each other. After all, their success depends on the continuing demand for the same product and a war between them could result in everyone being worse off than they were before.

Let us consider an example of pure conflict within an oligopolist situation involving two competing firms. Such a market is a special case referred to as a **duopoly**. As with a game of chess, the moves of one player, or firm, will affect the other's situation. Let us focus our attention on market share. Between them they satisfy 100 per cent of the market. Any increase in market share achieved by one must result in a loss of market share for the other. No matter what happens, the sum of the two market shares will always be 100 per cent. For this reason this type of game, the very simplest kind, is called a **constant sum** game.

Assume that what we are looking at is the market for petrol and that two companies X and Y satisfy the entire market between them. Company X is considering four possible strategies designed to maximize its market share. It must choose between them and it realizes that despite all its attempts at secrecy, its competitor Y will know its choice. The four possible strategies are:

1 giving stamps away with the petrol,
2 a new high-powered advertising campaign,
3 reducing the price of petrol,
4 opening new garages.

Table 4.2 shows the percentage share of the market that company X would expect to capture following each of the four separate strategies. For each strategy there are four possible outcomes depending on which of the four strategies company Y chooses to reply

Table 4.2   Percentage market shares for company X

Company X's strategy	Company Y's strategy			
	1	2	3	4
1	60	50	**45**	60
2	70	60	**50**	55
3	75	60	**55**	65
4	60	**40**	45	50

with. If for example X decides to give stamps with its petrol, that is strategy 1, and Y responds by reducing the price of its petrol, that is strategy 3, then X would end up with 45 per cent of the market. This would leave company Y with 55 per cent.

It would be a reasonable assumption on company X's part to expect company Y to respond to whichever strategy it opts for with the strategy that will minimize X's eventual market share. For example, if company X chose strategy 4, company Y would respond with strategy 2, as this would leave X with only 40 per cent of the market. Had Y responded with strategies 1, 3 or 4, this would have left X with 60 per cent, 45 per cent, or 50 per cent respectively, all in excess of 40 per cent. In other words, if company X assumes the worst, then the outcome that it would expect from each strategy would be the lowest market share in each row. These are shown in bold type in Table 4.2 and together are called the **row minima**.

Given all this what would now constitute rational behaviour, bearing in mind the uncertainty, interdependence, and conflict that exists within the situation? If company X is to assume that company Y will respond by choosing that strategy which is worst from company X's point of view, then company X should behave in accordance with the **maximin criterion**. That is, it will choose the best strategy from the worst possible outcomes, and this will be achieved by choosing the strategy that gives the highest figure in the row minima. In other words they would choose strategy 3, giving them 55 per cent of the market.

In reality, of course, oligopolistic competition is never as simple as this. To begin with

there will often be more than two participants, and there would rarely be a complete conflict of interests such as that assumed in the above example. As a result a degree of **collective decision-making** may result. Certain broad rules of behaviour may develop relating to price leadership, market share, investment, and so on. If such agreements between firms are embodied in a legally enforceable formal document, the group of firms involved has formed a **cartel**.

In both Britain and America cartels are illegal, as it is felt that their general effect is to restrict output, raise prices, and generally create monopoly conditions. As a result, where such behaviour does exist, it usually takes the form of vague informal agreements and for this reason it is difficult to analyse. Under these circumstances such collective agreements and mutual understandings between oligopolists are also difficult to enforce. Actions can easily be misinterpreted. There is always a possibility that uncontrolled 'warfare' might break out.

Some games try to be a more realistic reflection of oligopolistic competition. Needless to say they are much more complex than the two-person constant-sum game that we have outlined. As well as including more variables and scope for co-operation, they can introduce criteria on which to base a choice of strategy other than the maximin criterion that we used. In this way a game could assume that a group of oligopolists might 'agree' to link its prices to those of a particularly dominant firm, so as to avoid the potential dangers of price warfare. After all, price warfare may result in everyone's profits falling. This would leave them free to compete in terms of advertising, quality, service, and so on. Another possible area for co-operation would be that of market share. Firms could split the total market up between them and then concentrate on a joint effort to increase the size of the total market.

However, even the most sophisticated attempts at game theory fail to provide a complete general theory of oligopoly.

5 Conclusion

To conclude this work on the theory of the firm, we might ask what empirical evidence there is to support these new theories. In fact, very little empirical work has been done, certainly not enough to allow any one of the new theories to take pride of place. Indeed none of them result in the sort of clear-cut predictions generated by the traditional theory, although to be fair the ability to make such predictions is not always their aim. The traditional theory is particularly valuable in the examination of perfect markets, while the more recent alternatives undoubtedly add to the traditional understanding of oligopoly through the introduction of more realistic assumptions.

Examination questions

Data response question

'The classical theory of the firm relied heavily on the notion that firms are small, owner-managed organizations operating in highly competitive markets whose demand functions are given and where only normal profits can be earned. If the firm did not therefore maximize profits it would fail to survive under these conditions. Setting aside the question as to whether this ever was a valid description . . . it is certainly far removed from the actual characteristics of firms in many branches of economic activity today. It is only when the main features of the organization of modern corporations are taken into account that the questions of the goals of the firm and its decision processes can be effectively discussed.'
(J.F. Pickering, *Industrial Structure and Market Conduct*, Martin Robertson, 1974)

a) Explain, within the context of classical theory, how profit maximization is crucial for a firm's survival.
b) What 'main features of modern corporations' would you consider the author had in mind when he questioned the adequacy of the traditional theory of the firm? Giving your reasons, state whether you would agree that such theory is now obsolete. (*London A, 1980*)

Essay questions

1 Supposing that a perfectly competitive industry became a monopoly, what changes would you expect to see in:
   a) the price of the industry's good;
   b) the output of the industry's good;
   c) the average cost of production of the good; and
   d) the marginal cost of production of the good?
   Explain your conclusions. (*Cambridge A, 1981*)

2 'Monopolists charge higher prices and produce lower outputs than would perfect competitors.' Explain how this is possible. Discuss whether or not it matters. (*London A, 1982*)

3 If price discrimination merely transfers consumers' surplus to producers why is it considered undesirable? (*Oxford and Cambridge S, 1982*)

4 'The perfect competition model is such an extreme market form, and so unrealistic in its assumptions, that it has little to offer towards the theory of the firm.' Discuss. (*London S, 1981*)

5 What is the purpose of an economic theory? Evaluate the following statement: 'The most severe test of an economic theory is whether it realistically describes the economic activity to which it is applied.' Illustrate both parts of your answer with reference to the theory of the firm.
(*Joint Matriculation Board A, 1981*)

6 On what grounds is it argued that large companies pursue goals other than the maximization of their profits? What alternative goals might a company have? (*London S, 1983*)

7 What problems arise in the pricing decisions of nationalized industries? (*Oxford A, 1982*)

8 Why might there be a tendency in conditions of oligopoly towards price rigidity? How may an individual oligopolist attempt to increase his share of the market?
(*Associated Examining Board A, 1982*)

9 The hundred largest companies in the UK control over 40 per cent of manufacturing output. In view of this, do you think that current economic theories of the firm are able to provide an adequate explanation of the competitive process in product markets? (*Joint Matriculation Board S, 1980*)

10 How might an economist's views on the merits of monopoly be altered were sales maximization to replace profit maximization as the assumed objective of the monopolist?
(*Oxford and Cambridge S, 1981*)

11 'It does not matter whether we think the corporation should maximize the welfare of its stockholders or of its managers or of its workers or of some combination of these; the fact is that it cannot maximize anything.' Discuss.
(*Cambridge Colleges Entrance*)

12 Discuss whether incorporation of motives other than profit maximization into the theory of the firm has improved our understanding of firm's behaviour. (*Associated Examining Board S, 1981*)

Chapter 5 *Distribution theory*

The notion of a **factor of production** has already been introduced. Factors of production are used by firms in order to produce goods and services. They are sometimes described as the firm's **inputs**. Economists have traditionally categorized them under four headings: **land, capital**, **labour**, and **enterprise**.

Land covers all natural resources. As well as the space upon which productive activity takes place it also includes minerals, forests, farmland, fishing grounds, and so on. Capital covers all man-made resources. As well as machinery and equipment it also includes manufactured materials, factories, railways, and so on. Labour covers all human effort — physical as well as mental, unskilled as well as skilled, manual as well as managerial. Enterprise covers an aspect of human behaviour not included under labour. It involves the taking of responsibility and risk — the responsibility of establishing a firm and the subsequent risks involved in its continuing existence.

To clarify further these distinctions some common misunderstandings can be highlighted. The area of greatest confusion exists between labour and enterprise, sometimes thought of as the two **human** factors. It is important to realize that enterprise is not an organizational or managerial function. Administrators and managers are part of the labour force. Enterprise establishes the structure within which management exists, appoints the top management, and ultimately carries the risks associated with the success or failure of the firm. As the managing director of a company an individual provides a specialist type of labour which is embodied in his managerial skill. He would only provide enterprise in so far as he might also be a shareholder. As a shareholder he is a part-owner, and as a result he is providing enterprise. As a managing director he is an employee providing labour.

Land and capital can be thought of as **non-human** factors. To avoid confusion here it is necessary to keep in mind the distinction between natural and man-made resources. Failure to do this can result in factors such as steel and chemical fertilizers being categorized under land when both are examples of capital.

In order to use or employ a factor of production a firm must pay the owner of the factor a price. This price will constitute the owner's income. In this chapter our main concern is how these prices are determined.

Factor prices are important for two reasons. Firstly, they determine **how** goods and services are produced. The method of production, or combination of factors, used by a firm will depend, amongst other things, on the relative prices of the factors available. Secondly, they play a part in determining the distribution of income (hence **distribution theory**), and this in turn determines **for whom** goods and services are produced. In theory each member of the community will receive an income equal to the value of the factors of production that he owns, that is the price for which he can sell them. Most households have only labour to sell, and therefore their income will take the form of a **wage**. Others may own land which will earn them **rent** or capital that will earn them **interest**. Individuals who provide enterprise will do so in the anticipation of earning income in the form of **profit**.

The distribution of income will depend on both the incomes earned by the various factors of production and on the way in which these factors are shared out between members of the community. It is possible to identify three related questions with regard to the distribution of income within a community. They are: what is the distribution, why is it what it is, and is it what it ought to be? The first is largely descriptive, while the third is largely normative. While touching on these we shall concentrate on the second question. In order to answer this question an explanation of what determines factor prices is necessary, and economic theory can help provide us with such an explanation.

At this stage it may be useful to set this chapter in the context of the book so far. The traditional explanation of factor price determination is based upon the working of the price mechanism (see Chapter 1). Factors are bought and sold in markets and as a result their prices are, at least in part, determined by the forces of demand and supply. However, unlike the market for final products the suppliers are households because they own the factors, while the demanders are firms because they wish to employ factors. In this way the theory of factor supply can be seen as an extension of household behaviour (see Chapter 2), while the theory of factor demand can be seen as an extension of the firm's behaviour (see Chapter 4).

The first part of this chapter will apply the theory of the price mechanism to the market for a factor of production, assuming perfect market conditions. This will involve an analysis of both the demand and the supply of factors. The second part of the chapter will see how well a traditional application of the price mechanism fits the markets for labour, capital, enterprise, and land. Where market imperfections exist, alternative approaches to the theory of distribution will be introduced.

Part 1   *The traditional view of factor markets*

In this section we shall outline a general theory of factor markets without attempting to distinguish between different factors of production. We shall assume that factor markets display perfect market conditions and that when isolating the market of a given factor for analysis the employment of all other factors will remain fixed. As with product markets the study of factor markets will begin with the application of demand theory and supply theory.

1 *The derived demand for factors*

Because it is firms that do the demanding in factor markets, we must start by re-stating an important assumption regarding their behaviour: their aim will always be to maximize profit.

With this in mind, the firm will ask itself three questions when deciding how much of a factor to employ:

1 By how much would an extra unit of the factor increase output? That is, what is the factor's **marginal physical product**?

2 By how much will total revenue change as a result of the sale of this increased output? That is, what is the factor's **marginal revenue product**?

3 How much will it cost to employ an extra unit of the factor? That is, what is the factor's **price**?

The first two of these questions emphasize the **derived** nature of the demand for a factor: a firm's demand for a factor is dependent upon the demand for the final product it is producing. Each of the above questions will now be considered in turn.

1.1 *Marginal physical product*

The marginal physical product of a factor can be defined as the increase in total output that results from increasing the employment of the factor by 1 unit, while keeping the employment of all other factors fixed. For example, consider a single factory producing playing cards. If the employment of one extra worker increased the weekly output by 30 packs of cards, then the marginal physical product of labour for this factor is 30 packs of cards per week. What if the factory now employed a second extra worker? What would the marginal physical product be

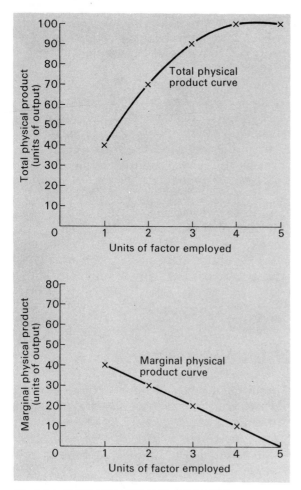

Fig. 5.1   Total and marginal physical product

Table 5.1   A factor's physical product

Units of factor employed	Total physical product (units of output)	Marginal physical product (units of output)
0	0	—
1	40	40
2	70	30
3	90	20
4	100	10
5	100	0

employing further units of the variable factor (assuming that the quantity of any other factor employed remains fixed). Indeed, if further units were employed the total physical product may actually fall, resulting in a negative marginal physical product.

1.2 Marginal revenue product

Not surprisingly, when deciding whether or not to employ an extra unit of a factor, the firm is interested in how much it can sell the increased output for. The marginal revenue product of a factor is the revenue raised by selling the increase in output brought about by the employment of one more unit of the factor.

If we assume that the firm in question is selling its final product in a perfectly competitive market, then calculating a factor's marginal revenue product becomes a straightforward operation. As the firm is facing perfect market conditions its output will be sold at the same price, whatever that output level might be. The firm is a price-taker, facing a horizontal demand curve and a constant marginal revenue that is identical with the market price (see Chapter 4, p.80).

Marginal revenue product (MRP) is calculated by multiplying the marginal physical product (MPP) by the constant price (P) of the final good (here the price is equal to the constant marginal revenue MR) so that

$$MRP = MPP \times P$$

Consider the firm represented in Table 5.1. Assume that the firm is operating in a perfect market and that it is faced with a constant

for each subsequent unit of a factor employed?

To answer this question we need to consider the **law of diminishing returns** (Note 2, p.140). The law states that, other things being equal, as the employment of a single variable factor increases, a point will be reached beyond which the variable factor's marginal physical product will decline. In the graphs in Fig. 5.1 the firm experiences diminishing returns throughout the range of employment possibilities. The total and marginal physical product curves have been plotted from the figures given in Table 5.1.

The implication of the marginal physical product curve falling to zero, as it does when 5 units of the variable factor are employed, is that it will be impossible to increase total output by

Table 5.2   *A factor's marginal revenue product*

Units of factor employed	Total physical product (units)	Marginal physical product (units)	Price of product (£)	Marginal revenue product (£)
0	0	—	2	—
1	40	40	2	80
2	70	30	2	60
3	90	20	2	40
4	100	10	2	20
5	100	0	2	0

market price of £2 per unit. The firm's marginal revenue product would be as shown in Table 5.2 and Fig. 5.2. As Fig 5.2 shows, when perfect competition exists in the product market, the *MRP* curve and the *MPP* curve fall at a proportional rate. The *MPP* curve slopes downwards in accordance with the law of diminishing returns, and as a result the *MRP* curve will also be downward sloping.

Had the firm not been perfectly competitive, the price at which it sells its product would decrease as the quantity sold increases. Whereas the competitive firm faces a horizontal demand curve and, therefore, a constant marginal revenue, the firm operating in an imperfect market is faced with a downward sloping demand curve. In order to sell additional output price will have to be reduced. This in turn means that marginal revenue will fall as output increases, so causing the marginal revenue product curve to be steeper and fall

more rapidly than the marginal physical product curve.

1.3 The factor's price

From the firm's point of view a factor's price is the cost of employing an additional unit of the factor — the marginal factor cost. If we assume that the factor market is perfectly competitive, then for any given firm the market price will remain constant no matter what quantity it employs.

Assume that a firm is confronted with a given factor price. How much of that factor will the firm employ? Given that the firm's aim is to maximize profit, it will go on employing the factor until its marginal revenue product falls to a level that is just equal to the marginal factor cost, i.e. the price of the factor. This enables us to determine the demand curve for a factor of production.

Fig. 5.2   *Marginal revenue product curve*

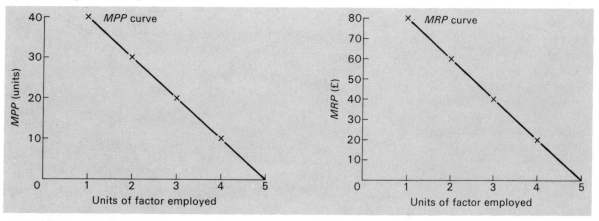

a) *Marginal physical product curve*   b) *Marginal revenue product curve*

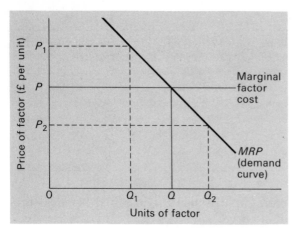

Fig. 5.3   *The single firm's demand curve for a factor*

1.4 A firm's demand curve for a factor

Fig. 5.3 helps illustrate more clearly the above profit maximizing condition and in turn enables us to draw a factor's demand curve.

If the firm employed anything less than Q of the factor, the marginal revenue product will exceed the marginal factor cost (or price of the factor). This means that the employment of a further unit could increase revenue by more than cost and so add to profit. As the firm is a profit maximizer the additional factor would be employed. By employing more than Q, marginal factor cost would exceed marginal revenue product and profits would fall. Clearly, with a factor price equal to P the firm would employ Q units of the factor. At this point marginal revenue product equals marginal factor cost and profit is being maximized.

In the same way if the factor price was P_1 then Q_1, units would be employed, while at a price of P_2 the firm would employ Q_2 units. From this we can see that the MRP curve indicates the quantity employed at each possible price, and this is exactly what we would expect a demand curve to tell us.

The demand curve for any factor of production is its marginal revenue product curve. As we have shown earlier, the curve will slope downwards from left to right (in accordance with the law of diminishing returns), so that more of the factor will be demanded at a lower price than at a higher price.

At this point it is worth re-stating our earlier assumptions. The above analysis will hold so long as only the factor of production under consideration is variable, and the firm is operating in perfect market conditions (see Chapter 4, p.80). This means that neither the price of the commodity produced nor the price or the quantity of any other factor employed will vary. In practice a change in the price of one factor of production will probably alter the employment of other factors.

1.5 Shifts in a factor's demand curve

The demand for a factor of production can either increase (D to D_1) or decrease (D to D_2) as shown in Fig 5.4. There are basically three causes of such shifts.

The first results from the derived nature of the demand for a factor. An increase in the demand for the firm's final product will increase the demand for the factor, other things being equal. An increase in demand for the final product will cause an increase in its price, which will in turn increase the factor's marginal revenue product and shift its demand curve to the right. A fall in the demand for the final product would have the opposite effect.

The second cause relates to changes in the

Fig. 5.4   *Shifts in the factor's demand curve*

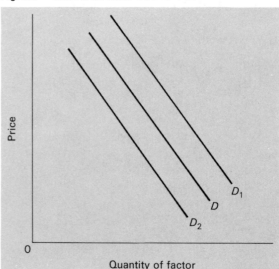

factor's marginal physical product rather than the price of the good produced. A technological change may increase a factor's productivity, so increasing its marginal physical product. This will have the effect of increasing the factor's marginal revenue product, thereby shifting its demand curve to the right. If a factor's productivity decreased, its demand curve would shift to the left.

A change in the price of other factors is the third basic cause. An increase in the price of a complementary factor would cause the factor's demand curve to shift to the left. An increase in the price of a factor that acts as a substitute would cause the demand curve for the factor in question to shift to the right. We recognize here the traditional analysis for complements and substitutes (p.12).

1.6 Elasticity of a factor's demand curve

As we know this refers to the responsiveness of the quantity demanded to a change in price. The demand for a factor will be more elastic:
1 the more elastic is the demand for the final product,
2 the more easily another factor can be substituted for it,
3 the larger the percentage of total costs accounted for by the factor.

1.7 An industry's demand curve

We saw in Chapter 1 (p.10) that the aggregate demand curve for a product can be arrived at by the **horizontal summation** of individual demand curves. Can we follow the same procedure in the case of a factor of production? Will the horizontal summation of the *MRP* curves of each single firm, such as the one shown in Fig. 5.3, represent the industry's demand for the factor?

For the answer to be 'yes', a further assumption must be made. We must assume that when the price and, therefore, the quantity of a factor employed by a firm varies, such a change does not affect other firms. In this way the output of all other firms and, hence the market price of the final product, will remain unaltered. Under such circumstances the *MRP* curve would

indeed represent the firm's demand curve for the factor, and the horizontal summation of such curves would give us the industry's demand curve for the factor.

However, in practice this is unlikely. When considering the firm at an aggregate level, it can no longer be viewed as an isolated unit. If the price of a factor changes for one firm, it will probably have changed for all other firms. An increase in the price of a factor will result in all firms employing less of it and producing less output. A single firm reducing its output would have no effect on the market price, but if all firms follow suit the market price of the final product will rise. This will shift each individual firm's *MRP* curve to the right, as *MPP* is now being multiplied by a higher price. The quantity employed by the individual firm will now be given by its new *MRP* curve (Fig. 5.5).

In Fig. 5.5 the factor's price has increased from P to P_1. As this price increase affects all firms, the industry's output will fall and the final product's price will rise, shifting the firm's *MRP* curve to MRP_1. At the new price, Q_1 units of the factor will now be employed. This decrease in employment (Q_2) is not as large as it would have been had the price of the commodity remained constant, thereby leaving the *MRP* curve unchanged.

This firm's demand curve (*DD*) can now be

Fig. 5.5   A firm's demand curve for a factor

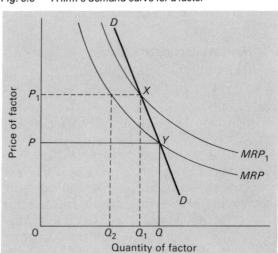

shown as the locus of points such as X and Y. It will clearly be steeper than the individual firm's MRP curve. If for each single firm the demand curve for a factor is worked out in this way, the horizontal summation of these steeper curves will give the industry's aggregate demand curve.

We can conclude that the MRP curve will constitute a firm's demand curve for a factor only if we assume that the price of the final product remains fixed even though output varies. If this assumption is dropped, as it ought to be in order to calculate the industry's aggregate demand for the factor, then a firm's demand curve will be as shown by DD in Fig. 5.5.

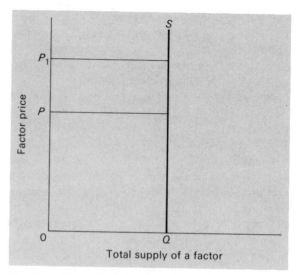

Fig. 5.6   A factor in perfectly inelastic supply

2 The supply of factors

It is difficult to discuss the supply of factors within a general framework, as the supply of each factor is subject to different influences. However, a few general observations can be made.

To begin with it is possible to distinguish between two ways of looking at the supply of a factor. Firstly, there is the **total** supply of a factor of production. Secondly, there is the **allocation** of the total supply of each factor between the various areas of economic activity. This second aspect of supply underlines how total supply is shared out between different industries and how, within a particular industry, it is shared out between the firms.

2.1 Total availability of a factor

The total supply of a factor is assumed to be fairly fixed in the short run. However, in the long run this assumption becomes less valid as the total amount available can increase over time.

The total supply of labour, measured in terms of man-hours (i.e. number of workers × hours worked) available per year, can vary with changes in the working population and the number of hours that make up the average working week. The stock of capital can increase over time if during a year an economy produces new equipment, machinery, etc. in excess of the amount of capital which wears out. In terms of total availability, land may seem particularly fixed in supply. However, 'unusable' land can be added to the supply of 'useful' land as a result of activities such as drainage, irrigation, and fertilization. Furthermore, as our definition includes all natural resources, the discovery of new resources and the exploitation of previously untouched reserves can also be viewed as increases in total availability.

To the extent that an economy's total supply of a factor is fixed, be it only in the very short run, the supply curve of the factor will be perfectly inelastic (Fig. 5.6). Given the perfectly inelastic supply conditions shown in the diagram, the quantity of the factor (Q) made available within the economy would be the same whatever the price, for example P or P_1.

2.2 Transferability of a factor

If the supply of a factor to a particular use was represented by a vertical curve such as the one in Fig 5.6, then as well as its total supply being absolutely fixed, this would also have to be its only use. In practice most factors have several possible uses and even within a single industry they can be supplied in varying amounts to competing firms.

This second aspect of supply involves looking at the supply of a factor to a particular industry or firm rather than at total supply. The supply to a given firm will clearly not be fixed. It can be increased by transferring factors from other firms within the same industry or from other industries.

At this stage we shall assume that factor owners want to earn as high an income as possible from the sale of the factors they own. This assumption allows us to predict that more of a factor will be supplied to a use where the relative price paid (i.e. income earned) is high. This implies that the supply curve of a factor to a particular use or firm will slope upwards from left to right as in Fig. 5.7.

At a price of P the owners of this factor will be willing to supply Q units for this particular use. At a higher price of P_1 this use will become relatively more attractive to the owners of the factor. As a result more units of the factor (Q_1) will be made available for employment in this use. These extra units (the distance between Q and Q_1) will have moved out of alternative uses, the rewards for which now seem relatively low.

The position of the supply curve will be influenced by the total availability of the factor. For example, if Fig. 5.7 referred to labour, an increase in the working population might shift the supply curve from S to S_1, signifying an increase in supply.

Fig. 5.7   *A factor's supply curve*

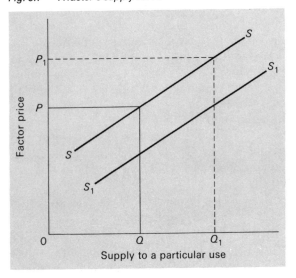

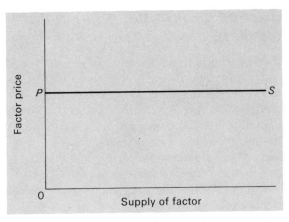

Fig. 5.8   *A factor in perfectly elastic supply*

The elasticity of a factor's supply will depend upon the extent to which and the speed at which factors can move between uses and firms in response to changes in relative prices. This is referred to as **factor mobility**. If a factor is mobile it can adapt to various uses and can move quickly between them. In this case its supply curve will be elastic. For a factor to have a perfectly elastic supply curve it must display perfect mobility and be in unlimited supply (Fig. 5.8). In this case firms and industries can employ as much of the factor as they like at the going price.

In order for a factor to move between uses it is sometimes necessary to move geographically from one part of the country to another. Hence we can distinguish between **occupational** and **geographical mobility**.

In terms of geographical mobility a plot of land is perfectly immobile. However, occupationally it can be put to many uses. Various crops could be grown on it, animals reared on it, factories built on it, and so on. A piece of capital equipment such as a typewriter can easily change location and industry, although its basic use is fixed. A large plant such as a steel foundry is clearly a fairly immobile piece of capital in all senses of the word. The geographical mobility of labour varies with age, family ties, the cost of moving, and so on. The occupational mobility of labour depends upon natural ability, training requirements, and a variety of social and institutional factors such as class barriers or closed shops respectively.

3 Price determination in factor markets

Having applied the theories of demand and supply to factors of production, it is now possible to bring them together and develop a theory of factor price determination. As we are assuming that factors are bought and sold under perfect market conditions, the mechanism of price determination will be similar to that outlined in Chapter 1, p.18.

In Fig. 5.9 the demand and supply curves relate to a given factor of production. The demand curve indicates a given industry's demand for the factor in question. The supply curve indicates how much of the factor its owners are willing to make available to the industry at each possible price. Under these circumstances a free market would produce an equilibrium price of P and an equilibrium quantity of Q. In other words, Q units of the factor would be employed at a price of P per unit.

If less than Q units were employed, the employment of an extra unit would earn more in revenue (as given by the demand curve) than it would cost (as given by the supply curve). The profit-maximizing firm would therefore increase the employment of the factor.

If employment increased beyond Q, the cost of the extra unit would be greater than the increase in revenue, thereby reducing profit. The firm would clearly not employ that extra unit.

In this industry the factor is earning a total income equal to the area OPEQ (i.e. $P \times Q$). By adding together the incomes (given by similar areas) that the factor is earning in all the industries that employ it, we would arrive at the total income earned by the owners of the factor within the economy. This would represent their share of the national income (Note 5, p.141). It is in this way that the price mechanism determines the distribution of income. Given the distribution of factors between households, the price mechanism determines the income to be earned by each unit sold and therefore, each household's income. This in turn will determine the allocation of final goods and services between consumers (see Chapter 3).

4 Shifts in supply and demand

We have already seen that various factors can cause the supply and demand curves to shift. Fig. 5.10 will help us to analyse the effects of such increases and decreases in the supply and the demand for factors. Assume that the diagram represents the demand and supply conditions for a factor within an economy. Equilibrium point A represents the original situation: the total income of the factor is equal to OPAQ.

If the factor in question was labour in the form of school teachers, what would be the effect of a fall in the birth-rate? The demand for the factor is derived from the demand for the final product, in this case education. A fall in the birth-rate will result in a fall in the numbers demanding education. Hence the demand curve for teachers will shift to D_1D_1, giving B as the new equilibrium point. Teachers' wages would fall to P_1, while the number employed would fall to Q_1. The share of the national income earned by teachers would fall to OP_1BQ_1.

If the factor in question was oil, what would be the effect of the discovery of a large new oilfield? The increase in supply would shift the supply curve from SS to S_1S_1, giving C as the new equilibrium point. The price of oil would

Fig. 5.9   Price determination in the market for a factor

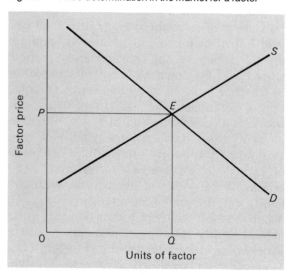

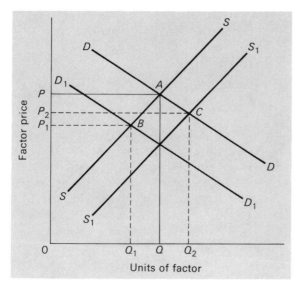

Fig. 5.10   *Shifts in supply and demand*

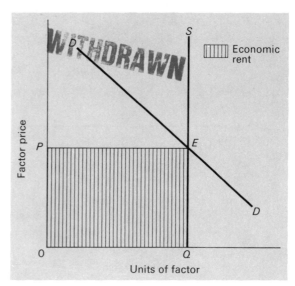

Fig. 5.11   *Economic rent: perfectly inelastic supply*

fall to P_2, while the quantity employed would increase to Q_2. Oil would now earn its owners an income of $OP_2 CQ_2$. This would represent an increase in income ($OP_2CQ_2 > OPAQ$), despite the fact that the price per barrel has fallen. This need not always be the case as the outcome depends on the relative elasticities of the two curves.

5 Economic rent and transfer earnings

In order to develop our understanding of factor incomes it will be necessary to distinguish between two elements which make up any such income.

Firstly, there is the minimum amount that a factor must be earning so as to prevent it from transferring to another form of employment. This is called the factor's **transfer earnings**. It represents the minimum earnings necessary to attract a certain quantity of a factor to a given use, remembering that a factor will always be attracted to that employment which offers the highest reward. As a factor's transfer earnings are equal to its next best earnings in any alternative use, they represent the **opportunity cost** of its present employment.

The second component of a factor's income

is made up of any income in excess of its transfer earnings. This is known as **economic rent**. It is possible to imagine extreme cases where a factor's income is entirely economic rent or entirely transfer earnings.

Consider a factor with a totally fixed supply, no production costs, and only one possible use. These conditions would produce a perfectly inelastic supply curve as shown in Fig. 5.11. The total supply of Q would be employed whatever the price. This is not surprising as there is no alternative employment for the factor. If a lower price than P were offered, none of the factor would transfer to an alternative use as there is no alternative use.

In this way there is no opportunity cost or transfer earnings and the total earnings of the factor will take the form of economic rent. The price is said to be totally demand determined, as it will depend entirely on the position of the demand curve for the factor. With a demand curve DD the equilibrium factor price will be P and its income, all economic rent, will be equal to the area $OPEQ$.

For a factor of production to have a perfectly elastic supply curve it must be in unlimited supply and have unlimited uses. Such a supply curve is represented in Fig. 5.12. Here the price paid for the factor is fixed by the price of the next most rewarding form of employment. The

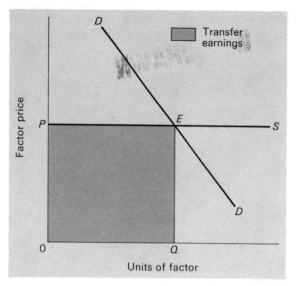

Fig. 5.12   *Transfer earnings: perfectly elastic supply*

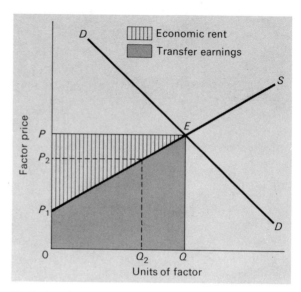

Fig. 5.13   *Economic rent and transfer earnings*

price paid need do no more than just prevent the factor from transferring to another use. All of the factor's income will be transfer earnings. In this case shifts in demand will only alter the quantity employed, leaving the factor's price unchanged. The factor's price (P) is said to be totally supply determined. With a demand curve DD the number of units employed will be Q and the factor's income (all transfer earnings) will be OPEQ.

In reality factors will usually have a limited variety of uses and some degree of variation in terms of total supply. This will result in an upward sloping supply curve as shown in Fig. 5.13. Here the factor's price will contain a demand-determined component and a supply-determined component. Of the total income earned by the factor OPEQ the area under the supply curve (OP_1EQ) represents the supply-determined component, while the rest (P_1PE) represents the demand-determined component.

In order to attract any of the factor to this use a minimum price of P_1 must be offered. The upward sloping nature of the supply curve tells us that higher rewards will have to be offered, if additional units of the factor are to be attracted to this line of employment. In order to attract Q units of the factor a price of P must be paid. This price will be paid to all units employed, so

that the first unit will earn an income that exceeds what would have been required to attract it into this use by P_1P. To attract this first unit into this type of employment it would have to be paid at least what it could earn elsewhere, so that P_1 is equal to its transfer earnings. (Any offer below P_1 would cause that unit of the factor to be devoted to an alternative use.)

Anything earned in excess of P_1 is economic rent, which in this case is equal to P_1P. As the quantity of the factor employed increases, so do transfer earnings. Each additional unit of the factor employed will earn a smaller amount of economic rent, so that unit Q_2 will earn an economic rent of P_2P. Unit Q will earn no economic rent, with P being exactly equal to its transfer earnings. In this way the total transfer earnings of Q units is the area OP_1EQ, while the total economic rent is the area P_1PE.

By looking at Fig. 5.13 it should be apparent that the more inelastic the supply curve the greater is the amount of economic rent and the smaller the amount of transfer earnings in any given income.

Still looking at Fig. 5.13 we might ask why the employer of this factor pays each unit an income of P. Why does he not pay the first unit P_1, unit Q_2 an income of P_2, and unit Q an income of P? The existence of transaction costs (see Chapter 1, p.34) involved in establishing each factor's transfer earnings goes some way to answering this question. Factor owners will further complicate matters by withholding the information as far as possible and by grouping together so as to offer the employer either the optimum number of factors at a price of P or no factors at all.

Some specific examples of the difference between economic rent and transfer earnings might serve to develop our understanding.

1 Consider a first-division footballer. A football club will have to pay him at least what he could earn playing for another club (assuming that we can ignore team loyalty and contracts). If this player is earning £600 a week while the best he could do with another club is £550 a week, then of his weekly income £50 is economic rent and £550 is transfer earnings. However, it is possible to assess his transfer earnings in a different way. What if, due to falling crowds (i.e. a decrease in the demand for the final product), all first-division clubs lowered their players' wages? If the player did not like the lower wages, he would have to leave football and do something else. Having left school at sixteen he may have no other skills or qualifications and manual work in a factory at a weekly wage of £150 may be the only alternative. He will presumably go on playing football until his wage falls below £150 a week. In this case £450 of the £600 can be thought of as economic rent, while the rest is transfer earnings. (NB: what economists call transfer earnings is not the same as the transfer fee paid by one club to another in order to gain the services of a player.)

2 Consider a pop singer who has had a string of recent chart successes. She may be earning £4000 a week for playing at the London Palladium. A year later her style of singing may be out of fashion, but she still performs in pubs and clubs for a fee of £300 a week. In other words, at least £3700 of the £4000 was economic rent. If she decided that when she could command a fee of only £200 a week she would give up singing, then this tells us that £200 a week constitutes her transfer earnings.

3 Consider a chocolate-bar dispensing machine that has been installed on the platform of a railway station. This is a piece of capital equipment. Unlike some other machines it is totally specific, i.e. it has no other use (assume that its physical nature means that it cannot be moved to another location). Once it has been installed, whatever the cost of installation, it is worth operating so long as it covers its operating costs. Whether it then earns £1 a year or £1000 a year, it will be kept in operation. This piece of capital will not be transferred to another use as it has no other use. As any net income is in excess of what is necessary to keep it in its present use, all of its income in any given year can be thought of as economic rent. The initial cost of installing the machine has already been covered and will not affect the present decision relating to its continuing use, i.e. bygones are bygones.

However, our view of this differs in the long run. In the long run the dispensing machine will wear out and a decision will have to be made about replacing it. Money will be invested in a new machine only if it is expected to earn its owner a sufficient return to make it worthwhile. If the previous machine has failed to provide this sufficient return, and if there are no anticipated market changes, the machine will not be replaced and the money will be invested elsewhere. Taking a long-run view, this sufficient return can be seen as the machine's transfer earnings.

Under these conditions all income can be classified as economic rent in the short run, while in the long run at least part of it can be seen as transfer earnings. Where factor income is seen as transfer earnings in the long run but economic rent in the short run, it is referred to as **quasi-rent**.

4 Consider a piece of urban land, unsuitable for any building development, which is being used as a car park. The payment made for the land must exceed what it could earn in its next most rewarding use — an open-air market. If anything less than this was paid, the land would cease to be a car park in preference to an open-air market. Assume

that as an open-air market the plot of land could earn £500 a week. A firm providing a car park would have to pay at least this amount. If as a car park the plot of land could earn far in excess of this, many firms would wish to employ the land for that use. Competition between these firms will pull up the price beyond £500 a week. The final equilibrium price might settle at £800 a week. Of this, £500 would be transfer earnings while £300 would be economic rent.

If planning permission was ever granted, the land may no longer be employed as a car park. A firm of builders may feel able to pay in excess of £800 a week. The earnings of a large office block or shopping centre may enable them to pay £1000 a week — of this, £800 would now be transfer earnings with £200 being economic rent.

It is unlikely that the plot of land would be used for agricultural purposes, e.g. allotments. The supply of urban land relative to the demand for it is much scarcer than the supply of agricultural land relative to its demand. Any of the payments mentioned would therefore be in excess of what would be necessary to prevent its transfer from an urban to an agricultural use. It is in this sense that the high prices paid for urban land can be seen in terms of economic rent.

These four examples have moved us away from the idea of a general factor of production towards specific types of factors. This movement will be continued in the second part of this chapter as we go on to look separately at the markets for labour, capital, enterprise, and land. In each case we shall consider the relevance of marginal revenue product theory, and whenever it is found wanting, alternative approaches will be suggested.

Part 2   *New approaches to factor markets*

It has already been made clear that a household's income is determined by the factors of production it owns and the prices it receives when making them available for use within the economy. We have explained in general terms how these prices are determined, on the assumption that factors are bought and sold in perfectly competitive markets.

We shall now turn our attention to the real world, where such markets are often far from perfect and where the resulting prices can become emotive social and political issues.

The market for labour displays more imperfections than most. For this reason we shall consider it first and in most detail. Through an analysis of labour markets we shall highlight many of the imperfections found in all factor markets. Labour markets display monopoly power in the form of trade unions, monopsony power in the form of single employers, or direct controls in the form of government intervention such as minimum wage legislation.

Following this a brief examination of the markets for capital, land, and enterprise will take place, enabling us to emphasize some of their specific characteristics.

1 *Labour and wages*

The determination of a wage rate in a world where all markets are perfectly competitive is a straightforward case of supply and demand analysis. Assume that the market for bar staff in the pubs of London is perfectly competitive. Large numbers of workers compete for the available jobs, while large numbers of employers compete to employ them. The result is that both are price-takers. Under these circumstances the employers' demand curve in the market will be the aggregate marginal

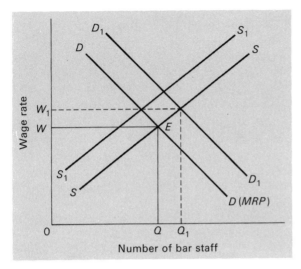

Fig. 5.14   The market for bar staff

outside the scope of this book as it raises too many political issues.

The relationship between a factor's income and its contribution to production (as implied by the MRP curve) emphasizes the importance of the demand for a particular type of labour in determining its wage rate. A given type of labour will be in great demand when it can produce a great deal of a highly priced output. An increase in demand for bar staff would shift the demand curve in Fig. 5.14 from DD to D_1D_1 and so increase the equilibrium wage to W_1. Such an increase might be due to hard work, enabling the bar staff to increase their productivity, or to an increase in demand for bar food, resulting in higher bar-food prices.

However, the demand for a unit of labour, as reflected in its marginal revenue product, provides only a partial explanation of wage determination. The rest of the explanation is to be found on the supply side of the market. The demand for doctors may be high, and as a great value is placed on their contribution they earn high wages. However, it is possible to envisage a situation where the supply of doctors is so great that they are not able to command very high earnings for their services. Indeed, we might ask why low-paid workers, such as bar staff, do not switch to being highly paid doctors? The decrease in the supply of bar staff (SS to S_1S_1 in Fig. 5.14) would increase their wage (W_1), while the increase in the supply of doctors would decrease their wage. This would continue until bar staff and doctors earned exactly the same wage. In fact, if this went on in all the different labour markets, everyone would earn exactly the same wage.

The fact that this does not happen is evidence of the many imperfections which exist in the markets for all types of labour. To begin with we shall consider possible imperfections on the supply side of labour markets, on the assumption that perfect conditions exist on the demand side and in the market for the final product. Following this we shall consider possible imperfections on the demand side of labour markets, assuming that perfect conditions exist everywhere else. Finally, we shall briefly consider the implications of imperfections on both sides of labour markets.

revenue product curve. As already explained the law of diminishing returns (Note 2, p.140) will result in this being downward sloping. The supply curve will be upward sloping as higher wages will attract more people into this line of work (Fig. 5.14).

With supply and demand conditions given by SS and DD, there would be an equilibrium wage of W with Q people being employed as bar staff. The total wages earned by bar staff in London would be $OWEQ$. In a world where the markets for both factors and final goods are perfect, we have already shown that marginal revenue product is equal to the factor's marginal physical product multiplied by the price of the final good. As each factor's income will be exactly equal to its marginal revenue product, the wage earned by each unit of labour will be equal to the value of its marginal physical product. In other words, it will be equal to its contribution to production.

Some see this as the 'fairest' way of distributing income. Others question this, pointing to the fact that the distribution of factor ownership is far from being 'fair'. A more fundamental criticism argues that the distribution of goods and services should not be determined by incomes based on productive contribution, but that it should be a function of people's 'needs'. However, this type of debate falls

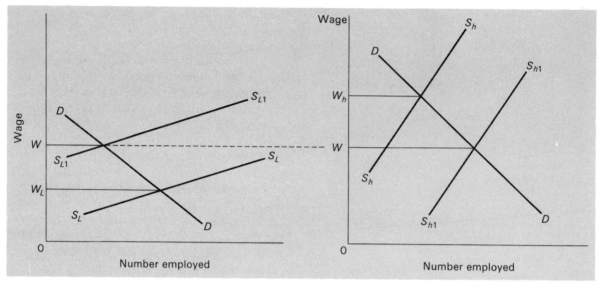

Fig. 5.15   Low wage area

Fig. 5.16   High wage area

1.1 Imperfections in supply

The immobility of labour

The fact that labour is far from mobile helps explain why workers do not move easily from one geographical location to another or from one occupation to another in search of the highest possible rewards.

Geographical immobility can be explained in terms of the cost involved, lack of accommodation, and social and family ties. In theory, perfect geographical mobility would eliminate wage differences between regions. Workers would move away from low wage areas towards high wage areas (Figs. 5.15 and 5.16).

Fig. 5.15 shows the supply curve shifting from S_L to S_{L1} as workers leave the area. As a result the equilibrium wage increases from W_L to W. In Fig. 5.16 the arrival of extra workers shifts the supply curve from S_h to S_{h1}, so lowering the equilibrium wage from W_h to W.

As far as occupational immobility is concerned the obvious constraint of natural ability is but one factor. The occupations open to an individual can be limited by social and family background. Such a constraint is not only to be seen in terms of social class. Discrimination against black workers and female workers provides further examples. Where such workers are forced to take low-paid jobs, the jobs will tend to remain low paid as the workers' inability to switch to higher paid jobs will ensure a high supply.

The need for extensive training and further education can act as a further restriction on the supply of labour to certain trades and professions. The number of places offered on apprenticeships and courses may be limited, thereby restricting the supply. A fixed number of places exists in teacher-training colleges, so that only this number of new teachers can enter the market each year. Assume that the demand and supply conditions for new teachers are as shown in Fig. 5.17.

The equilibrium number of new teachers would be Q_e with each earning a wage of W_e. However, what would happen if only Q places were available in teacher-training colleges? As the supply of new teachers will be limited to this number, they would each earn a higher wage of W. The teacher-training colleges would have to turn away XY applicants each year.

The time and cost involved in acquiring skills and qualifications can also restrict entry into many occupations. Skilled trades often require long apprenticeships while professions in law, medicine, architecture, and accountancy require long periods of study and examination. Much of the cost involved can be seen as an opportunity cost: the money that could

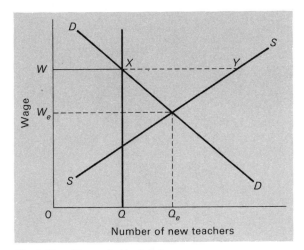

Fig. 5.17   The market for teachers

ist in a product market there is no one single goal, such as profit maximization. It is possible to identify several alternative objectives.

Fig. 5.18 highlights the main objectives. In this labour market the supply and demand conditions are represented by SS and DD. The free market forces would establish an equilibrium wage of W_3 with Q_3 workers being employed.

1 If the union's aim is to maximize the number of workers employed, and therefore its membership, there would be no incentive for it to move away from this equilibrium wage. A higher wage rate would result in a contraction of demand, while a lower wage would contract supply. Either way fewer workers would be employed.

2 However, maximizing the number employed may not be its aim. The union may use its monopoly power to push the wage rate above its equilibrium level. If, as in Fig. 5.18 the demand curve is inelastic (see Chapter 1, p.13) at the point of competitive equilibrium, the total income earned by the union's members (OW_3EQ_3) can be increased by raising the wage. If the union's aim is to maximize the

Fig. 5.18   Possible aims of trade unions

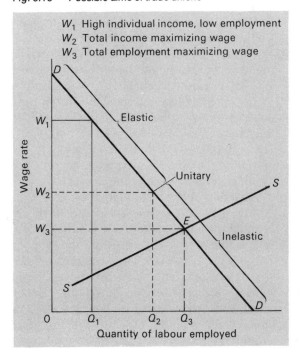

have been earned by working. Even though the long-term return in the form of higher potential future earnings may more than compensate for lost earnings during the training period, many families may be unable to finance the short-term cost.

Financial barriers may also restrict entry to occupations where initial capital is required. The individual who would like to be a shopkeeper needs premises and stock, the builder needs equipment, the solicitor needs a partnership, etc.

Monopoly power — trade unions

In assuming that labour markets are competitive we have ignored the existence of trade unions. In many labour markets the supply of labour is controlled by a union. The union can be thought of as a monopoly seller of labour, and as with monopolists in the market for goods (see Chapter 4, p.84), they have the power to choose either the price (wage) or quantity (number employed) given market demand.

As well as trying to increase wages and safeguard jobs, unions have pursued many other objectives on behalf of their members. Working hours have been reduced, health and safety conditions improved, pension funds set up, and the views of workers generally have been brought to bear. However, it is the goals which specifically relate to wages and employment that interest us here. Unlike the monopol-

Fig. 5.19 Union strategies

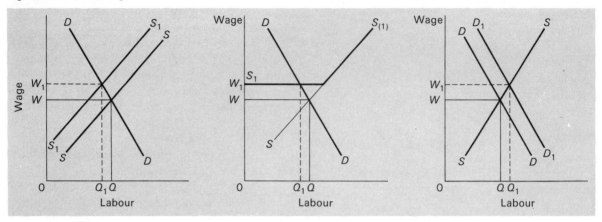

a) *Restrict supply*   b) *Fix minimum wage*   c) *Shift demand curve*

total earnings of its members, it will go on increasing the wage up to W_2. This wage rate coincides with the point of unitary elasticity on the demand curve. To increase the wage rate above this point would reduce total income, as the demand curve will now be elastic.

It is important to notice that increasing the wage rate from W_3 to W_2 can only be accomplished by reducing the number employed from Q_3 to Q_2. We saw in Chapter 4, p.85 how the monopolist must reduce his output to push up his price. In the same way the union must reduce employment to push up the wage.

3 A further possible union objective might result in the wage rate being pushed above W_2. By restricting membership and employment to a very low number, the union may achieve a very high wage rate (W_1) for its very limited membership (Q_1).

Fig. 5.19 suggests three basic strategies that a union might adopt to alter wage rates. For example, it might want to increase a competitive wage rate of W to the higher level of W_1.

1 In Fig. 5.19a the union has successfully restricted the entry of workers into this line of employment, thereby shifting the supply curve from SS to S_1S_1. This would clearly be easier where some form of closed shop exists, i.e. only unionized labour can be employed. Achieving a higher wage rate in this way would reduce the number employed.

2 In Fig. 5.19b the union has in effect imposed a minimum wage of W_1. The union's demand for a minimum wage could be backed up by the threat of a strike. If the employers do not pay at least a wage of W_1, no workers will be available for employment. This is shown by the new 'kinked' supply curve. If the employers feel that they must accept the union's minimum wage, they will only do so at a lower level of employment. As in Fig. 5.19a the number employed will fall from Q to Q_1, but this time the fall is a contraction in demand on the part of the employers not a decrease in supply on the union's part.

3 In Fig. 5.19c we have a situation where the union has increased both wages and employment opportunities. This has been achieved by shifting the demand curve for labour to the right. In order to bring this about the union could either increase the productivity of its members or increase the demand for the final product. Productivity might be increased by the introduction of new conditions of work, while union pressure on the government might result in import restrictions increasing the domestic demand for the final product. An alternative approach is to increase the demand for workers by forcing employers to take on workers who are not really necessary. This is sometimes called **feather-bedding**. An example would be a rail union forcing management to keep 'firemen' in the cabs of diesel and electric trains.

In identifying some possible union goals and strategies we have highlighted the trade-off which often exists between higher wages and lower levels of employment. However, as yet we have not managed to identify an optimum wage/employment position that a union might aim for. If an analogy is to be shown between a union and the profit-maximizing monopolist in a product market, we need to identify what unions are seeking to maximize. Suggestions have included the maximization of wages, employment, and, in an attempt to combine both elements, the total income earned by members. In fact, there is no such easy answer. Even taking the union-monopoly analogy to its extreme fails to provide any clear-cut conclusions about the impact of unionization.

As shown in Chapter 4, p.85 the monopolist will set his sales at that level that equates his marginal cost with his marginal revenue. This will result in maximum profits being earned. If the union is to be seen as a monopoly seller of labour, it will aim for a level of employment that equates labour's marginal revenue with its marginal cost. It can be shown graphically that this will maximize the economic rent earned by labour. In Fig. 5.20, SS and DD represent the competitive supply and demand conditions in a given labour market. Under perfect market conditions, the market wage rate would be W with Q workers being employed.

Let us consider the implications of unionization. The union has labour to sell and finds itself confronted by the demand curve DD. This demand curve represents labour's average revenue curve (AR) and its downward sloping nature tells us that to increase the quantity employed, a lower wage rate will have to be accepted. In other words, the corresponding marginal revenue curve for labour (MR) will fall below it.

The supply curve SS represents the marginal supply price, i.e. the wage necessary to attract each additional unit of labour to this form of employment. The area under the supply curve represents the opportunity cost of the labour employed, i.e. what it could have earned in its next most rewarding line of employment. This was referred to in the first part of this chapter as its transfer earnings (p.109). The transfer earn-

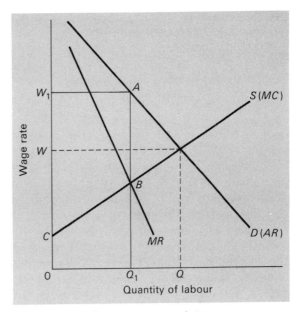

Fig. 5.20   Monopoly in a labour market

ings of each additional unit of labour employed can be thought of as its marginal cost (opportunity cost). In other words, the supply curve SS corresponds to labour's marginal cost curve.

In accordance with the monopoly model the union, acting as a monopolistic seller, will fix the level of employment at Q_1 so as to equate its members' marginal revenue with their supply price (marginal cost). This will generate a wage rate of W_1. The unionization of labour has pushed up the wage rate and reduced the number employed so as to maximize labour's economic rent, i.e. that part of total income that exceeds transfer earnings. In Fig. 5.20 economic rent is being maximized and it is equal to the area CW_1AB, leaving transfer earnings equal to $OCBQ_1$.

The weakness of this model rests on the supply side of the analysis. As the union does not actually produce the labour provided by its members, it fails to incur costs in the same way as a firm in a product market. The union itself stands to gain nothing directly from maximizing its members' economic rent. In addition, it will find itself under pressure from those union members who are being forcibly kept out of work so as to maximize the economic rent earned by those who are lucky enough to have jobs. Given this pressure and the fact that the

117

union itself stands to gain very little from such an outcome, the model fails to provide convincing predictions.

The backward-bending labour supply curve

Although this is not so much an imperfection as a peculiarity, it is a phenomenon worthy of note. In choosing how much of his labour to supply, an individual is simultaneously making a decision about how much leisure time he will have to enjoy. An extra hour of work will mean an hour less of leisure. The 'price' or opportunity cost of leisure can be thought of as the hourly wage rate that has to be sacrificed.

Now consider the effect of a wage increase on the demand for leisure in terms of the **income** and **substitution effects** introduced in Chapter 2, p.58. The income effect of a higher wage rate will be an increase in the demand for most commodities, including leisure. The higher wage rate also means that leisure has become more expensive relative to other commodities, so that the substitution effect would result in a fall in the consumption of leisure, i.e. an increase in the number of hours worked.

The final outcome will depend on the relative sizes of these two effects. The available evidence would seem to suggest that for lower

wage rates the substitution effect outweighs the income effect, so that more work is undertaken as wage rates rise. However, as wage rates continue to increase, people will eventually reach a point beyond which the income effect will outweigh the substitution effect. Wage increases beyond this point will be 'spent' on extra leisure time, so that less work will be undertaken as wage rates rise. This will result in the individual's labour supply curve being **backward-bending** as in Fig. 5.21.

Despite this, it is probably true to say that the aggregate supply curve for a particular type of labour will usually be upward sloping throughout its length. Any tendency for existing workers to work less when faced with a higher wage will usually be more than offset by new workers being attracted into that line of work.

1.2 Imperfections in demand: monopsony

Monopsony is said to exist when only one buyer is present in a market. For a given labour market this means that one firm is the sole purchaser or employer of the type of labour in question. In the real world it is difficult to find examples of pure monopsony. However, the National Health Service has a degree of monopsony power over the employment of doctors, while the National Coal Board has an even greater degree of monopsony power over the employment of miners.

Consider a monopsonist operating in a labour market that displays perfectly competitive conditions on the supply side. What does it cost him to employ an extra worker? If the buyer's side of the market had been perfectly competitive, a single firm could employ an extra worker at a cost equal to the existing market wage rate. However, as the monopsonist is the only buyer, he is confronted by labour's upward sloping supply schedule.

In other words, he can only attract an additional worker by offering a higher wage rate, which must then be paid to all employees and not just the extra one. The marginal cost of employing an additional unit of labour is equal to the resulting increase in the total wage bill. This will be equal to the wage paid to this extra worker plus the amounts paid to existing

Fig. 5.21   *The backward bending labour supply curve*

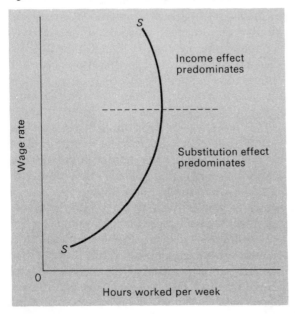

Income effect predominates

Substitution effect predominates

Wage rate

S

S

0

Hours worked per week

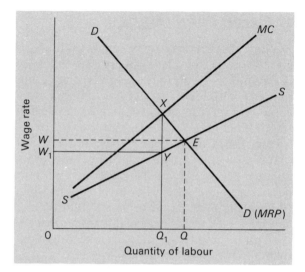

Fig. 5.22   Monopsony in a labour market

employees to increase their wage rate to the new higher level. For this reason the marginal cost of employing an extra worker will exceed the wage rate paid to that worker. This in turn means that the marginal cost curve for labour will be above and steeper than the supply curve for labour (Fig. 5.22).

Given the market situation shown in Fig. 5.22 we now need to ask what quantity of labour the monopsonist will employ. Assuming that the firm is a profit maximizer, we can apply our usual marginal analysis. The firm will employ workers up to the point where the cost of employing one extra worker equals the extra revenue generated by its employment. In other words, the firm will go on increasing the number employed until the marginal cost of labour is equal to its marginal revenue product.

In Fig. 5.22 the equilibrium point is X, giving a profit-maximizing level of employment of Q_1. Having established an employment level of Q_1, it is a simple matter of looking up to the point of intersection with the supply curve (Y) to find the wage rate that the monopsonist will have to pay (W_1).

Before leaving Fig. 5.22 it is worth pointing out that point E, respresents the equilibrium point in a perfectly competitive market, would provide both a higher wage rate (W) and a higher level of employment (Q) than does the profit-maximizing monopsonist.

1.3 Bilateral monopoly

A bilateral monopoly is said to exist in a market when both the seller and the buyer exercise monopoly power. Both the union and the single employer may feel strong enough to put forward 'take-it-or-leave-it' offers. The union can threaten strike action, while the employer can threaten a lock-out. This can then develop into a bargaining process, the outcome of which is impossible to predict. However, the analysis used so far can predict a range within which a settlement will probably occur.

This involves bringing together our earlier views of the monopoly seller (Fig. 5.20) and the monopsony buyer (Fig. 5.22) in the following way (Fig. 5.23). The monopoly analysis concluded that the union would seek a wage of W_2 with Q_2 units of labour being employed as given by point A on Fig. 5.23. This would equate labour's marginal revenue with its supply price as given by the supply curve SS. The monopsony analysis concluded that the employer would employ Q_1 units of labour with a wage rate of W_1 being paid as given by point B. This would equate the marginal cost of labour with its marginal revenue product as given by the demand curve DD.

Fig. 5.23   Bilateral monopoly

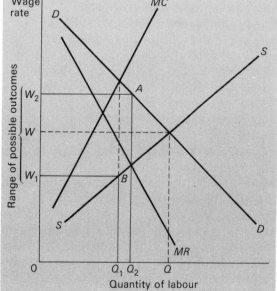

Both the monopoly union and the monopsony employer aim to restrict employment below the competitive level of Q. The union is trying to push the wage rate above the competitive wage of W, while the employer seeks to set it below the competitive rate. The union is trying to maximize the economic rent of its members, while the employer is trying to maximize his profit.

The best that the theory can do is specify a range of possible outcomes. The final wage rate will lie somewhere between W_1 and W_2, and so the number of workers employed will lie between Q_1 and Q_2. The exact wage rate will depend upon the relative strength and skills that the two sides can bring to bear on the **collective bargaining** process.

1.4 Summary

In analysing the market for labour we have identified the basic imperfections that exist. Labour markets can be further complicated by the existence of traditional differentials on which some workers insist long after they have ceased to be justified, and non-monetary factors such as fringe benefits and job satisfaction. In the face of imperfections the government may be justified in intervening. Such intervention can take the form of legislation aimed at regulating the behaviour of both unions and employers. In the field of collective bargaining independent arbitrators and conciliators can be appointed and minimum and maximum wages set. In the UK the Monopolies and Mergers Commission, the Advisory Conciliation and Arbitration Service (ACAS), and Wage Councils all represent attempts at government intervention, as does any general attempt at incomes policy.

Next, we shall consider briefly the markets for factors other than labour. In doing so we shall identify forms of income other than wages. Interest will be earned by capital, rent by land, and profit by enterprise. Together these only constitute about a quarter of total income, with the other three-quarters being accounted for by wages. Nevertheless they perform an important part in the processes of both resource allocation and income distribution.

2 Capital and interest

Capital is the factor of production that includes all man-made resources. This simple definition is twofold: not only does it imply that capital plays an important part in the production of goods and services, but also that capital itself is the product of human activity.

Once this is understood, it becomes apparent that capital will earn an income not only for the owners of capital goods such as buildings, equipment, and so on, but also for those who finance the production or acquisition of such capital goods. In both cases this income can be thought of as **interest**. However, this common denomination can be misleading.

Interest on **real capital**, i.e. capital or investment goods, refers to the **market return** earned by capital goods such as machinery, plant, etc. For example, the businessman who owns a machine, or is thinking of buying one, will expect a return out of what he earns by selling the machine's output.

Those who finance the production or acquisition of real capital, own **money capital**, i.e. their savings. Interest on money capital simply refers to the price at which funds are lent and borrowed in order to finance investment in real capital. For example, in order to finance the purchase of a new machine the businessman will need to borrow an amount of money capital equal in value to the original monetary value of the machine. The lender who grants the loan will expect a price for his services in the form of interest on the money capital borrowed.

The income earned by the real capital, in this case a machine, should at least cover the interest payable on the money capital borrowed for the machine to be purchased. Any income earned by the machine in excess of this is profit and will be considered later (p.126).

The points made so far are essential for a good understanding of the following theories.

2.1 The loanable funds theory

This analysis of the determination of the rate of interest and the level of investment focuses our attention on the market for money capital or

loanable funds. In essence it is a traditional application of the price mechanism. Supply will be seen in terms of the availability of loanable funds. The demand for loanable funds will be directly derived from the demand for capital goods. And the demand for capital goods will, in turn, be derived from the expected returns in the market for the final product.

On the supply side of the market, money capital is made available for borrowing by those who are willing to lend their savings. Saving is any income not spent on present consumption. Saving involves a sacrifice in terms of the loss of utility that this non-consumption of goods and services entails. The borrowers have to pay the lenders a price that will induce them into forgoing this utility. This price is referred to as interest. The higher the rate of interest is, the greater is the inducement to postpone consumption and save. The higher the savings are, the higher is the amount of loanable funds available for investment in real capital. In fact, the theory assumes that all savings will be used in order to buy new real capital. In this way the supply curve will be upward sloping from left to right.

On the demand side borrowers' demand for money capital is derived from their demand for real capital or investment. The demand for real capital will depend upon its marginal productivity. Other things remaining constant, as more capital is employed, so the productivity of an extra unit of capital will fall. In other words, the law of diminishing returns will apply to capital in the same way as it does to all other factors.

What is meant by the productivity of capital is best illustrated by an example. Consider a road haulage firm about to add to its stock of vehicles by purchasing a new lorry. This additional piece of capital will cost the firm £50 000. Allowing for inflation, operating costs, and depreciation, the anticipated annual net income from the lorry must now be calculated. Assume that this net income is expected to be £2500 a year. The productivity of this piece of capital, that is the rate of interest it will earn, is given by expressing £2500 as a percentage of £50 000, i.e. 5 per cent. This yield is often referred to as the **marginal efficiency of**

capital (*MEC*), and it will fall as additional units of capital are employed.

Whether or not this firm would decide to buy the lorry will now depend on the rate of interest that will have to be paid in order to borrow the £50 000. If the required money capital can be borrowed at a cost (i.e. at a rate of interest) of anything up to 5 per cent it will pay the firm to buy the lorry. If the cost of borrowing is in excess of 5 per cent, the investment in this particular piece of real capital would not take place.

The firm has an alternative to borrowing in the form of using its own funds. However, an opportunity cost is incurred in terms of the interest that these funds could have earned. The analysis is identical to that for borrowed funds, with investment taking place as long as the expected return is in excess of the interest forgone.

In more general terms firms will go on borrowing money capital in order to finance investment up to the point where the falling marginal productivity of real capital is reduced to a level equal to the marginal cost of borrowing, that is until the marginal efficiency of capital is equal to the existing rate of interest paid on borrowed funds or the forgone interest on their own funds. In this way the downward sloping *MEC* curve will represent the demand curve for capital.

As the rate of interest payable on borrowed funds falls, so investments that previously looked unprofitable become profitable. The lower the rate of interest is, the greater is the demand for loanable funds.

We are now in a position to show how supply and demand in the market for capital determine the rate of interest, and how in arriving at this equilibrium point, saving will be exactly equal to investment (Fig. 5.24). This diagram can first be used to highlight the two different aspects of interest. If a firm was employing Q_1 units of capital, the last unit employed would earn a rate of interest equal to i_1. This is a measure of its productivity. In order to borrow the funds necesary to purchase this last unit a rate of interest of i_2 would have to be paid. The return earned by the real capital (i_1) is clearly greater than the interest paid on the

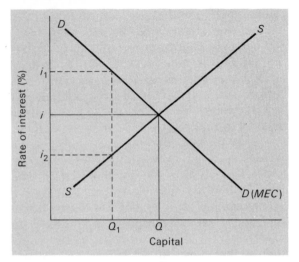

*Fig. 5.24   The determination of interest:
loanable funds theory*

money capital (i_2) borrowed in order to finance its purchase. In other words, additional investment in capital goods will take place as it will add to profit. This will continue until Q units of capital are being employed.

At this point the return on real capital (i.e. its marginal efficiency) is exactly equal to the rate of interest paid in order to borrow money capital. This equilibrium point will give the market rate of interest (i). No further units of capital will be employed as their net income will fail to cover the interest paid on the borrowed funds needed to purchase them. The resulting equilibrium position can be seen to equate savings (the supply of money capital) with investment (the demand for real capital) at what is sometimes called the **pure** rate of interest.

2.2 How useful is this analysis?

There is undoubtedly some truth in the traditional theory, but overall it would seem to oversimplify the process involved and overemphasize the importance of the rate of interest in determining the supply of and the demand for capital.

As with much of the classical theory it provides a useful analysis as long as perfectly competitive conditions exist. Capital markets are no different from other markets in that perfect conditions rarely do exist, with mono-

polistic tendencies and government intervention being easily identifiable. Doubts can be expressed about the validity of the classical analysis of the market for capital on both the demand and the supply sides of the market.

The demand side of the market

The classical theory assumes that the demand for loanable funds is totally derived from firms' demand for new real capital. In fact, both households and the government are major borrowers and the funds they borrow are not always used to buy **new** real capital. Households may borrow to buy consumer durables, existing stocks and shares, and second-hand houses. Governments may borrow to pay wage bills or pensions. Changes in such borrowing will have an impact on the market for loanable funds independently of any change in the marginal efficiency of capital.

The classical theory also overlooks the fact that the demand for money can include more than just the demand for loanable funds. People may also demand money 'to hold' in the form of cash. This is where money is held as an asset in its own right without there being an immediate intention to use it. This is sometimes referred to as **hoarding**, and this motive for demanding money will be returned to shortly (see liquidity preference theory, p.123).

It is also argued that the loanable funds theory overemphasizes the impact of interest rate changes on the demand for capital. Such changes may have some impact, but more important influences are often at work. For example, investment decisions are greatly influenced by business expectations regarding future levels and techniques of economic activity. An increase in interest rates may not deter an investment decision, if businessmen anticipate the continuation of boom conditions in the economy. If a depression is anticipated, even low rates of interest may fail to stimulate investment. In other words, shifts in the *MEC* curve due to expected changes in productivity may well have a greater influence on investment levels.

Similarly, we can question the impact of changes in the interest rate on the investment decisions of households. Personal factors (such as the arrival of a baby) may influence household investment decisions, while social and political considerations may have a strong influence on decisions of public authorities.

The supply side of the market

The classical theory assumes that loanable funds are equal to savings. In other words, all savings are made available to those wishing to invest. This assumption oversimplifies actual events as the total amount of savings will not necessarily be lent out. Under certain circumstances firms, households, and even the government may hold on to their savings in liquid form, i.e. in the form of cash. The amount of money available as loanable funds will also be affected by the attitudes and activities of the state's monetary authorities and the country's banking system. The state can print money, while banks, subject to state regulations, can create money through their lending activities.

As with demand, there is also evidence to suggest that the level of saving is influenced by factors other than the rate of interest. For many households the most important influence on their level of saving is their income. People tend to save a higher percentage of their income, the greater their income level is (see Chapter 3, p.65). Nor do households see the earning of interest as the only reason for saving. Social attitudes may result in habitual saving, while a society's financial framework may provide for a great deal of contractual saving, e.g. through insurance companies and pension funds. Where households are saving in order to accumulate a given sum (e.g. the price of a holiday), the rate of interest may well have little impact. In fact, what impact there is may be in opposition to that predicted by the classical theory. Higher interest will mean that less has to be saved in order to reach the desired target.

Firms and governments too may save for reasons other than the achievement of interest. Firms save as a safety measure against a future decline in demand for their product as well as to provide funds for future expansion or capital replacement. When governments feel that purchasing power is too high, they might counteract this by making their revenue from taxation exceed public sector spending.

There are clearly many questions surrounding this classical theory of interest determination. An alternative approach has been suggested by J.M. Keynes who sees the whole process rather differently. For Keynes it is the supply and demand for **money** rather than loanable funds that is relevant. A brief outline of this theory will follow, although it is not central to our understanding of the market for capital. This theory suggests that the forces influencing interest determination are to a degree separate from those at work in the market for capital.

2.3 Keynes's liquidity preference theory

Keynes argued that money is not simply demanded so that it can be spent on new capital goods. He focuses our attention on the demand to hold money in the form of cash rather than in any other type of asset, e.g. securities, cars, buildings, etc. Cash is described as a very liquid asset, as it is readily accepted in exchange for goods and services. Keynes argued that this **liquidity preference** (i.e. demand to hold money or cash) stems from three basic motives:

1 Transaction motive: This money is held to finance day-to-day spending. The amount held for this purpose will normally vary directly with changes in both income and the price level.
2 Precautionary motive: This money is held to cover any unexpected spending, e.g. a wedding, a journey, a car accident, etc. Keynes called the money held for these two motives **active balance**. He argued that they would be fairly stable in the short run and not at all susceptible to changes in the rate of interest.
3 Speculative motive: Any money held in excess of the amount required to satisfy the transaction and precautionary motives is described by Keynes as an **idle balance**. At first sight it may seem rather strange that anyone would want to hold such balances as they will earn no income. Keynes provided an answer to this in the following way.

Imagine that the alternative to holding money is to use it to buy government securities or bonds (Note 6, p.141). Liquidity would be sacrificed in return for a secure income-earning asset. However, although there is a guaranteed fixed income in the form of interest, there is a risk involved. A fall in the market price of the bonds will result in a capital loss. If bond prices are expected to fall, people would rather hold money than buy bonds. The demand for money will be high. If bond prices are expected to rise, people would rather be holding bonds. The demand for money will be low.

The current rate of interest earned by a bond will vary as its market price varies. If bonds are expensive, this in effect means that the interest they earn is low and vice versa. In this way, if interest rates are low (i.e. bond prices are high) and are expected to rise (i.e. bond prices fall), people will hold money rather than bonds so as to avoid capital losses. Alternatively, if interest rates are high (i.e. bond prices are low) and are expected to fall (i.e. bond prices increase), people will hold bonds rather than money so as to benefit from capital gains. This sort of behaviour is clearly **speculative** in nature, and the speculative demand for money will vary inversely with the rate of interest.

The liquidity preference curve

The total demand to hold money (i.e. liquidity preference) can be calculated at any given time by adding together all 'active' and all 'idle' balances. Active balances will not vary, while idle balances will vary inversely with interest rate changes. This is shown in Fig. 5.25. It is worth commenting on the fact that the downward sloping liquidity preference curve will eventually flatten out and become horizontal. This is explained in terms of there being a minimum level of interest necessary to persuade people to give up the liquidity and security associated with the holding of cash.

The supply of money

Having represented the demand to hold money in terms of the liquidity preference curve, Keynes went on to consider the supply of money. Unlike the classical theorists he did not see this simply in terms of the level of current savings. In addition to savings governments can print money, and within limits banks can create money. Keynes saw the supply of money as being fixed in the short run by the state's monetary authorities and therefore used a curve such as that labelled M to represent it (Fig. 5.26).

Fig. 5.25   The liquidity preference curve

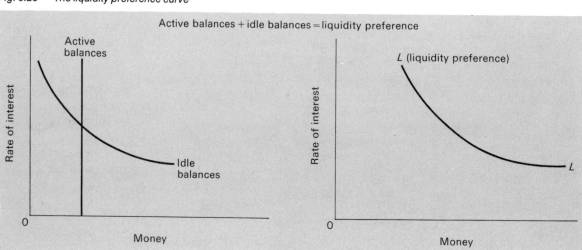

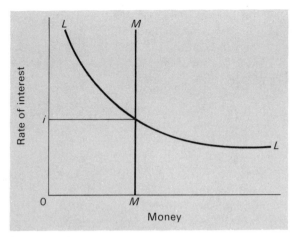

Fig. 5.26   The determination of interest: monetary or liquidity preference theory

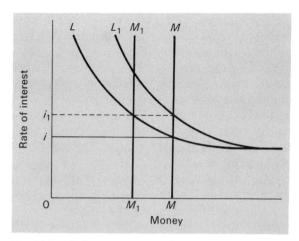

Fig. 5.27   Shifts in demand and supply

The determination of interest

From here Keynes went on to explain the determination of the rate of interest in terms of the intersection between the demand curve for money and its supply curve. In Fig. 5.26 the rate of interest would settle at i.

Had it been above this level, households would have found themselves holding unwanted money. In order to rectify this they would use the excess holdings to buy bonds or other assets. The effect of the increase in the demand for bonds would be to increase their price and therefore lower interest rates. This would continue until the rate of interest settled at i.

A rate of interest below the equilibrium level (i) would leave households with less money than they would like. They would try to rectify this by selling bonds or assets. This increase in the supply of bonds would lower their price and hence increase interest rates. Once again this would continue until the market was back in equilibrium with the demand to hold money being exactly matched by the supply.

Fig. 5.27 shows the effects of changes in liquidity preference and the money supply. With a liquidity preference represented by the curve L and a supply of money equal to M, the rate of interest would be i. An increase in the rate of interest to i_1 could have been caused by either a fall in the supply of money to M_1 or an increase in the demand for money to L_1.

Whatever the cause is, the higher rate of interest and the reduced availability of credit would result in a fall in investment activity.

2.4 Uncertainty as an imperfection

Much of our discussion so far has ignored the existence of uncertainty. The returns on capital will be spread over the future and uncertainty surrounds events in the future. The lender of money capital cannot be certain of repayment. The borrower who invests in real capital cannot be certain of how much income it will earn him in the light of changing demands and technology. Uncertainty about the future rate of inflation complicates the whole area of interest determination.

The problem can be seen in terms of the difference between the **money** rate of interest and the **real** rate of interest. If you pay me £10 interest at the end of a one-year loan of £100, the money rate of interest is 10 per cent. However, if the rate of inflation for that year was 6 per cent, the real rate of interest would be only 4 per cent. If I had anticipated this, I would have charged you 16 per cent interest and so finished up with a real rate of interest of 10 per cent as originally expected.

But, what would happen if my anticipated 6 per cent rate of inflation turns out to be a wrong estimate? If it is greater than this, borrowers will gain as the real rate of interest will be lower than 10 per cent; if it is less than 6 per

125

cent lenders will gain as the real rate of interest will be greater than 10 per cent. The ways in which people respond to this uncertainty regarding the real rate of interest will have implications for the determination of the money rate of interest.

The existence of varying degrees of uncertainty explains another feature of capital markets that we have so far ignored. There is in fact no such thing as **the** rate of interest. The capital market can be seen as a series of sub-markets each with different degrees of uncertainty and, therefore, different rates of interest. Uncertainty varies with the **credit-worthiness** of the borrower, the **marketability** of the loan or security, and the **duration** of the loan. These qualities are highlighted in the following examples:

1 Lending to the government or large well-established companies is seen as safe. The likelihood of default is slight and their credit-worthiness is said to be good. Borrowers with such a high credit standing will tend to be charged lower rates of interest.

2 Governments borrow by selling securities such as Treasury bills or long-term stock, while companies can sell shares and debentures. These securities are described as marketable when they can easily be sold. In other words, such assets have the attraction of liquidity. The greater their marketability or liquidity is, the lower will be the rate of interest they earn.

3 The longer the duration of the loan is, the greater the risk of default will be and, therefore, the higher the rate of interest.

This last way of subdividing the market for loans enables us to introduce the distinction that exists between the money market and the capital market. The money market is basically the market for short-term loans, while the capital market is the market for long-term loans. It is interesting to note the suggestion that the Keynesian explanation of the determination of interest rates, in terms of the supply and demand for money, is most meaningful in the context of the money market, while the traditional theory based on savings and investment provides a more useful explanation of events in the capital market.

So far we have emphasized uncertainty from the point of view of the lender, i.e. the supply side of the market. On the demand side the borrower is also confronted with the risks associated with uncertainty. The traditional theory has suggested that investment in real capital will take place when the rate of return is at least equal to the interest paid on the loan necessary to finance the investment. This would be all very well if there were no risk involved and the firm could be sure that its anticipated rate of return will materialize. Given that there is no such guarantee, the firm's decision-makers will only undertake the investment, if the expected rate of return is in excess of the rate of interest at which they can borrow. In other words, the anticipated yield of the investment must cover not only the interest charges but also an additional payment for the risk that is being taken.

This additional payment or risk premium can be thought of as a separate cost of production. Those who are willing to put themselves at risk are said to be providing enterprise and the risk premium they expect to earn in return can be thought of as profit. This can now be looked at as a separate factor of production.

3 Enterprise and profit

3.1 Pure profit

There is some confusion over what exactly constitutes profit. The accountant will calculate a firm's profit by substracting costs from revenue, where costs are taken to include:

1 factor payments to workers, suppliers of capital, and any other resource owners.
2 the cost of components.
3 the depreciation of existing capital, e.g. machines, buildings, etc.
4 premium payments to cover against insurable risks, e.g. theft, etc.

However, **net profit** calculated in this way is not what economists mean by **pure economic profit**. This net profit belongs to the owners of the firm or the entrepreneurs, but part of it can be seen as a return to any managerial or organizational functions they might provide (i.e. labour), while a further part includes the normal rate of return on any capital supplied plus the opportunity cost of using natural resources provided by owners. When these implicit costs are subtracted from the accountant's net profit, what remains is the economist's **pure profit**. It is this pure economic profit which constitutes the income earned by enterprise or entrepreneurship.

In practice this sort of calculation is very difficult to carry out with any certainty. The isolation of pure profit from other factor incomes is not easy. Furthermore, as a factor price it differs from other factor incomes in that it is a residual item which cannot be fixed in advance. It is prone to considerable fluctuations and it can even be negative. The very concept of entrepreneurship provides further problems. It is intangible and as a result not easily subjected to quantitative measurement.

For these reasons any attempt to apply normal supply and demand analysis to the market for enterprise will invariably break down. There would seem to be no single explanation of why firms earn pure economic profit, let alone what this level of profit should be. We shall identify two basic explanations or theories of profit that have been put forward.

3.2 Theories of profit

Uncertainty

Here profit is seen as the reward that entrepreneurs receive for bearing **uncertainty**. It is important to differentiate between uncertainty and **risk**. Uncertainties that can be insured against, such as a cargo being lost at sea or a factory destroyed by fire, are classified as risks. In taking out insurance policies to cover such risks, the uncertainty is being passed on to the insurance company and the premium paid can be seen as one of the firm's costs.

However, the major uncertainties of business activity cannot be eliminated in this way. Uncertainty surrounds future events regarding changes in demand, technological progress, the behaviour of competitors, factor prices, government policies, and so on. As long as such uncertainties cannot be insured against, they must be borne by the entrepreneurs. In return for carrying the burden of uncertainty they stand to earn profit.

Innovation

Innovation can be seen in terms of the development of a new product, the implementation of a new production technique, or the introduction of a new marketing strategy. The entrepreneur who succeeds through undertaking such activities will be rewarded in the form of profit. As others follow his lead by undertaking similar activities, so this profit will be eaten away. However, this will take time, especially where barriers to entry exist, and in the meantime the original entrepreneur may be earning large profits. Such barriers might take the form of a **patent**, where the state confers an exclusive right on a firm to produce a new invention for a given period.

3.3 Normal and excess profit

Pure profit can be subdivided into **normal profit** and **excess** or **surplus profit**.

Normal profit is the minimum return necessary to guarantee that an entrepreneur will continue to bear uncertainty and provide initiative within an industry. It must be equal to his best possible alternative rewards and can, therefore, be viewed as an opportunity cost or transfer earnings.

Where pure profit is more than just normal profit the difference constitutes excess or surplus profit. As excess profit is in addition to the entrepreneur's transfer earnings, it is clearly a form of economic rent. If excess profit exists under perfect market conditions, it will attract new entrepreneurs into the industry, with the resulting increase in supply lowering the market price until only normal profit is once again being made. While excess profit can be earned in the short run, only normal profit can be earned in the long run under perfect market conditions. Where imperfect market conditions exist and entry can be restricted, excess profits can go on being earned, and in the case of the monopolist they can go on being earned indefinitely.

3.4 Enterprise

Although the usual supply and demand analysis does not seem to work for enterprise, it is still useful to think of it as a separate factor of production. Like other factors its supply is scarce — not everyone is willing to take on the uncertainty involved nor is everyone able to be innovative. The supply of enterprise will also be greater, the higher the potential return is. When potential profits seem to be high, more businessmen will be willing to bear uncertainty and seek out and develop new ideas.

Within both market and mixed economies there is a need for enterprise (in a command economy enterprise will be provided by the state). Without it productive activity will not take place, despite the existence of land, labour, and capital. Someone must take the initiative to co-ordinate these other factors. This is undertaken by the entrepreneur. As his aim is to maximize profit, he will see to it that maximum efficiency is achieved through an optimum combination of factors. It is in this way that profit plays an important role in resource allocation.

4 Land and rent

A discussion of rent as an income to land cannot proceed until we have an exact understanding of the word's various meanings. These vary with the context in which the word is being used.

4.1 Contractual rent

This relates to the use of the word 'rent' in everyday speech. It is the payment made for the use of an asset that is owned by someone else, e.g. a car, a flat, a TV set, a plot of land, an office, etc. This particular meaning is not of great interest to us as economists. The economist would see the rent paid on a flat, for example, as also including elements of wages, interest, and profit.

4.2 Economic rent

For the economist this use of the word rent is fundamental. In fact, we have already come across it (p.109). In this context it refers to the income earned by any factor of production that is in excess of its transfer earnings. In other words, it is a payment over and above what a factor could earn in its next most rewarding employment, i.e. over and above its opportunity cost.

An element of any factor's income will take the form of economic rent, whenever its supply is anything other than perfectly elastic. The more inelastic the supply is, the greater will be the economic rent as a proportion of total income. Where supply is perfectly inelastic, all income earned can be thought of as economic rent (Fig. 5.28).

The high earnings of individuals with some unique talent can best be thought of as a rent earned on talent rather than wages earned on work. The high earnings of very specialized equipment can best be thought of as rent on its scarcity rather than interest earned on capital.

Classical economists such as David Ricardo saw the supply of land as being perfectly inelastic as in Fig. 5.28c. For this reason all the income earned by land was seen as economic rent. As we shall see this is perhaps an oversimplified view of the supply of land, but it has resulted in the term being used in a further way — to describe the total return to land.

4.3 Rent: the return to land

The classical view

Early economists defined land as the natural productive powers of the earth. They went on to argue that this productive power was fixed in supply and that it was provided by 'nature' at zero cost. As it costs nothing to produce it, it would be employed at any positive price, and the entire return to land was seen as **unearned**. The further assumption that land has only one use enabled them to represent the supply of land by a perfectly inelastic supply curve. In other words, there was no supply price or opportunity cost involved, and the total

Fig. 5.28   Economic rent

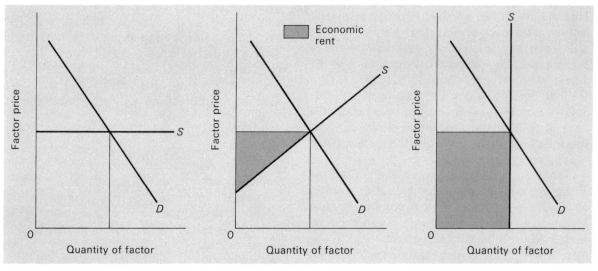

a) *No economic rent*   b) *Some economic rent*   c) *All economic rent*

income earned by land was looked upon as economic rent, i.e. no transfer earnings.

This view of land led to the conclusion that its income was entirely determined by its marginal revenue product, or demand. Any change in the demand for land would leave its supply unaltered and change only its price.

Consider an island where sheep farming is the only use to which the land can be put (Fig. 5.29). The scarcity of land for sheep farming on the island is represented by the supply curve S. The land's productivity is represented by its demand curve (*MRP*). The original equilibrium point is given by E.

If the original rent charged had been higher than R, some of the available land would not have been put to use. As it costs the land-owners nothing to provide the land and as it has no alternative use, the rent would have fallen as landowners competed with each other in an attempt to find sheep farmers. If the rent had been lower than R, sheep farmers would have demanded more than was available. Competition between the sheep farmers for the fixed amount of land available would have pushed rents up. The price of land would settle at R, giving a total income to the landowners of OREQ, all of which can be classed as economic rent.

If wool were now to become an increasingly fashionable material, the demand for it and hence its price would rise. This would in turn cause the *MRP* curve to shift to the right as far as MRP_1, giving a new higher equilibrium level of rent at R_1. The total earnings of land will now have increased to OR_1E_1Q, all of which will be economic rent.

Fig. 5.29   Classical view of the market for land

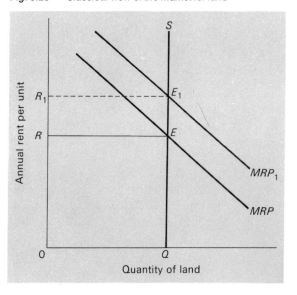

The modern view

The classical approach overlooks two related facts regarding the use of land:

1 A given area of land may have various uses.
2 Land can be converted from one use to another.

Where a piece of land has an alternative use, only part of the 'rent' is actually pure economic rent. Only the income earned in excess of what it could earn in its next most rewarding use will be pure economic rent.

Consider our island at present being used for sheep farming. A firm of developers may come along and see the island as a potential centre for tourism. The whole island could be converted for use as a holiday complex. If the island were put to this alternative use, the marginal revenue product of land might be as represented by MRP_2 (Fig. 5.30).

From the positions of the two marginal revenue product curves we can see that the land will be more productive if devoted to tourism rather than to sheep farming. As the landowners will seek the highest possible return (R_2), the land will be converted to use as a holiday complex. The total return to the land, usually referred to as rent, will be equal to OR_2E_2Q. However, only $R_1R_2E_2E_1$ of this will be pure economic rent.

Looking at Fig. 5.30 it appears that any price in excess of R_1 would result in the land use

being transferred from sheep farming to tourism. If this were the case, why would the developers pay a price as high as R_2? The answer is to be found in terms of the scarcity of the land relative to the demand for it. Tourism is clearly profitable, and potential developers will compete with each other for the available land. This competition will push the price up to R_2.

It will be useful at this stage to bring out the idea that the amount of rent that appears as economic rent rather than transfer earnings varies depending on the standpoint adopted.

Even if the island could only be used for sheep farming, part of the rent paid by an **individual** sheep farmer will appear to him as transfer earnings, i.e. the price that he must pay to prevent the land being transferred to a competing sheep farmer.

From the sheep farming **industry's** point of view, there are no transfer earnings as long as the land has no other use. However, if the land has several uses, the price paid by the industry to prevent it from being transferred to another use can be thought of as transfer earnings. In this way the supply of land to an industry, where the land has more than one use, will be as shown in Fig. 5.31.

The supply curve S represents the supply of

Fig. 5.30   Modern view of the market for land

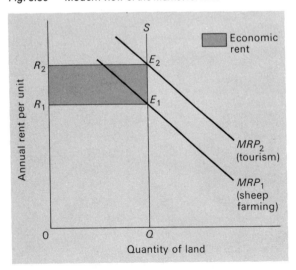

Fig. 5.31   The supply of land to an industry

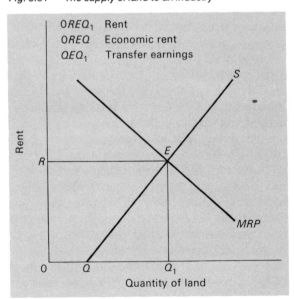

land to sheep farming. Q units of land have no other use and, therefore, no transfer earnings. If sheep farmers want to employ land in excess of Q, they must at least pay an amount equal to what the land could earn in its next most rewarding use, say, growing potatoes. If sheep farmers use Q_1 units of land, then QEQ_1 of the land's income would represent its transfer earnings. This would be needed to attract the land away from other uses.

From the point of view of the **economy** as a whole, land can be thought of as a non-producible resource that is totally fixed in supply. Viewed in this sense its provision involves no opportunity cost and its entire income is unearned. Such earnings are pure economic rent. It was from this last standpoint that classical economists viewed land and hence they were able to conclude that the return to land was entirely made up of (economic) **rent**.

4.4 Quasi-rent

This concept of rent highlights the importance of the time framework under consideration. As we have seen rent stems from the scarcity of a factor. Any factor with a less than perfectly elastic supply will earn some economic rent, while the entire earnings of a factor with perfectly inelastic supply will be economic rent.

In earlier sections of this chapter we have seen how in the very short run the supply of most factors is perfectly inelastic. The office space available in a town cannot be increased that quickly. New buildings could not be constructed immediately to satisfy a sudden increase in the demand for offices. The short-run impact of such an increase in demand can be seen in Fig.5.32.

The original equilibrium point E means that Q units of office space are earning a total income of $OPEQ$. Demand now increases from D to D_1. In the short run, supply is fixed (S_s) so that this increase in demand will increase the earnings of the existing office space by PP_sE_sE. As this extra income is a result of the inelastic nature of supply, it would seem reasonable to think of it as economic rent. The owners have done nothing to earn this extra income.

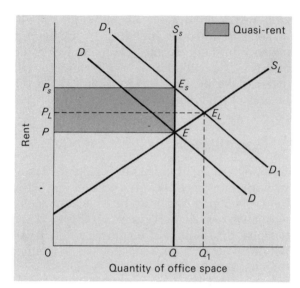

Fig. 5.32   Quasi-rent

However, in the long run, additional office space can be provided (S_L). As the quantity available increases towards Q_1, so the price and, therefore, the economic rent falls. Such economic rent is not pure economic rent. Temporary rent of this nature is referred to as quasi-rent.

4.5 Rent as a factor income

The traditional view that sees land in terms of economic rent (i.e. unearned income, all of which is unnecessary to maintain land in employment) is rather misleading as it suggests that the return to land has no economic function. However, where at least a part of the return to land is seen as a transfer payment it will serve to allocate land between different uses. Land will only be employed in a particular use when its productivity in this use is at least as high as in any alternative uses.

As the economic rent earned by land or any other factor is not strictly necessary to maintain it in its most efficient use, it is often seen as an ideal object of taxation. As economic rent is an unearned surplus, it can be taxed without altering resource allocation. The whole of the tax would fall on the resource owner, so that market prices would not change.

This argument would certainly seem to apply to land where the total supply is fixed. Rising land prices often come about without land-owners having done anything to justify this increase in their income. The mere fact of an increasing population, for example, will increase the demand for land and hence the income of landowners.

5 Conclusion

The first part of this chapter discusses factor incomes in terms of positive economics, while the second part has introduced a number of normative issues. Not least of these is the personal distribution of income, i.e. the distribution of income between households rather than between factors.

In terms of the total income earned by all factors in the UK, by far the largest share goes to labour in the form of wages — approaching 80 per cent. Because of the difficulty in differentiating between them, official statistics include interest along with profit. Together they make up about 14 per cent of total income. This leaves slightly less than 7 per cent in the form of rent.

Changes in percentage share do not always reflect changes in the relative marginal productivities of factors. More likely explanations are to be found in terms of the changing bargaining power of labour and employers along with government attempts at intervention.

Government intervention is usually designed to alter the distribution of income between persons that has been generated by market forces. Along with setting maximum or minimum levels for the various income types, the government can attempt to redistribute income through the use of both taxation and transfer payments, such as wage supplements and subsidies. In this way some households will receive less than the marginal productivities of the factors they own would seem to justify, while others will receive more. Taxation can result in income received being less than income earned, while transfer payments can result in income received being greater than income earned. Progressive taxation is perhaps the most obvious example. This type of taxation results in increasingly large proportions of extra income failing to reach households as their earned incomes grow.

Some crucial questions can arise out of this type of government intervention:

1 to what extent can income be redistributed in this way without distorting the market's signals regarding efficient resource allocation?

2 to what extent will redistributing income discourage effort and enterprise?

These questions serve to remind us that factor prices are not only important in terms of income distribution but also in terms of productive efficiency. Traditional distribution theory argues that factor prices set under competitive market conditions will result in the most efficient possible combination of factors being employed. Firms will achieve optimum efficiency by employing factors so that the following will hold true:

$$\frac{MRP \text{ of labour}}{\text{wage}} = \frac{MRP \text{ of land}}{\text{rent}} = \frac{MRP \text{ of capital}}{\text{interest}}$$

This chapter has provided several criticisms of this view. In looking at any given market, the necessary assumption that conditions elsewhere can be held constant is unrealistic. It is also unrealistic to assume that the productivity of different factors can be isolated. Where factors are complements rather than substitutes, this is not always possible.

The existence of market imperfections and the employment of factors by the public sector further undermine a theory based so heavily on the assumption of perfect markets. This criticism is particularly true of the market for labour, where collective bargaining between unionized labour and dominant employers is often built upon such intangible concepts as differentials, comparability, and relativity.

Perhaps the most fundamental criticism of the conventional theory is that it assumes a given initial distribution of income. The theory itself fails to provide an explanation of this initial distribution. Indeed none of the new approaches seems to provide an explanation and for this reason it can be argued that there is still no satisfactory theory of distribution.

Examination questions

Data response question

'The protagonists of the free market system explicitly state its advantages as freedom and efficiency . . . They regard men and women as primarily motivated by individual economic self-interest. The laws of supply and demand are held to operate because individuals are so made that they seek to sell to the highest bidder and buy from the cheapest (supplier). It follows that a person's income or wealth reflects his economic worth. Thus, man is seen as economic man . . .'

(R. Holman, *Poverty: explanations of social deprivation*, Martin Robertson, 1978)

a) In what sense does the the behaviour of economic man lead to efficiency in the free market system?
b) Discuss the assertion that an individual's productivity is a sound basis for determining the distribution of income. (*London A, 1980*)

Essay questions

1 What are the main components of the marginal productivity theory of distribution? How would a rising trend in the share of wages in national income be explained in terms of this theory? (*Oxford and Cambridge A, 1980*)

2 Discuss the proposition that if the prices of factors of production were set in completely free markets then national income would be larger and less unequally distributed. (*Oxford S, 1982*)

3 Explain how rates of pay are determined in a competitive labour market. Discuss why differences in pay are likely to exist between workers
a) within a single firm and
b) in different industries.
(*Joint Matriculation Board A, 1982*)

4 Discuss the relevance of marginal productivity theory for the determination of wages in a mixed economy. (*London A, 1982*)

5 What part would you expect differences in ability to have in explaining the personal distribution of earnings from wages and salaries?
(*Cambridge Colleges Entrance, 1981*)

6 What factors may influence the supply of labour
a) to a particular occupation or industry and
b) to the economy as a whole? (*Welsh A, 1982*)

7 'If nothing is done to curb the monopoly power of unions we have to accept more inflation and more unemployment, probably much more of both than would be present in a competitive market' (Professor G. Haberler). Examine the reasoning that might lead one to this conclusion.
(*Associated Examining Board A, 1980*)

8 'If a trade union increases the wage level in an industry then, other things being equal, the level of employment in that industry will fall.' Discuss.
(*London A, 1984*)

9 What effects will a rise in interest rates have on:
a) business investment,
b) the demand for money? (*Oxford A, 1982*)

10 Outline and evaluate a theory of profit.
(*Oxford and Cambridge A, 1981*)

11 Define economic rent and explain how it is determined. To what extent does the theory of rent help us to account for the changing pattern of urban land use and development?
(*Joint Matriculation Board A, 1981*)

12 Why have we no satisfactory theory of distribution?
(*Oxford and Cambridge S, 1981*)

Conclusion

To begin with we shall return to the distinction made in the Introduction between **microeconomics** and **macroeconomics**. It was made clear that in microeconomics we study the behaviour of individual decision-making units. Throughout the subsequent chapters we have therefore focused our attention on the behaviour of individual households and individual firms.

A household's behaviour revolves around decisions about how best to earn an income, how much of it to spend, and what to spend it on. In other words, its behaviour can be analysed in terms of factor ownership, consumption, and saving.

The behaviour of a firm involves decisions about what to produce, how much of it to produce, and how to go about producing it. Its behaviour can be analysed in terms of factor employment, output, and investment.

Microeconomic theory is concerned with how and with what consequences these decisions are co-ordinated. Macroeconomics is concerned with the aggregate impact of these decisions on the economy as a whole. In this way the macroeconomist would be involved with the total size of national output, while the microeconomist would be inclined to take this as given and concern himself more with its make-up and distribution. Both standpoints are important and valid. For example, it is desirable to increase the size of the economy, but there would be little point in producing goods and services that consumers do not want.

Having established the area covered by microeconomics, we can now assess how well the preceding chapters have developed our understanding of it. Three basic concepts have repeatedly emerged. These will now be restated as they provide the key to a full understanding of the subject matter.

1 Basic concepts in microeconomics

1.1 Opportunity cost

Running through most of economics is the fact that resources are scarce. When making decisions households, firms, and governments are faced with the constraint of limited resources. This scarcity can be reflected in many ways, such as shortages of money, physical resources, and time.

The existence of scarcity means that whenever a decision or choice is made, a cost is involved. The concept of cost is crucial to any economic decision, as costs will always arise when choices have to be made between the alternative uses of scarce resources.

Economists take a broader view of costs than the straightforward monetary cost emphasized by the accountant. For the economist the cost of any activity is represented by what has been given up to acquire it, i.e. the **opportunity cost**. The cost of any activity is the loss of the opportunity to pursue the most attractive alternative given the same time and resources.

This can often be seen as a straightforward money cost. For example, the opportunity cost of spending £4 on a cinema ticket is the lost opportunity to spend that same £4 in some other way. In terms of time, an evening spent reading this book means an evening less for watching television.

A further way of assessing opportunity cost is shown through the following example. What is the cost of a sixth-form education to the student involved? The cost may seem quite low. A few supplementary books, pens and pencils, and perhaps bus fares to and from school or college. However, from the economist's point of view this calculation would have omitted an important opportunity cost. The economist would also include the amount the student could have been earning if, rather than staying on at school, he or she had taken a job. The student who chooses to stay on at school for an extra two years must feel that the benefit of greater potential future earnings and the personal satisfaction gained from study will outweigh all the opportunity costs involved.

The simple fact that having more of one thing involves having less of something else is central to economics. This fact is embodied in the concept of opportunity cost and for this reason the concept plays an important part in much of the analysis of this book. It is implicitly involved in many of the theories, with its relevance being particularly obvious in analyses such as the production possibility curve, the budget line, and transfer earnings.

1.2 The margin

As we have just seen the idea of opportunity cost highlights the fact that choices have to be made regarding economic activity. The concept of the **margin** reminds us that most of these choices involve small or marginal increases and decreases in economic activity. Very rarely do we make 'all or nothing' decisions. It is almost always the case that we consider the effects of relatively small adjustments at the boundaries of our present economic activity.

The consumer does not choose between eating meat or never eating meat. In the light of changing prices and preferences, he will decide whether to consume rather more or rather less meat relative to other foodstuffs than he is doing at present.

The firm manufacturing canned meat will consider increasing or decreasing its weekly level of output. Will the extra income earned by the sale of an extra 1000 cans a week be greater than the cost of producing them?

The worker will choose whether or not to work a few extra hours of overtime. Will his increased earnings more than compensate for his loss of leisure time? The household will have to decide how much to save each month. Will the extra interest earned by increased savings outweigh the sacrifice of present consumption?

The aim of each decision-making unit is to find its optimum pattern of economic behaviour. For the individual this can be seen in terms of maximizing his utility. For the firm it involves maximizing profit. It is worth remembering that the optimum level of any economic activity is that where any small increase or decrease in the level of activity will cause the value of whatever is being maximized to fall.

Before leaving the concept of the margin, here are some of the applications of marginal analysis that we have introduced: marginal utility; marginal cost and revenue; marginal social costs and benefits, the marginal propensity to consume; the marginal rate of transformation; the marginal rate of substitution; marginal revenue product; the marginal efficiency of capital.

1.3 Diminishing returns

This final concept tells us what to expect as we alter the level of any particular economic activity: there will always come a point beyond which the 'return' to any activity will begin to diminish.

1 As an individual increases his consumption of a good by equal increments, so each additional unit will yield smaller and smaller increases in total satisfaction (diminishing marginal utility).

2 As an individual consumes more of a good, so a given reduction in the consumption of it can be compensated for by smaller and smaller quantities of other goods (diminishing marginal rate of substitution).

3 As a firm increases the employment of a factor by equal increments, the employment of other factors remaining fixed, so a point will be reached after which the resulting increases in output will get smaller and smaller (diminishing marginal productivity).

4 Finally, as the output of one good is reduced by equal increments, so the resulting increase in the output of other goods made possible by this will get smaller and smaller (diminishing marginal rate of transformation).

2 Government policy and microeconomics

Taken together these three concepts — opportunity cost, the margin, and diminishing returns — are crucial to an understanding of microeconomics. Once understood they provide a framework within which microeconomic policy can be discussed.

Now is the time to draw together some of the threads of government policy in this field that have been introduced as part of each chapter.

2.1 Policy aims

The concern of microeconomics is basically that of resource allocation. When governments feel that the free market forces are failing to provide an optimum allocation, they argue that intervention is both necessary and justifiable.

The price mechanism is clearly failing to allocate resources efficiently if it fails to provide the goods and services people want or if it fails to produce them in the most cost effective way. We have shown that where market imperfections and externalities exist, the price mechanism cannot be relied upon to achieve the goal of **efficiency** in either product or factor markets.

Related to the goal of efficiency is that of **equity**. The price mechanism takes the existing distribution of income and wealth as given, but is the existing distribution necessarily fair? What constitutes 'fair' in this context is very much a matter of opinion. However, when governments see the existing distribution as being 'unfair', they may decide to intervene. The economist will be at hand to predict the effects on distribution of different government policies, although the final choice of policy will be made by politicians.

The whole area of government intervention is further complicated by the interrelated nature of these two basic policy aims of efficiency and equity. If in the name of equity incomes are redistributed in terms of people's needs rather than as a reward for their productive contributions, the result may be a loss of efficiency. For example, while redistributing

income a progressive tax system may reduce the incentive for hard work and enterprise.

While not advocating total equity, many would see a greater degree of equality as a desirable aim, even if there is a cost measured in terms of a loss of efficiency and a fall in total output. This is a valid position to take, although there is at least a theoretical danger of more equal shares of a much smaller national output leaving the poor less well off then they were before.

2.2 Policy instruments

Having identified some policy aims, we now need to ask how might governments try to achieve them. What can governments do when faced with market failure?

Two broad possibilities have emerged. Governments can either tinker with the price mechanism in an attempt to increase its efficiency or they can replace it with an alternative method of resource allocation. Examples of both approaches can be found throughout the earlier chapters.

Tampering with the price mechanism in an attempt to increase the efficiency with which it works can be achieved through the imposition of taxation and subsidies, the setting of minimum and maximum prices, and the introduction of legislation. All of these can be used to affect output and consumption decisions and so alter resource allocation.

Where external costs exist taxation may be the answer, while activities that generate external benefits may be subsidized. Minimum wages may be set in the labour market to offset monopsony power, while maximum price levels may be used to try and increase the output of monopolists. Government legislation can also be used to influence economic activity. Education is made compulsory, discrimination is made illegal, behaviour is monitored by institutions such as the Monopolies and Mergers Commission, and codes of practice are established for many industries. It is worth remembering that these direct and indirect attempts at influencing economic activity will not always achieve the desired outcome. As with the 'free market', the results of govern-ment intervention must be critically assessed in terms of both efficiency and equity.

In the face of extreme market imperfections an alternative approach is to replace the price mechanism with the central planning of the state. Production and distribution decisions are made by some central authority rather than by the interaction of market forces. The most obvious example of this is when a whole industry is nationalized. When the state takes on this responsibility for selected markets within an economy, we are said to have a **mixed** system. In a **command** system the state exercises this allocative control throughout the economy.

In the mixed economies of the West govern-ment control is common where markets are **natural monopolies** or where the products involved display some of the characteristics of either a **public good** or a **merit good**. In the UK many public utilities, such as gas and electric-ity, can be seen as natural monopolies. Public goods would include defence, roads, and the police, while education and health services can be thought of as merit goods.

Serious problems surround the pricing pol-icies of goods and services provided by the state. Should they be provided free of charge, with the taxpayer covering all the costs involved? Alternatively, should the consumers be charged a price, and if so what should the price be? Answering questions such as these is not easy in the absence of the price mechanism. In cases such as defence and the police it is clearly not practical to charge individual users. However, services such as education and health pose more complex pricing problems.

Other doubts about complete government control relate to excessive bureaucracy, uncer-tain objectives, and less vigorous management in the absence of a meaningful profit motive.

3 A final comment

At its simplest the broad aim of this book has been to understand and evaluate the price mechanism as a system of resource allocation. Economic activity is clearly never as simple as

any theory suggests. It is both complex and varied and for this reason theories have to simplify the real world. However, good theories must strive to maintain a basis in reality.

Where fairly competitive market conditions exist, the price mechanism seems to provide an efficient means of co-ordinating output. Under these circumstances it remains the basis of economic decision-making in mixed econ-omies such as the United Kingdom. On the other hand, we have seen that there are certain conditions under which it fails to provide generally acceptable outcomes. Shortcomings in the price mechanism have resulted in it failing to cope with inequalities of income, externalities, and monopoly. As a result most mixed economies suffer from problems such as poverty, pollution, and exploitation. For these reasons the public interest is said to require government intervention. The fact that these problems continue to exist reminds us that government intervention is itself often less than perfect.

A final comment takes us beyond the realms of this particular book. There are those who would argue that a close link exists between the economic freedom of the market and political freedom. They argue that a causal relationship exists between the interplay of free market forces and the development of democratic institutions. Conversely, it is argued that the inherent imperfections of the market system inevitably lead to great inequalities of income and wealth, which in turn lead to inequalities in terms of political power.

This debate clearly encompasses more than pure economic theory and serves to remind us of the scope that exists for interdisciplinary study within the broad spectrum of social science.

Appendix

Optimal allocation of resources: a marginal analysis

The traditional argument in favour of perfect competition rests on its ability to produce an optimum allocation of resources. This argument was presented in Chapter 1 in terms of the price mechanism maximizing the community's surplus. In the light of concepts introduced in Chapters 2 and 4, we are now in a position to offer an alternative explanation.

Chapter 2 shows how under perfect market conditions a consumer's marginal utility schedule for a good constitutes his demand curve for the good (Fig. A.1). For this to hold we must assume that the consumer's aim is to maximize utility.

Chapter 4 shows how under perfect market conditions a firm's marginal cost schedule constitutes its supply curve (Fig. A.2). For this to hold we must assume that the firm's aim is to maximize profit.

We are now in a position to view the market situation as shown in Fig. A.3. Equilibrium in this market will produce a price of P and a quantity of Q. The market price is equal to both the marginal cost of producing the good and the marginal utility derived from its consumption. In other words, when a perfect market is in equilibrium, marginal utility equals marginal cost.

Fig. A.1   Marginal utility and demand

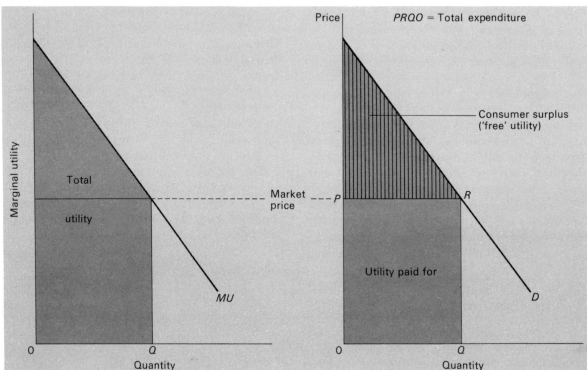

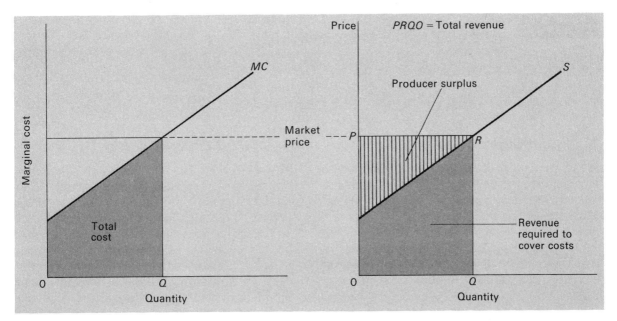

Fig. A.2   Marginal cost and supply

Looking at Fig. A.3 we can see that any output less than Q will mean that marginal utility is greater than marginal cost, so that any increase in output will provide the community with utility in excess of the extra cost — the community's total satisfaction will be increased. Any output level greater than Q will mean that marginal cost is greater than marginal utility, so that any further increase in output will produce costs in excess of the extra utility — the community's satisfaction will fall.

This enables us to conclude that when marginal cost is equal to marginal utility the community's total utility or satisfaction (welfare) cannot be increased by altering the output of the good in either direction. In theory the price mechanism will produce such a situation in the market for every good and service, thereby producing an optimum allocation of resources.

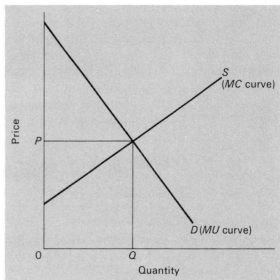

Fig. A.3   Equilibrium in the market

Notes

1 *Real income*

In this context we are talking about real income as opposed to money income. The amount of income earned may increase in terms of money taken home, but the extent to which this is a real increase depends upon changes in the value of money. The value of money varies with the price level: as the price level increases, the value of money falls and vice versa.

If, as money income increases by 10 per cent, the overall price level also increases by 10 per cent, then real income will have remained unchanged. The implication is that there has been no change in the quantity of goods and services that can be bought. An increase in real income means that more goods and services can be bought: money income has increased by a greater percentage than have prices.

2 *The law of diminishing returns*

This law explains the U-shaped nature of both the average variable cost curve and the marginal cost curve. The law might be expressed briefly as follows: If, at a given point in time, the quantity employed of one factor of production is increased by equal amounts, the quantities of the other factors remaining fixed, the resulting increases in output will eventually become less and less.

Consider the law in relation to marginal costs. Assume that the variable factor is labour and that it can always be bought at the same wage per unit. The reason why the marginal cost of increasing output will rise is because the extra output being added by each successive unit of labour is going down in accordance with the law of diminishing returns.

3 *Economies of scale*

This is sometimes referred to as 'increasing returns to scale'. The use of the word 'scale' implies that all factors of production are being varied. Thus the situation being analysed differs from that analysed by the law of diminishing returns where some factors remain fixed.

The argument is that when the productive capacity of a firm or industry expands, total production costs will increase less than proportionally with output, i.e. average costs will fall. The expansion in scale will permit more scope for rationalization, specialization, mechanization, automation, and so on. However, the economies to be gained by large-scale production will not continue indefinitely with continuing increases in output. There is a danger that **diseconomies of scale** will result in long-run average costs increasing. These diseconomies will often result from management or administrative difficulties related to co-ordinating activities on a large scale and the growth of bureaucracy.

4 *Elasticity at a point*

A common mistake is to confuse the slope of the demand curve with its elasticity. This results in the misconception that a steep demand curve must be inelastic and a flat one elastic. The point to realize is that the slope depends on absolute changes in price and quantity, while elasticity depends on percentage changes. A straight-line demand curve has the same absolute slope throughout its length. However, towards the top of the curve price is high and a small absolute change will represent a very small percentage change. At the same point on the demand curve, quantity is very low and even a small absolute change will result in a very large percentage change. The result will be a very high degree of elasticity at this point.

In fact, any point above the mid-point on a straight-line demand curve is elastic, any point below it is inelastic, and the mid-point itself displays unitary elasticity.

5 National income

This refers to the money value of the total flow of goods and services produced in an economy over a given period. It will be equal in value to the total flow of incomes paid out to the factors plus any profit retained by firms. The United Kingdom's national income in 1981 was £181 179 million.

6 Securities

In this context we can best think of a security as any income-yielding document that can be bought and resold. Securities are issued for sale by central and local government, firms, banks, etc. in order to raise funds. There are many types of securities depending on the amounts involved, the time-period, who is issuing them, the form the income takes, etc. **Bonds** are usually long-term fixed interest securities and the holder is a creditor. Ordinary shares are issued by companies and carry variable interest; the holder is an owner. Gilt-edged securities are any issued by the government. These are just some of the distinctions to be found.

Reading list

General

E. G. Dolan, *Basic Microeconomics*, Dryden Press
R. Dorfman, *Prices and Markets*, Prentice-Hall
G. Hewitt, *Economics of the Market*, Fontana
R. G. Lipsey, *Positive Economics*, Weidenfeld & Nicolson
B. V. Marshall, *Comprehensive Economics*, Longman
P. A. Samuelson, *Economics*, McGraw-Hill
H. Speight, *Economics: The Science of Prices and Incomes*, Methuen

Chapter 1

K. Hartley, *Problems of Economic Policy*, Allen & Unwin
R. Sugden and A. Williams, *The Principles of Practical Cost Benefit Analysis*, OUP

Chapter 2

H. J. Green, *Consumer Theory*, Penguin
M. B. Johnson, *Household Behaviour*, Penguin

Chapter 3

F. S. Brooman, *Macroeconomics* (Chapter 5), Allen & Unwin
G. F. Stanlake, *Macroeconomics: An Introduction* (Chapter 5), Longman

Chapter 4

G. C. Archibald, *The Theory of the Firm*, Penguin
K. J. Cohen and R. M. Gyert, *Theory of the Firm*, Prentice-Hall
M. C. Sawyer, *Theories of the Firm*, Weidenfeld & Nicolson

Chapter 5

D. Sapsford, *Labour Market Economics*, Allen & Unwin
H. Williamson, *The Trade Unions*, Heinemann

Index